Samuel Beckett

Samuel Beckett

Laughing Matters, Comic Timing

Laura Salisbury

EDINBURGH
University Press

Edinburgh University Press Ltd
The Tun – Holyrood Road
12 (2f) Jackson's Entry
Edinburgh EH8 8PJ
www.euppublishing.com

First published in hardback by Edinburgh University Press 2012

Typeset in 10.5/13 pt Sabon by
Servis Filmsetting Ltd, Stockport, Cheshire,
and printed and bound in Great Britain by
CPI Group (UK) Ltd, Croydon, CR0 4YY

A CIP record for this book is available from the British Library

ISBN 978 0 7486 4748 4 (hardback)
ISBN 978 1 4744 0140 1 (paperback)
ISBN 978 0 7486 4749 1 (webready PDF)
ISBN 978 0 7486 4970 9 (epub)

Contents

Acknowledgements

One of the things this book suggests is that in things taking their time, a space for the experience of being obliged to others might be preserved. Perhaps coincidentally, perhaps not, this book has itself taken a long time to complete; as such, it finds itself happily indebted to the many others who have shared with me the time of its thinking and writing.

Birkbeck College has been and remains a place where my work has been supported, challenged and changed by the ideas of others. My colleagues on Birkbeck's MA in Modern and Contemporary Literature – Rebecca Beasley, Joe Brooker, Roger Luckhurst, Carol Watts and Joanne Winning – alongside our astonishing, irrepressible students, have transformed my understanding of modernism and modernity. I have also benefited from having had time to read in groups, and the students and colleagues at Birkbeck with whom I have read Derrida, Hegel and Freud have all contributed in substantial ways to the thinking within this book. Anthony Bale, Isabel Davis, Aoife Monks, Gill Partington and Sue Wiseman at Birkbeck all offered intellectual sustenance, friendship and much practical support, as did Mary Brewer, Rachel Christofides, David Cunningham, Liz Farr, Stacy Gillis, Paul Lawley, Catherine Laws, Ronan McDonald, Kaye Mitchell, Andrew Shail, Russell Smith and Angela K. Smith at other institutions. Particular thanks are due and gladly offered to Paul Hendon and Min Wild. Always attentive to the rhetorical nuances of philosophical texts, reading with them over many years has taught me how to think through metaphor.

One of the key ideas in this book that Beckett's famous 'obligation to express' should be understood in terms of compulsion and drive owes a particular debt to conversations with Paul Sheehan and Shane Weller. I would also like to thank present and past members of the London Beckett Seminar, particularly Liz Barry, Garin Dowd, Tom Mansell, Ulrika Maude, Sinéad Mooney, Stéphanie Ravez and Derval Tubridy for their company. Daniela Caselli's rigorous, analytical eye has, from the start, had a profound influence on my work on Beckett. She has also persistently shown me how the most serious intellectual demands and humour might sit together.

At various points during its writing, this book has been read by Peter Boxall, Mary Bryden, Simon Critchley, Andrew Gibson and Leslie Hill. Their searching analysis and generous, serious engagement with the work has benefited it in very considerable ways. Jackie Jones at Edinburgh University Press believed in the work and her clear-sighted professionalism has earned both my gratitude and respect. My greatest intellectual debt is owed to Steven Connor, who was always able to find in my work the beginnings of a conversation that would lead it beside and beyond itself. His influence on my thinking and encouragement in the shaping of my own critical voice has been incalculable.

Extracts from Samuel Beckett's unpublished material – 'Whoroscope Notebook', 'Psychology Notes', the manuscript drafts of *Molloy*, *Come and Go*, *Quad* and *That Time*, and letter to Thomas MacGreevy dated 2 January 1932 – all reproduced by kind permission of the Estate of Samuel Beckett, c/o Rosica Colin Ltd, London. Early incarnations of work in Chapters 2, 4 and 5 have previously appeared in Russell Smith's edited collection *Beckett and Ethics*, *Samuel Beckett Today/Aujourd'hui* and *Parallax* respectively. The publishers are gratefully acknowledged.

Joanne Peters and Gabriel Rogers were true friends in offering emergency proof-reading, and to those other family and friends who didn't give a damn about Beckett but cared enough about me to ring me, distract me and remind me what having a sense of humour is all about – thank you. Adam Turnock was there at the beginning and throughout, caring about this project simply because it was mine. More than any other, I am obliged to him. Ursula Turnock, however, was the one whose coming in the shadow of this book's going helped me finally to make an end. This book is dedicated to her – with love.

Abbreviations

CDW   Samuel Beckett (1990) *The Complete Dramatic Works*. London: Faber & Faber.

CSP   Samuel Beckett (1995) *The Complete Short Prose: 1929–1989*, ed. S. E. Gontarski. New York: Grove Press.

D   Samuel Beckett (1983) *Disjecta*, ed. Ruby Cohn. London: John Calder.

LSB   Martha Dow Fehsenfeld and Lois Overbeck (eds) (2009) *The Letters of Samuel Beckett, Vol. 1: 1929–1940*. Cambridge: Cambridge University Press.

NO   Samuel Beckett (1992) *Nohow On: Company, Ill Seen Ill Said, Worstward Ho*. London: Calder Publications.

T   Samuel Beckett (1994) *Molloy, Malone Dies, The Unnamable*. London: John Calder.

Introduction

It makes sense to start a book on Samuel Beckett's comedy with an exemplary joke. Maybe something from *Waiting for Godot* would do, that early and perhaps most securely comic of all of the dramatic works. And yet, despite the fact that critics of all persuasions – from Ruby Cohn to Carla Locatelli, Simon Critchley to Alain Badiou, Theodor Adorno to Wolfgang Iser – speak with a resounding though discordant voice affirming that Beckett is funny, it is hard to pull out a juicy one-liner, a punchy joke with a securely tied up comic finish or payoff, to stand as evidence to confirm this apparently secure reputation. Unlike Groucho Marx or Oscar Wilde, Beckett rarely appears in joke books or collections of witticisms, for there are very few jokes or verbal gags that function as moments of comic relief that might lend themselves to being pulled, whole and alive, as it were, from the form that surrounds them and through whose surface they sometimes break. Even in the early satirical essays, Beckett's verbal comedy is neither so reassuringly discrete nor assimilable into a digestible list of comic payoffs. Beckett's texts are perhaps more like obsessively weakened and etiolated situation comedies, punctuated by the occasional faded vaudeville gag and enlivened with a frisson of excess, than they are collections of standard joking forms or one-liners.

One might argue, of course, that jokes and comedy are not identical. Jokes are a kind of short circuit between elements; they are determined by a certain brevity, and always marked in and by the final instant in which the humorous payoff occurs. Comedy, on the other hand, allows pleasurable release right from the start; but it stretches initial incongruities, folding them into new configurations through forms of rhythmic accretion, hesitation and deviation. So maybe Beckett produces comedy but not the easy reproducibility of jokes. But this isn't quite right either. Beckett's work is persistently concerned with jokes, but it homes in on those that are the clichéd and shop-worn. Beckett likes old chestnuts that appear failed, or at least failing – as if their timing is all wrong – and he is able to squeeze a little further humour from that. Certainly, much of Beckett's work has elements that fit the description of comedy – one might think of Winnie in *Happy Days*, an ironic diva of bourgeois respectability 'stuck up to her diddies in the bleeding ground' (*CDW*: 156), or the protagonist of *First Love* who inscribes the name of his beloved into 'an old heifer pat' (*CSP*: 34) – nevertheless, somehow these scenes are disturbed and distended by insecurity too. Beckett's comic moments are indeed hard to extract and describe precisely because the rhythms of the work seem at different times to exceed the boundaries of proportionate comic construction, buckling out into the straight flat land that surrounds the set piece, while also somehow falling short of the requirements of humour, as though the timing mechanism for the placement of misplacement has long ago wound itself down.

An example. In the first part of Beckett's *Trilogy*, Molloy, like a good intellectual wrapped in his *Times Literary Supplement*, calculates his rate of flatulence:

> Three hundred and fifteen farts in nineteen hours, or an average of over sixteen farts an hour. After all it's not excessive. Four farts every fifteen minutes. It's nothing. Not even one fart every four minutes. It's unbelievable. Damn it, I hardly fart at all, I should never have mentioned it. Extraordinary how mathematics helps you to know yourself. (*T*: 30)

Despite the extraction from the larger comic scene, this is clearly funny. But it is not simply the absurd situation that elicits a comic response; rather, the comic appears within the suggestive lack of fit between the event of farting and the language with which it is described and determined. Such a structure seems close to Beckett's comic signature: a form of syncopation in which action is rendered out of step with words as verbal desire or ability falls out of phase with physical incapacity or incontinence, or action becomes too quick for the sluggish materiality of language. But as soon as one becomes attentive to this syncopation in Beckett's work, the limits of the comic become disturbingly distended. Almost every sentence or phrase, from the early bombastic essays to the final bleached vocables, seems to contain squeezed and compacted shards of comic matter – 'bit[s] of all right' or 'smithereens[s]' (*CDW*: 97) – that are thrown up by the minimised and often suggestively idiomatic maladjustments of fit that remain endemic within the texts. Perhaps, then, if one were to imagine writing the compendium of Beckett comedy, it would be all too possible that if one could get started at all, it might prove impossible to stop, as pages could be filled with nothing but long transcriptions from his texts. This imagined book wouldn't quite fit the bill in terms providing condensed and quotable comic matter, but it would nevertheless retain those trembling movements and rhythms that assume the signature of a writing that is recognisably 'Beckettian', just when all authorising possibilities appear to be announcing their disappearance.

So this 'Beckettian' signature is not to be found most clearly in the comic themes of Beckett's work, although there are notably humorous thematics that can be traced across portions of the *oeuvre*. Instead, this book argues that many of what come to be regarded as the most aesthetically, philosophically and critically significant aspects of Beckett's work inhere in its formal rhythms, recursions and interruptions – in what might be thought of in another way as its particular comic timing. Axiomatically, comedy is always all in the timing – the correct (mis) placement of words, images, movements and the sharing of a joke in an appropriate context – although, remarkably, there has been no philosophical account of comedy that places temporality at its heart. The fundamental argument of this book, however, is that it is precisely the vital, determining significance of temporality within the comic that Beckett's work obsessively illuminates and explores. In turn, it is because Beckett's texts remain profoundly concerned with processes of gathering time into themselves and materialising this concern at the level of consciousness – exploring that it matters and why it matters – that comedy makes its insistent, repetitious return. Temporality is no longer simply the passive environment of existence that is the ground for all experience, not just the textual; rather, Beckett develops a style fixated on syncopations, hiccups, and on limping and hindered progression to materialise as affect the complex, often abrasive, sensation of time passing. For there is little sense of being carried along on a seamless fabric of given narrative or theatrical time here. Beckett's funny peculiar texts instead force their temporality on audience or reader, impressing and eliciting a time-consciousness and forms of affective temporal experience seemingly at odds with the smooth enjoyments of art as a simple pastime. And it is precisely within this grainy resistance of temporal form, I will argue, that Beckett's oft-noted yet seemingly rather unthematisable concerns with the ethical obligations of art find their hesitant, wary, often merely whispered, articulation.

Human Humour

So Beckett's texts may not be replete with easily describable comic moments; nevertheless, they do conspicuously and self-consciously aspire towards comic effect. This self-consciousness manifests itself as the knowing manipulation of recognisable comic forms and strategies; but there are also occasions when characters offer comment on the compulsions of the comic that remain within these bleached and bleakened fictive and theatrical scenes. In fact it is precisely within these moments, as the comedy on page and stage is suddenly rendered conscious of itself and its seeming evanescence, that it becomes clear that Beckett's comic timing is concerned with producing sets of pleasures that are fundamentally passing. For despite the undoubted comic effect upon the audience of *Waiting for Godot*, discomfort is also elicited as characters manifest their awareness of playing parts in a comedy with which they no longer feel themselves to be in sync. Only a minimised and uncertain humour remains for Vladimir and Estragon, just a little laughter erupts unexpectedly from Didi but it dies on his lips. In the midst of this hopelessness and failure, the duo 'daren't even laugh any more', they can '[m]erely smile' (*CDW*: 13). In *Endgame*, although Hamm remarks to Clov '[t] he whole thing is comical, I grant you that. What about having a good guffaw the two of us together?', Clov simply states, '*[a]fter reflection*', 'I couldn't guffaw again today' (122). Nagg '*chuckles cautiously*' at Hamm's hammed up and pompous declamation that there is '[a] heart, a heart in [his] head', but Nell admonishes him: 'One mustn't laugh at those things, Nagg. Why must you always laugh at them?' (100–1), causing any complacent audience laughter to stagger. Of course, she then concedes that a gagged and stifled humour is possible: 'Nothing is funnier than unhappiness, I grant you that . . . Yes, Yes, it's the most comic thing in the world . . . we still find it funny, but we don't laugh any more' (101). So although, as Hamm states, for the characters within Beckett's texts '[t]his is not much fun. But it's always the way at the end of the day' (98), maybe for the audience some humour can be found this 'unhappiness'. Perhaps, when faced with a vision of life purposively going on when all going on is purposeless, you've got to laugh.

Now this is the most common critical reading of Beckett's comic work, as the dictum '[n]othing is funnier than unhappiness' is read as both an explanation of the humour that insists within the texts and an aesthetic maxim. Critics repeat Nell's dictum straight-faced, as it were. As such, the laughter that occurs both within the texts and as an effect of them has tended to be read as a way of facing up to this unhappiness and of acknowledging the inevitable futility of the 'human condition'. There is, of course, a long and venerable tradition of reading humour as the locus and limit of the human. Aristotle writes that man is 'the only animal that laughs' (1984b: 1049) and, as Simon Critchley puts it, 'this quotation echoes down the centuries from Galen to Pophyry, through

Rabelais to Hazlitt and Bergson' (2002: 25). In *Molloy*, Father Ambrose and Molloy agree, despite their differences, that humour is human, and Beckett makes a wry joke of this:

> What a joy it is to laugh from time to time. Is it not? I said. It is peculiar to man, he said. So I have noticed, I said. A brief silence ensued . . . Animals never laugh, he said. It takes us to find that funny, I said . . . Christ never laughed either, he said, so far as we know. He looked at me. Can you wonder? I said. (*T*: 101–2)

For readers of Beckett who have sought to find in his work an investigation of the vicissitudes of the human condition, the persistence of the comic has indeed offered enticing lifelines. Before the 1980s, when the dominant accent within Beckett criticism could still be thought of as 'existential humanism', the comic aspects of the work seemed to function as both an instigator and an underwriter of that most essential Beckettian thematic. If, as the presentation speech had it, Beckett won the 1969 Nobel Prize for literature for a body of work that 'transmuted the destitution of modern man into his exaltation' (Ellmann 1989: 235), comedy and laughter was seen to function as the means by which the human condition could be wearily acknowledged and endured. As Paul Sheehan puts it in his reading of this humanist criticism:

> to face the void so unflinchingly . . . even to adopt a fierce comedy towards it, makes such humour as there is cathartic, therapeutic, and heroic. And from therapeutic heroism it is but a small step to an ethic of redemption. Humour, then, is the chief means whereby the transmutation of destitution (antihumanist pessimism and alienation) into exaltation (humanist heroism) can be gleaned most clearly. (2002: 153)

So it is not a question of the work providing a little comic relief; it is more that, through humour, shards of humanity and dignity are still to be found amid the ruins of narrative and the detritus of a post-apocalyptic theatre space. Ruby Cohn's very early and influential work on Beckett's comedy suggests such a reading: 'Beckett's comic heroes are limp rags of life lost in a stone cold universe' (1962: 291); they demonstrate a hobbled and humbling stoic heroism, the gritty residue of the human at the moment of its dissolution. 'Seeking sense and sensibility in an indifferent cosmos, reflecting the Absurdity of the Macrocosm in the absurd details of the microcosm, the Beckett hero cries out in the frustration of humanity, which is our own' (Cohn 1962: 290), she states. This comedy is not, however, what Critchley describes as a Nietzschean 'laughter of tragic affirmation . . . that rails in the face of the firing squad' (2002: 105) or what Cohn refers to as the 'black laughter' of the surrealist hero who defies and transcends his fate by 'triumphantly expelling a laugh with his last lungful of breath' (1962: 287); rather, the laughter of both characters and audience becomes a stifled, anguished, weary acknowledgement of that shared and endured fate: 'It defies no one and transcends nothing' (Cohn 1962: 287).

As Beckett suggested, when directing *Happy Days* at the Schiller-Theater in Berlin, if 'black' laughter is impossible, a certain kind of humour might yet persist – a 'rire jaune' (Pfister 2001: 50). The early short story 'Yellow' (1933) considers just this impossibility of barking forth tragically heroic laughter on the brink of the void.[1] Belacqua, in hospital for an operation to remove a boil on his neck and a portion of his toe, attempts to 'laugh himself out of this weakness' (Beckett 1970: 172). In this world of tragic negation, '[w]as it to be laughter or tears? It came to the same thing in the end, but which was it to be now?' (175). He decides, in the end, that he must

> efface himself altogether and do the little soldier. It was this paramount consideration that made him decide in favour of Bim and Bom, Grock, Democritus, whatever you are pleased to call it, and postpone its dark converse to a less public occasion. (176)

He decides in favour of the 'Stalinist comedians' (as Beckett was to refer to Bim and Bom in early drafts of *Godot* (Bair 1978: 670, n. 4)), the clown who feigns failure and the laughing philosopher, because 'weeping in the charnel house would be misconstrued' (Beckett 1970: 176) as a sentimental lament at the prospective loss of his own life rather than a reaction to the tragic 'follies of humanity at large' (176). But the laughter he achieves is resolutely ineffective; it has none of the triumphalism of 'black laughter' that laughs in the face of death. His jokes fall flat or miss their mark; he dies with neither tragic nor heroic affirmation, but rather from a medical blunder: 'They had clean forgotten to auscultate him!' (186). Belacqua's 'black' laughter, offering itself up like '[s]mears, as after a gorge of black berries' (177), becomes the 'yellow' laughter of the text that laughs at his misplaced triumphalism. In this world where heroic laughter is no longer possible, the comedy that remains within the text – laughing at the impossibility of laughing triumph – seems both to demonstrate and exemplify the possibility of grinning and bearing it.[2]

But if Beckett's work has been a resource for thinking through questions of the human, the *oeuvre* has, more recently, been recast as a rigorously persistent exploration of the newly deformed configurations of subjectivity traced out by the philosophical antihumanisms that came to dominate continental philosophy post-1968 and Anglo-American literary theory within the 1980s and 1990s. During this time, a number of critical works appeared that attempted to establish Beckett's credentials as the anticipator and guarantor of various forms of antihumanist thought. Connor (1988), Hill (1990), Trezise (1990) and Locatelli (1990), followed by McMullan (1993), Katz (1995), Begam (1996) and Uhlmann (1999) in the next few years, all wrote monographs that explored poststructuralist approaches to Beckett's work, while many others produced articles and chapters in books on the relationship between Beckett and diverse forms of philosophical antihumanism. Using the work of Maurice Blanchot, Gilles Deleuze, Jacques Derrida, Michel Foucault and Julia Kristeva, in particular, critics began to read Beckett's work as a resource for exemplifying precisely what it meant to decline the ideas of the human that, with their precipitate and weary certainties and totalities, found a groping salvation within the mess of modern existence.

With this new theoretical apparatus, however, the tendency to read Beckett's work as a tragic comedy (or comic tragedy) began to fade out. Despite an emphasis in poststructuralist readings on tropes of repetition, interruption, disjunction and difference, on what might be thought of as important resources for the comic, antihumanism and humour began to assume the appearance of antitheses. In *Beckett's Dying Words* (1995), Christopher Ricks – famously and resolutely anti-literary theory – used the comic (or the Irish bull, as he terms it) that inheres within Beckett's self-styled 'syntax of weakness' as a device to explode what he represented as the complacencies within deconstruction that had been so influential in the reshaping of Beckett studies. In Ricks's terms, if all language is 'a bull anyway, unremittingly engaged in self-contradiction' (1995: 199), then the specific power and affective structures within the comic leach away under the all-consuming antitheses of the poststructuralist reading of language. Against the 'pyrrhic and pyrrhonist victory' (Ricks 1995: 199) of deconstruction and its linguistic idealism, as Ricks has it, the insistence of the comic in Beckett's work denies any postmodern waning of affect or shrug of relativism to reveal how words are still capable of relating to and illuminating 'life and reality' (201). Of course, Critchley rightly objects that Ricks's claims are 'advanced on the unargued assumption and availability of such items as reality and life' (1997: 170), but it is not simply fortuitous that Ricks recruits Beckett's comedy as a bastion of the real and the human in his war against his conception of the complacent idealism of deconstruction. For Ricks, humour is humane – it is generous and communicative – while deconstructive antihumanism is left with the onanistic pleasures of play, where it offers any pleasure at all.

Although Ricks tacitly acknowledges the reflexive play, irony and textual high jinks within deconstruction, he, quite rightly, suggests that Beckett's comedy has a rather different flavour. And it is indeed significant that most poststructuralist readers of Beckett, concerned with the serious questions of the deconstruction of meta-narrative, the appearance of linguistic uncertainty or the construction of an unstable and reflexive self, avoid much extended discussion of Beckett's comedy. If an exception is required to prove a rule, Carla Locatelli's early poststructuralist study of Beckett, *Unwording the World* (1990), precisely engages with the question of whether humour and certain forms of philosophical antihumanism can be thought together in terms other than as simple antitheses. She declines to read Beckett's humour as an illumination of the tragic heroism of the human condition; rather, the tenacious trace of the comic that remains when all other affect has waned beyond any certain recognition functions as a critique of the authority of those meta-narratives that continue to rattle within an almost corpsed humanism. Locatelli rescues the humour within a poststructuralist account of Beckett's work by emphasising the deconstruction of hierarchies of value that seem immanent within various form of the comic. As suggestive as this reading is, though, Locatelli's study never seems quite to come to terms with the idiom of Beckett's humour that Ricks so effectively illuminates nor, more specifically, with why Beckett's deconstruction of meta-narrative should be affectively funny rather than simply paradoxical.

In the 1990s, however, it became clear that a significant strand of deconstructive literary criticism had begun to weary of appearing to reproduce a mode of reading that focused upon the textual games that are the explicit target of Ricks's critique – games that seemed to suggest an ethical relativism and a coded political retreat. As a response to the putative ahistorical formalism and resistance to questions of value found within deconstructive literary theory, a new generation of critics worked to illuminate how Derrida's long-standing and insistent engagement with the philosophy of Emmanuel Levinas could been seen as a resource for developing a reading practice informed by, and in some way demonstrative of, the necessity of certain ethical obligations.[3] Although many critics remained suspicious of this most glacial enclave of 'high' theory, seeing it as a form of linguistic idealism or complacent scepticism that froze out questions of value and thus of the ethical in its critique of the metaphysical foundations upon which such terms are based, philosopher-critics like Simon Critchley, among others, worked to retrieve deconstruction from its implication in seemingly disinterested forms of gaming and play by suggesting that 'an ethical moment is essential to deconstructive reading and that ethics is the goal, or horizon, towards which Derrida's work tends' (1999b: 2).

The return to ethics in deconstructive literary practice that ensued, to questions of value and to the relationship between selves and others, seemed, in one sense, like a stepping away from a formalism that had become lodged in the theory and the returning of literature to its multiple contexts. It was also a mode of analysis that required a much stronger acknowledgement of deconstruction's own family history, and the ways in which it was drawn from a postwar and, more specifically, a post-Holocaust historical context in which models of humanism, accounts of subjectivity, and even Enlightenment knowledge itself, had seemingly become philosophically implicated in atrocities they had not only been powerless to prevent, but they had actually seemed to abet. Shane Weller crisply describes the mode that traces a strong genetic link between various postwar philosophical antihumanisms as 'the attempt to think a saving alterity' (2006: 2). Whether the culprit is Enlightenment knowledge or phallocentrism, thought is insistently revealed to be logocentric, something that seems compelled to turn all alterity, through a transformative violence, into an object of knowledge, forcing a distorting presence onto things that should be allowed to persist in their temporal particularity and difference – in their multiplicity and otherness. The work of Levinas, Blanchot, Deleuze, Derrida and Lyotard, but also those philosophies of Kristeva and Irigaray informed by Lacanian psychoanalysis, can indeed all be seen, in necessarily distinctive ways, as fundamentally concerned with excavating modes of thought in which forms of otherness can hesitantly appear. This genetic connection can also be extended to Theodor Adorno who, more explicitly than any of the others but coming from a rather different intellectual context, relates the seeming violence within Enlightenment knowledge and philosophy to the historical event of the Holocaust in which the demand to respect alterity and the call to allow otherness to exist in and for itself had found its most systematised abrogation. But it is significant to note that it is Beckett's work that, for Adorno, opens up a mode in which the difference of the world can be preserved in the face of systems of thought and economics that would seek to reduce everything to sameness. Although, as we shall see, Adorno has a specific philosophy of art that enables a glimpse of a world in which otherness could be allowed to inhere, very many of these thinkers turn to language, and even to literature, sometimes even specifically to Beckett, as a place where alterity might find its minimal conditions of shelter.

Over the last two decades, it has been the thought of Levinas that has proved most influential on the attempt within literary studies to consider the potential of aesthetic texts to create spaces and non-violent economies in which otherness could be solicitously preserved. There have been a number of cogent and persuasive accounts of the ways in which Levinas's philosophy and Derrida's ethics of deconstruction that he draws from Levinas can be applied to literature (despite the former's devastating suspicion of the literary and the rhetorical); it therefore seems unnecessary to rehearse the argument again here.[4] But it does make sense briefly to summarise the structure of Levinasian ethics and to indicate the ways in which the demands and duties illuminated by that philosophical project have found a voice within Beckett studies.

In a manner somewhat similar to Heidegger's retrieval and reposing of the forgotten question of being in order to illuminate a fundamental ontology (1962: 21–35), Levinas seeks to render explicit an elided yet fundamental ethical structure that underpins human experience and subjectivity. But where most philosophical systems ask ontological or epistemological questions of the subject – questions concerning its place within and relation to the world and its ability to know or to judge – Levinas uses the relationship between the subject and an other as a way of calling into question the *res cogitans* and its acts. He suggests that before the self is an ego, an intentional consciousness, it is sentient, affective and effected – in other words it exists in relation to others. In this sense the relationship with another human being precedes Heidegger's project of fundamental ontology. Ethics does not come second, as a task for the self to choose, as it does for Heidegger; rather, ethics is first philosophy. As John D. Caputo puts it in his insistent refrain, 'obligation happens' (1993: 6, 24, 192). Levinas explicitly critiques the self that would seek to reduce all otherness, everything that is outside of itself, to its own project and self-presence, to the Same, and affirms: '[w]e name this calling into question of my spontaneity by the presence of the Other ethics' (Levinas 1969: 43). This spontaneous self always risks losing sight of the other, or of seeing the other too clearly and turning it into the object of its powerful, representing gaze; but the relation with the other precedes and thus cannot be reduced to such comprehension. Levinas's magnum opus, *Totality and Infinity* (first published in 1961), consists of a description of how the self and its 'joyous possession of the world' (1969: 75–6) is precisely put into question by the presence of the other. For the other is close to the self, but its proximity can never be collapsed into absolute identity. In the small difference between self and other, there is an infinite distance. As Critchley puts it, 'I *face* the other and keep my distance, for distance implies respect' (1999b: 286). Perhaps most significantly for the argument to be advanced here, Levinas explicitly states that the ethical relationship with the other is not simply to be found within the time that a relationship between self and other takes; rather, the relationship between self and other is the very ground upon which temporality grows. 'Is not sociality something more than the source of our representation of time: is it not time itself?' (1988: 93), he demands.

One of the reasons why this work seems so paradoxically suggestive for literary studies is that, for Levinas, 'the *relation* between the same and the other . . . is language' (1969: 39). 'Not every discourse is a relation with exteriority' (Levinas 1969: 70), however. Levinas's linguistic ethical relation is a 'conversation', seemingly a form of phatic communication that says little other than 'Bonjour' or 'après vous, monsieur'. Rhetoric or the manipulation of language for effect, even the specific content of the conversation, 'consists in corrupting this freedom' (Levinas 1969: 70), though – reducing the temporal addressivity of language to the abstractable presence of content. In one sense, then, the form of language or conversation is always being contaminated by a content that binds the conversation within the language of ontology. Levinas's later work, *Otherwise than Being, or Beyond Essence* (first published in 1974), concentrates on precisely this problematic distinction between what might provisionally be called the form and content of ethical language, the Saying and the Said, as he effects what Critchley describes as a 'linguistic or deconstructive turn' (1999b: 8). As Jill Robbins explains:

> Ethical language is described . . . in terms of the operative distinction between the Saying and the Said, which corresponds roughly to the kind of speech that foregrounds the relation to its addressee, and a denotative speaking that absorbs alterity into thematization. (1999: xiv)

The ethical relation is described by Levinas in this later work in terms of trauma, wound, of being held hostage, persecuted and subjected to the call of responsibility, but the terms he uses to trace out this relation always risk being turned into 'being' or 'essence' in the language of philosophy, as their Saying becomes the Said. Levinas thus attempts to describe ethics through a language that stutters, repeats, disrupts and interrupts itself, as 'a saying that must also be unsaid in order thus to extract the *otherwise than being* from the said' (1998: 7). The effect of this stuttering uncertainty is, in Critchley's terms, 'a performative disruption of the language of ontology, which maintains the interruption of the ethical Saying within the ontological Said' (1999b: 8). As a 'performative enactment of ethical writing' (Critchley 1999b: 7) that is a deconstruction of ontology rather than its transcendence, *Otherwise than Being* seems to describe and enact what Caputo terms a powerful 'poetics of obligation' (1993: 79).

Now this ethical turn within deconstruction seemed to offer much to Beckett studies, as Beckett's stuttering texts continue to suggest uncertain yet serious demands upon the textual subject, audience and reader, even as all seems subject to deconstruction. It offered, in particular, a way of thinking about language as informed and determined by particular obligations. In Beckett's work, words may 'indicate the very impossibility of moving beyond language', as Linda Ben-Zvi has it (1980: 188), but there is no complacent shrug to be found, no retreat into the comforting space of a linguistic idealism, free from external and internal demands, compulsions and shudders of painful and pleasurable experience. Anthony Uhlmann, using the Levinas of *Totality and Infinity*, indeed describes how the problems of saying 'I' that insist in *The Unnamable* at once enact a relationship of non-violence or 'justice' – 'the infinite relation between the same and the other in Levinas' – and the violence or 'injustice' that inheres within language and representation – 'the infinite non-relation, or failure to relate, between a shadowy same and an equally shadowy other in Beckett' (1999: 165). Another articulation of the possible relationship between Levinas, language and Beckett is Ewa Płonowska Ziarek's reading of *How It Is*. She describes how the tortured space of *How It Is* enacts the 'nightmarish aspect of communication' (1996: 180) as the other is violently constituted by language and even subject to mathematical calculation. In a powerful unravelling of the optimism of 'communicative reason' (Ziarek 1996: 180) and the promise of a rational linguistic community described by Jürgen Habermas, she nevertheless articulates the text's insistence on the 'impossibility of *eliminating otherness* completely' (192). The text thus performs a relationship between self and other that is one of irreducible difference and distance 'that is not resolved in the production of *sensus communis*' (193). A few years later, and this time using Levinas's distinction between the Saying and the Said, Andrew Gibson illuminates an ethical interruption of the totalising language of ontology that finds an apogee, of sorts, in Beckett. Concentrating on Beckett's late trilogy of *Company, Ill Seen Ill Said* and *Worstward Ho*, he finds an enactment of an ethical Saying in which '"saying about" repeatedly reveals itself as a "saying to"' (Gibson 1999: 143). In these texts, he discovers a persistent addressivity and an explicit desire to unsay or at least leave the scene 'half-said, to let [it] be in some dim hinterland where [it] is not brought to full presence and seen and articulated with clarity' (144). For Gibson, this temporal rhythm of ill-saying disarticulates the violence within representation, allowing otherness to persist, at least temporarily, in and as itself.

But none of these readings is particularly suggestive of the humour that reverberates within Beckett's work, from the early sarcastic short stories to the groaning pun of the almost final *Worstward Ho* (1980–1). Of course, there is little that is comic, either in form or effect, about Levinas's ethical obligation and the experience of trauma, of being held hostage, which cuts through and dislocates the self rather than confirms its plenitude. In his early 'Is Ontology Fundamental?' (1951), Levinas does find a potential for comedy in the way the intentions of the self will necessarily be interrupted by the facticity, the otherness, of the body and its material environment that cannot be subsumed into intention or comprehension. But such comedy is always shuddering towards the affect of the tragic, even as the interruption of the subject's self-possession is the ground for ethics:

> The comedy begins with the simplest of our movements, each of which carries with it an inevitable awkwardness. In putting my hand out to approach a chair, I have creased the sleeve of my jacket. I have scratched the floor, I have dropped the ash from my cigarette. In doing that which I wanted to do I have done so many other things I did not want. The act has not been pure, for I have left some traces . . . Sherlock Holmes will apply his science to the irreducible coarseness of each of my initiatives and thereby, the comedy may well turn tragic. When the awkwardness of the act turns against the goal pursued, we are at the height of tragedy. (Levinas 1996: 4)

Comedy may point towards the ground of the ethical, but Levinas's post-Holocaust demand that otherness be preserved is hardly funny, and it seems, at first glance, very far indeed from the robust and often libidinal forces mobilised in Beckett's joking – forces that cluster as much around drive as any clearly articulated ethical obligation. Locatelli's early and brief attempt to effect a rapprochement between Beckett and Levinas suggests that Beckett's epistemological deconstruction of 'logocentrism' is broadly 'congruent' with an ethics that would seek to return the Said to the Saying; but she remains silent as to how such a Saying, or 'unwording' (in her terms), relates to her earlier assertion that the 'comic in Beckett is the locus of doubtful discourse . . .the arch-enemy of logocentrism' (1990: 31). Because Locatelli does not address the question of how humour is constructed to be affective it becomes hard to know why the process of 'unwording' in Beckett's work should be, at one moment, an occasion of trauma and wounding, while offering comic pleasure at another. One of the questions this book will ask is whether the insistence of the comic in Beckett's work might use its own seizure of time to articulate and act out a compulsive fear of representational violence, while simultaneously exploring forms of writing that offer a sufficiently resistant shape that otherness might be preserved. But it will also attempt to think through the affective structure of the comic. And if, for Levinas, the human subject is affective and affected, traversed by the temporality of its relationship to an other before it is a thinking ego, just as for Adorno, as we will later see, the world is populated with material bodies and objects that cannot simply be abstracted into ideas, this study will ask whether the temporal, peculiarly passing, experience of the comic that Beckett's work elicits can be related to a historically specific hope for an ethics of the aesthetic.

Fun and Trembling

Laughter and amusement are one of the psychological and physiological givens of the human. Apart from those who have suffered specific kinds of neurological damage, all humans laugh and amuse themselves. Despite the clear fact that humour is profoundly cultural and jokes remain notoriously resistant to translation, the universality of human laughter suggests it might be important to define and explore what elements remain common to the formal and affective qualities of humour and the comic. I am not going to assert a firm difference between humour and comedy; instead, it is perhaps sufficient to state that the topics under investigation are those forms within Beckett's work that create amusing effects and the affective structures produced when readers or audiences find a particular form funny.

Comedy demands variety and innovation, for defeated expectation is one of the most significant formal elements within the production of humour. But if there are no truly new jokes, just old jokes subject to makeovers with more or less successful results, there might be an underlying formula with which most comic instances agree. John Morreall has drawn attention to the consistently narrow theoretical modelling that has underpinned the philosophy of laughter and humour, suggesting that there have been only three explanations offered for the production of humorous effects: the Superiority Theory, the Relief Theory and the Incongruity Theory (1987: 5–6). The majority of philosophical considerations of humour have been dominated by one model only, however – the Superiority Theory that maintains that laughter is usually directed at someone with a derisive or scornful intent. People who speak inappropriately or without measure, those who act in a way that is out of step with their social position or their status as human beings, are laughable. Even if we laugh at ourselves, it is with a sense of superiority over our own previous position. Although the idea of laughter as an expression of malice or irrationality is there in the work of Plato and Aristotle, it is Hobbes who, in 1651, offers the Superiority Theory its moment of condensation, stating that laughter is the effect of a feeling of 'sudden glory arising from some conception of eminence in ourselves, by comparison with the infirmity of others, or with our own formerly' (1839: 46). Although there is no explanation why such infirmity should produce humour or indeed why its production should be so erratic, it is this morally stinging account of laughter as aggressive that serves to explain the persistent neglect of the comic as a philosophical topic until the mid-eighteenth century.

The Relief Theory suggests, however, that amusement appears due to a kind of physiological hydraulics in which laughter becomes 'the venting of excess nervous energy' (Moreall 1987: 6), and is most famously explicated by Sigmund Freud in *Jokes and Their Relation to the Unconscious* (1905). There, he suggests that jokes short-circuit the necessary for the modification and repression of sexual and dominating instincts in the subject who is to function in society;[5] consequently, the energy that would have been spent on this repression is momentarily liberated and discharged as laughter, with the *'yield of pleasure correspond[ing] to the psychical expenditure* [on inhibition] *that is saved'* (Freud 1905: 117). But although Freud borrows elements from both the Superiority and the Incongruity theories to describe jokes as constructions, he is finally more concerned with the effects within the psyche that cause such amusement, and thus with the subjective experience of the comic, rather than the structure or form of jokes.

This is to get ahead of things, though, in terms of tracing a history of the comic. For in 1725, the philosopher Frances Hutcheson was explicitly to critique Hobbes's aggressive and self-aggrandising model, thus fashioning the beginnings of an Incongruity Theory of humour that aimed at socialising laughter and seems closest to capturing the essential features of comic form:

> the cause of laughter is the bringing together of images which have contrary additional ideas, as well as some resemblance in the principal idea: this contrast between ideas of grandeur, dignity, sanctity, perfection and ideas of meanness, baseness, profanity, seems to be the very spirit of burlesque; and the greatest part of our raillery and jest is founded upon it. (1994: 53)

Although much comedy is still based upon social inequalities, here Hutcheson's shifting of attention from the self-assertion of ridicule to the perception of the aesthetically incongruous and defeated expectation marks an important point in the philosophical rehabilitation of laughter; indeed, Kant, Schopenhauer and Kierkegaard will all go on to posit their own Incongruity theories of humour. The bodily and psychological pleasures of laughter may always be accompanied by an exercising of power but, Hutcheson states, such power need not be ultimately totalitarian: 'Ridicule, like other edged tools, may do good in a wise man's hands, though fools may cut their fingers on it, or be injurious to a unwary bystander' (1994: 61). Hutcheson reminds his reader, however, even as he aestheticises humour, that it is pre-eminently a social affair and thus subject to questions of ethics. But instead of finding an inherent irresponsibility or even irrationality in the impulse to laugh, he reads the responsible use of humour as an integral part of rational social relations.

So Hutcheson's work on humour marks the end of the totalitarian domination of the Superiority Theory in its formalist account of incongruity; significantly, though, it is not an obviation of the rule of power or the necessity of an ethical response to its expression. In their aesthetic theories of comic incongruity, however, Kant and Schopenhauer mask the effects of power in laughter. It is indeed remarkable that these accounts of incongruity, where there is, as Schopenhauer puts it, a 'paradoxical and unexpected subsumption of an object under a conception that is in other respects heterogeneous to it' (1966: 91), so frequently have recourse to racist jokes in their attempts to illustrate what is supposedly a purely formal aesthetic theory. Kant's 1790 joke of defeated expectation rather than superiority runs thus:

> Suppose someone tells us this story: An Indian at an Englishman's table in Surat saw a bottle of ale being opened, and all the beer, turned to froth, rushing out. The Indian, by repeated exclamations, showed his great amazement. – Well, what's so amazing in that? asked the Englishman. – Oh, but I'm not amazed at its coming out, replied the Indian, but at how you managed to get it all in. (1987: 203)

For modern eyes it is difficult to see such a joke as working through the actions of incongruity at all, as the choice of Englishman and Indian as protagonists seems politically charged in the most explicit fashion.[6] But maybe perceptions of superiority and incongruity are never all that distinct. An extreme example of the way incongruity can slide into the most pernicious assertions of superiority can be found in the remarkable development of the Ku Klux Klan. Having started out as a rambunctious drinking club of ex-Confederate troopers who played 'spooky' gags on all their neighbours, they progressed to 'scaring' newly freed slaves by playing practical jokes such as offering a hand to shake and then riding away leaving what turned out to be a false arm in the other's grasp (Wade 1987: 32–7). That they then moved on to the most extreme abuses of power is well known, but what is both striking and suggestive is how choosing a target for joking and playing with incongruity can lead so seamlessly to the assertion of the butt of the joke as a truly degraded other.

There is something important and potentially critically valuable about the ways in which, under analysis, the distinctions between the Superiority Theory and the Incongruity Theory begin to lose their clarity. For while incongruity marks an occasion and action of power because it is based on notions of value (one can only assert a lack of fit if one understands what it means for something to fit 'properly', thus asking the question who or what decides such propriety), all superiority and attempts to wield power through humour are, I would suggest, simultaneously based upon a certain perception of incongruity and defeated expectation, in other words upon a loss of absolute power. Humour might be, then, the location where power ineluctably asserts itself, but where it also submits to loss.

As a site where relationships of power are negotiated, humour and the comic describe a necessarily social space. In *Comedy: The Mastery of Discourse*, Susan Purdie (1993) presents a usefully demystifying account of humour that negotiates the questions of power hinted at above by marrying the Freudian insistence upon humour and joking as a social occasion to Lacanian models of the construction of subjectivity that appear through language use. Joking utterances, as she terms them, are discursive acts that occur in a moment of exchange between a Teller and an Audience. Importantly for Purdie's argument, all joking involves a discursive exchange in which the capacity to use language and to claim its power is negotiated. Purdie asserts, following Freud, that the pleasure of funniness comes from breaking the rules of propriety and the law; but she notes that there seems to be more at stake in joking than simply the expression of high spirits, for joking remains such an integral and valued part of common social discourse. Instead of marking a peripheral moment to the social scene, she suggests instead that laughter and joking negotiate a fundamental use and exchange of power where the capacity to define and assert subjectivity is both restated and risked.

The fundamental law that is transgressed during any joking utterance, Purdie argues, is that which defines the 'proper' use of language. Using Saussure's suggestion that the bond between signifier (the sound/image) and signified (the concept/idea) is determined by convention rather than intrinsic, she explains that in any linguistic act one signifier need not, necessarily, be clipped, singly, to one signified. Of course, the operation of making sense limits this potential or play within language, ensuring that, on many occasions, one signifier is seen to generate just a single set of meanings. But it is just this sense-making rule, Purdie states, that is broken in those 'aberrant' uses of language such as poetry and joking that encourage and manipulate the multiple generation of signifiers/signifieds. As Lacan indeed confirms in *Seminar IV*, '[i]n playing with the signifier man brings into question, at any moment, his world, all the way to its very roots. The value of the joke . . . is its possibility to play on the fundamental non-sense of all usage of sense' (Lacan 1994: 294; quoted in and trans. Zupančič 2008: 142). What makes joking funny rather than simply troubling, however, is the possibility of retrieving an instant of sense from such moments through a marking of the law in the act of transgression. Purdie indeed warns that 'unless this excess generation is then recuperated in some way, all "meaning" threatens to disappear' (1993: 21). Because joking is recognised by an other (an audience) as a conscious and temporary manipulation of language rather than an unconscious and aberrant transgression of the law, it asserts a Teller's capacity both to break and to recognise the fundamental rules of language and communication.

What remains so useful about Purdie's account of the construction of humour is her careful deconstruction of the discrete integrity of the Superiority and Incongruity theories. By noting that the transgression of the rule of language is simultaneously its marking, its reinstatement as meaningful, and an assertion of the Teller and Audience's ability to use the law (in)appropriately, there is a reinsertion of issues of power into even the most putatively formal expressions of incongruity. And if, as Lacan suggests, subjectivity's place in the Symbolic Order is determined by the ability to use language appropriately, to exchange meaning effectively and thus be confirmed in its correct use of language by an other, then it is subjectivity itself, the possibility of being counted as a meaningful human being, that is at stake within such incongruity. Equally, though, Purdie's reworking of the Superiority Theory, where the butt of a joke is a 'misuser' of language or unable to engage appropriately in discursive social exchange, crucially serves, by implication, to evacuate absolute power from such expression of superiority. Purdie indeed suggests that situations involving either absolute power or absolute degradation are not funny, perhaps because they cannot be understood as working within a social economy of exchange at all. Only the butt who somehow has the potential to threaten one's position is worth degrading, for we must be able to seize the power they lose. Similarly, there is little possibility of degrading a truly fearful, absolutely powerful figure. The laughter of a slave at his/her master can only occur as their unquestionable authority undergoes slippage and the master is coded, at least momentarily, as illegitimately possessing and ineptly wielding their power.

Perhaps, though, comedy determines and demands a far more radical trembling of power than Purdie's assertion that a degraded butt is never totally powerless requires. She suggests that in competent linguistic exchange we swap the capacity to construct each other's identity as meaningful, whereas in inept exchange, represented by the butt of the joke, it is precisely the claim to full subjectivity that is most sharply at stake. In Purdie's account, although comedy '*confirms* (rather than suppressing or opposing) our dependence on Symbolic observance and the interpersonality which that implies . . . in creating us as masters of discourse, it removes the subservience from our subjection' (1993: 107). This may well be so, but Purdie's claims of mastery are somewhat premature. By reading joking as a social occasion, any mastery is always threatened by the possibility that the other may mistakenly or purposefully withhold the laugh that confirms the joker as someone who can mean and be a subject within the Symbolic Order. As Wittgenstein puts it:

> What is it like for people not to have the same sense of humour? They do not react properly to each other. It's as though there were a custom amongst certain people for one person to throw another a ball which he is supposed to catch and throw back; but some people, instead of throwing it back, put it in their pocket. (1980: 83)

Telling a joke always puts the Teller at risk of having the terms of his or her game refused. But, more fundamentally, recognition by the other does not lead to any easy coming into presence within Lacan's model of subjectivity. It is here that Purdie's account of the recognition by the other as it receives the teller's joke and the reconstruction of the subject as the 'master of discourse' is simply inattentive to the ways in which the relationship between self and other is incongruous and menaced by misrecognition and lack within Lacan's system. There is a desire for full presence, but that is precisely what the other can never give. As the self opens itself to the other, the very possibility that such recognition would offer anything more than a trembling, transient, stability seems questionable.[7] The anxious repetition that joking demands in the social scene, the insistent and paranoid demand for recognition by the other again and again, indeed reveals the impossible fragility of such 'mastery'.

It is clear, then, that comedy is a powerfully informed structure, in that its formal relationships of incongruity or asymmetry are always being constructed, traversed and deformed over time by questions of power. A comic performer might make a pun or exploit a moment of linguistic instability; a clown might unexpectedly slip over or fall through a paper wall that had seemed solid; but even reduced to its barest formalism, comedy only pierces and punctures expectation as it transgresses limits of propriety, whether they are social, sexual, physical or linguistic. But, as Purdie has argued, comedy does not shatter the power that informs and constructs the limits of congruity; indeed, the comic seems both to advertise and to make pleasurable the use of something that is always implicit within any act of transgression. As Michel Foucault has powerfully demonstrated, the transgression of a limit can never be an assertion of absolute freedom from the restrictions of enclosure: 'The limit and transgression depend on each other for whatever being they possess: a limit could not exist if it were absolutely uncrossable and, reciprocally, transgression would be pointless if it merely crossed a limit composed of illusions and shadows' (1980: 34).

Now this movement of transgression and marking, unbinding and binding of the law or the limit, is rendered particularly explicit within the realm of humour. The transgressive pleasure experienced within the comic would never be felt if the limit was absolutely impermeable; but equally, there would be no frisson, no pleasure to be gained from stepping outside of the law if that law was not felt, at least momentarily, to be constrictively real. Comedy distorts the limits of propriety and expectation, but because this transgression can only be felt and experienced if those limits are held to be effective and affective, they are implicitly (if not permanently) reinstated. Indeed, perhaps comic transgressions are pleasurable rather than terrifying or abysmal because this overstepping of the limit is usually recognised to be contingent – passing. Carnival turns the world on its head, proving that the power of that order is never total, but because its rule-breaking antics are marked as temporary inversions, hierarchical limits are deformed but are not broken. Neither a space of absolute freedom from the law nor of binding restriction, then, comedy both shatters and preserves the limit by its temporal action of crossing and recrossing – it simultaneously confounds and confirms. As Beckett himself put it in a lecture on Racine and Molière given at Trinity College Dublin and transcribed by Rachel Burrows in 1930–1: 'Comic spirit: oscillation between equilibrium and lack of it' (Le Juez 2008: 66). Within such comic play, conventions and expectations become like a skipping rope that is jumped over but whose encircling climate cannot be left as long as play persists. The limit is not strong enough to resist the deforming impact of the comic transgression, but it is not sufficiently weak to shatter upon contact; instead, the comic could be thought of as a force and a form that might make that threshold reverberate and tremble.

The quivering of this membrane or limit within comedy indicates the action of a conflictual form that pits the inside – the space of conservation and conservatism – against the deforming impact of the outside – the radical break that threatens to shatter these confining conditions. And at the point at which these opposites meet and determine but do not completely outstrip one another, these forces cause an event of trembling. Neither force nor form has sufficient mastery to have victory over its other; neither is weak enough to cede to its opposite. Trembling thus could be seen as the physical manifestation of forces that are acting in opposition, but whose movements are held in the same space. Imagine a two pence piece that has been sent spinning on a table. While it is replete with rotational force, the coin is seen to resist the force of gravity and the action of friction that would seek to return it to a flat, still condition. But as that rotational force begins to fall away due to the interference of friction and gravity, there is a moment before the coin drops when it is held in a trembling oscillation. The rotational force is no longer strong enough to transcend this interference, but it is not yet weak enough to relinquish its revolutions completely. This moment of trembling indicates a lack of coincidence between force and form, movement and matter that cannot be brought into balance by either the victory of strength over weakness or of a coincidence of contraries. Trembling fades out as conflictual forces become equivalent; it gathers strength as a lack of coincidence within its conflictual form grows (although if this disequilibrium becomes too great, if strength is victorious over weakness or vice versa, trembling will also disappear). Trembling may look as if it is dialectical, but there can be no synthesis, no victory for either side, no transcendence of the temporal motion, if it is to remain as trembling.

Of course the joke or the comic instant would seem to be slightly more stable, a little less susceptible to oscillations and vicissitudes, than the movement of tremor; it is a transgression always to be followed by a marking. Secure comedy is, after all, precipitated by a moment of understanding, as if it has, momentarily, lifted up its materials and bound them under a higher comic principle of congruity. But, as we have seen, the joke or the comic moment always risks the possibility of misrecognition, of dissolving back into unmarked incongruity – an incongruity that is pre-comic, although also comedy's very possibility. Comedy never fully transcends incongruity, dialectically, as it were, for the movement of transgression requires the resistance of powerfully informed asymmetries in order for it to be experienced as such. But if good or securely tendentious jokes work to still the reverberations of uncertainty and incongruity, I would suggest that one tunes into Beckett's jokes and comedy at a different kind of frequency. Instead of representing moments that mask the instability immanent within their construction, Beckett's comedy seems to advertise failure and uncertainty. The work is indeed replete with jokes or comic moments that couldn't properly be called witty – jokes which hold back from the instant of the comic payoff but are bound to the quivering temporality of the almost. And the aesthetic significance of the off-colour joke, the joke that is subject to interference and seems to be approaching funniness – for these jokes are not simply unfunny – but stumbles before achieving it, or falls through a trapdoor at the other end, is considerable for Beckett. As Walter Redfern notes of the early texts, 'it is perversely logical that a writer boasting that he specialised in failure should home in on failed jokes' (1998: 102). These comic instants are perhaps not quite 'failed'; rather, they are failing, subject to a gathering of terms that almost ends up in wit but never quite achieves that momentary, specious certainty.

'That's not moving, that's *moving*'

Let's go back to Beckett. Here is a joke the eponymous Murphy tells to Celia:

> 'Why did the barmaid champagne?' he said.
> 'Do you give it up?'
> 'Yes,' said Celia. 'Because the stout porter bitter.' (Beckett 1993: 81)

This is not a great joke; in fact it is rather far from even being a good one. Certainly Celia is not very taken with it, but Murphy finds humour there:

> It amused Murphy, that was all that mattered. He always found it most funny, more than most funny, clonic . . . He staggered about on the floor in his bare feet, one time amateur theological student's shirt, dicky and lemon bow, overcome by the toxins of the simplest little joke . . . The fit was so much more like one of epilepsy than of laughter that Celia felt alarm. (Beckett 1993: 81)

He finds himself in fits – in the 'clonic' spasms of disorganised muscular contractions. Despite the fact that this joke doesn't really work, for why would the barmaid need to sham pain if she really had been bitten, Murphy finds himself moved by the comic business. And his overwrought and somewhat incongruous reaction rather rescues the humour for the reader, whose initial response is more likely to resemble Celia's than Murphy's; it becomes amusing that this slight form causes Murphy to be rendered so explicitly beside himself. Although there may be little levity in the joke, and it may go down like a lead balloon, some humour can be salvaged from the unexpectedly exaggerated reaction. Beckett shows that a lead balloon, at least on one level, might be thought of as a mechanism that goes down well.

The clonic effect of the bad joke is not straightforward, however, for any laughter at Murphy's laughter is not given much space to resound. Within the reader, the comic effect quickly fades and fails, just as Murphy soon comes to the sense that his laughter 'was unnecessary, the fit was over, gloom took its place' (Beckett 1993: 81). If the orthodoxy of humanist readings of Beckett's humour suggests that if it is not a cure for the human condition it is at least a tonic,[8] a clonic effect is rather different. A clonic contraction is, after all, the antithesis of those continuous and organised spasms that attach to a physiological definition of the tonic. Clonic laughter indeed suggests an effect that is far more unpredictable and a way of being moved that does not necessarily bolster the ability of the self to mark transgression from its own still centre. This book will go on to argue that, in numerous configurations, the comic instants in Beckett's work precisely oscillate between an overdetermination and underdetermination of elements, rendering comedy and affect threateningly uncertain. As such, it will suggest that it is the passing effect of clonic laughter, rather than the production of anything tonic, that describes the compulsive compact between strength and weakness, between a failure that is never quite achieved and a success that is never fully sustained, that the texts are concerned to explore and evoke.

As Murphy's 'clonic' reaction shows, the comic, like the movements of trembling or shaking that seem to describe its formal qualities, is persistently affective: it is described by a form of movement that is itself moving. Just as non-pathological physiological trembling and quivering are instances where feeling (fear, anticipation, pleasure) finds itself inscribed on or in the body as movement, the comic might also be thought of as a space where form and feeling are necessarily brought together. For comedy to be said to exist within a text at all, someone must find themselves moved. The reaction from a reader or an audience might not be quite like Murphy's; nevertheless, as formal incongruities undercut, displace and reconfigure the expected movements within language or physical actions to produce comedy, audiences and readers also might find themselves moved in unexpected and unpredictable ways. Although it seems as if there is an elision in the argument in the suggestive symmetry between form and affect, the comic cannot be said to exist without the effect to which it lends its movements; amused laughter is an effect that necessarily takes the shaken form of the engine that drives it. The comic is an instance of trembling in which form and feeling come to resemble each other, to fall into each other's rhythms, through a reverberative contagion.

So the comic emerges as a space in which the feeling of form and the form of feeling are brought into a chiasmus, but it is also a space where thought and feeling become implicated with one another. For the feeling of amusement and physiological comic affect, as we have seen, both depend upon a certain moment of comprehension. As Jonathan Miller sees it: '[comic] laughing matter is cognitive; we have to understand the situation before we can be tickled into laughter, or embarrassed into blushing' (1987: 7). Despite the necessity of this comprehension, though, laughter remains under weak conscious control; it does not necessarily submit itself to the intentional ego. 'Get a hold of yourself', they say, as you find yourself subject to a bout of infectious laughter, laughing your head off. Laughter is an area of the involuntary for we cannot simply laugh when we feel like it and once we have started it can be hard to stop; but it also belongs to the province of will for it can be suppressed.

Now some forms of poststructuralism, particularly the mode of deconstruction practised in literary studies by Paul de Man and his followers, have appeared suspicious of feeling and its imbrications with the category of the aesthetic, despite never quite being able to give up the frissons of affect within the play of textual *jouissance*. As Isobel Armstrong has demonstrated, Derrida's reading of Hegel and De Man's reading of Kant both imply a construction of a category of the aesthetic contaminated by notions of affect and sensation felt by a seemingly unified, self-present, subject. In these readings, the aesthetic becomes

> the last bastion of the private self hubristically conceived as omnipotent creator. The aesthetic harboured and justified the ultimate aggrandizement of the transcendent subject as master of its world. Aesthetic ideology was the 'pure' essence of economic individualism, which it duplicated and endorsed. (2000: 46)

Critics who have taken deconstruction into Beckett studies have also often ceded discussion of affect, with a somewhat raised eyebrow, to those who still wanted to talk about the 'human condition'. An 'existential humanist' approach is certainly still the dominant accent in popular representations of Beckett's work, as it is frequently found to be full of ordinary human feeling that no critical or academic understanding is required to appreciate. As a result, it has been uncommon to find theoretically inflected discussions of feeling and affect within Beckett studies. At the risk of reducing both positions to caricatures, it seems that within Beckett studies deconstruction has not wanted to respond to the realm of feeling, and existential humanism, having already had its aesthetic responses that confirm the dignity of the human subject, has not found it necessary explicitly to critique them.

But are poststructuralism and discourses of feeling and affect really so inimical to one another? Rei Terada has suggested, using the work of De Man and Derrida in a rather different way to Armstrong, that the Enlightenment conception of the coherent subject should not be seen as the guarantor and repository of feeling; rather, emotion can be seen to operate, as it does for Freud, as 'a differential force within experience' (Terada 2001: 9) that effects a deconstruction of that autonomous rational subject. Terada suggestively describes how emotions are configurations of ideas, feelings and sensations that inhabit the marshy hinterland between a Cartesian mind/body dualism. As Ronald de Sousa explains, because emotions are experienced physiologically they 'drag us from our dreams of pure reason', 'yet just as surely they are mental phenomena' (quoted in Terada 2001: 21). Terada articulates further implications of mind and body, suggesting that perhaps one feels and perceives physiological sensation as emotion, rather than simply as affect, only as it is filtered through representation and minimal forms of cognition. For Terada, then, to suggest a rethinking of feeling and emotion is not to hope for a return to unmediated experience, for '[w]e are not ourselves without representations that mediate us, and it is through those representations that emotions get felt . . . [T]he Cartesian would-be subject feels when it represents itself to itself, when it reads its self-representation' (Terada 2001: 21). To analyse emotion, then, in Terada's poststructuralist account, is already to stage a deconstruction of that glib distinction between thought and feeling that Armstrong suggests is required to 'rethink the power of affect, feeling and emotion in a *cognitive* space' (2000: 87), and to bring necessarily subjective literary affect into a newly reconfigured relationship with seemingly objective formal structures. For Armstrong, the fact that feelings 'cross categories, [are] experienced in consciousness and registered by the body, that they belong to the mind and the soma, straddling conscious and unconscious just as they straddle mind and physiology' (108), opens up the aesthetic as a radical place where complex imbrications of cognition and bodily sensation that seem to fly below the radar of sociolinguistic analysis could be delineated and explored.

Terada does not adhere, as Brian Massumi does in 'The Autonomy of Affect', to a strong distinction, drawn initially from psychoanalytic discourse, which represents 'emotion' as something that requires a reasonably coherent subject and 'affect' as something that does not (Massumi 2002: 28). Where Terada explores the complex interference of cognition and sensation within both emotional and affective experience, Massumi suggests that affects are less structured according to conventional ideas of narrative, or goal-directed interpretations of the personal, than those affects that are marked by intensity but exert fewer cognitive pressures and are less likely to be tied to intention and action. By Massumi's analysis, the experiences produced by Beckett's comedy, traced through with sensations of uncertainty, delay, suspension, would perhaps be more affective than emotional. Nevertheless, the cognitive component vital to sensations of humour remains in Beckett's work, suggesting a gathering up of experience into at least a minimal sensation of 'mine', even as the idea of easily catalogued, distinctly filed, sets of emotional experience seems hard to sustain. Beckett's later writing indeed seems particularly obliged to stage, through the interaction of comic form and affect, the compact between organised, directed and intentional aspects of human experience and those compulsive, intense and unintentional elements that drive both individual and social life. To return to a discussion of the affective qualities of Beckett's comedy is not, therefore, to claim that its effects are universal, suggestive of a facile subjective coherence or inattentive to those historical and material conditions which people will experience both cognitively and through embodied sensation (although this book is not a cultural history of the feeling of the comic in relation to specific performances and appearances of Beckett's texts). Rather, it is to say that the texts offer both a space for these diverse mediations to take place and, perhaps, the conditions under which such portions of experience might be materialised and explored.

So, as we shall see, Beckett's comedy – indeed his work as a whole – is concerned with the fact that neither thought, feeling nor sensation are certain; instead, the texts remain obsessed with producing effects as places of passage where both cognition and affect find themselves mapped and moved – rendered beside themselves. But perhaps one of the reasons why comedy inheres in Beckett's work at the very places where its most serious concerns are also staged is precisely because it is always affectively on the move. Comedy has no direct emotional concomitant: it does not always produce joy, and even less frequently the sustained effect of happiness; feelings of triumph or simply a good-willed shrug at the collapse of sense are both equally likely to mark the appearance of comic laughter. And if this shifting quality is part of comedy's nature, then a comedy obsessed with its own passing over will illuminate the shuddering vicissitudes of feeling experience even more clearly. In attempting to map this territory of the passage between such sensations as those of pleasurable mastery, perhaps through meta-feelings like the shame one might feel about such laughter of superiority, through the possibility of a euphoria in seeing meaning and sense set aquiver, towards feelings of disconcertedness and then affective indeterminacy – being confused about what one is feeling, whether it has an object, whether it is active or passive – this book hopes to describe the specificity of Beckett's preservation of certain portions of temporal, passing experience that find themselves rendered grittily resistant as they extrude into consciousness.

Of course, the soliciting of affects which stage a place of passage, an occasion where thought, feeling and sensation fade in and phase out, performs a trembling of categories and resistance to certainty – whether of cognition, feeling or affect – that Beckett's work also suggestively describes. Within many of Beckett's texts, mind and body persistently seem to be comically tripping each other up, producing unexpected collocations of control and its lack in which the thinking ego is suddenly rendered out of step with an interruptive materiality. In *Molloy*, the eponymous narrator's ideas won't settle in the mind but shudder into the body: 'Oh they weren't notions like yours, they were notions like mine, all spasm, sweat and trembling, without an atom of common sense or lucidity' (*T*: 68). At other times it is the body and its movements that offer some semblance of order and control. In *Footfalls*, the voice of a mother asks the slowly pacing daughter: 'Will you never have done . . . revolving it all? . . . It all. In your poor mind' (*CDW*: 400). The little consolation offered is suggested by the ordered movement of matter as it is represented to the body: 'No, Mother, the motion alone is not enough, I must hear the feet, however faint they fall' (401). But these descriptions or representations are never simply formal; they are, instead, always on the way to being something else, as they materialise similarly porous and passing feelings and affects in the bodies and minds of their readers. Between form and feeling, text shades into an experience of texture.

Laughing Matters

Crucially for the argument to be made here, this concern with the materialisation of the shifting quality of affect, the attempt to render explicit the shuttling back and forth between cognition and sensation, mind and body, both within the texts and their reception, never seems fortuitous in Beckett's work. If May '*must* hear the feet', if seeing the old woman in *Ill Seen Ill Said* is held against a strong sense that she must be preserved from such knowledge and approached 'gently', if speaking becomes a reflex in the *Trilogy* as much as an expression of an intending mind, this exploration of the passage of affects that are shaped by cognition and moulded by the demands of the material body is marked by a repeated, compulsive quality – an oddly passionate insistence whose very force represents and evokes an abrasive and displacing excess to rationality. And, I argue, it is this compulsion to undermine the seemingly impervious security of knowledge, thought, intention and will which, though appearing to whisper of universality and the human condition, actually binds Beckett's aesthetic to a particular historical frame. Indeed, it binds Beckett to the intellectual context of a modernity become suspicious of Enlightenment values that had its moment of condensation in the experiences of the Second World War. Beckett's mature work must indeed, I think, be understood as bound to the particularity of postwar thought and its attempts to understand ethics as something that would permit the persistence of forms of otherness and difference in the face of an account of knowledge that seemingly seeks, often violently, to flatten out the material texture of the world. Where Levinas finds an ethics in language's capacity to hold open a non-violent temporal relationship between self and other, and an ethics in the subject's capacity to feel and experience an obligation to the other that precedes knowledge, where Adorno, as we will later see, finds in art the conditions for the preservation of difference in a late capitalist world where everything is exchangeable and seems reduced to the same, Beckett explores through art a suggestively congruent, although much more uncertain, suspicion of the virility and mastery of knowledge which finds its alibi in forms of presence. Beckett's art remains bound by a sense of the concerns at stake within specific versions of ethics emergent at this historical moment; nevertheless, it retains little confidence, knowledge or belief that the work could offer up any graspable ethical position for itself.

Perhaps the most influential recent characterisation of Beckett's comedy has sought precisely to examine its humour alongside an ethics drawn implicitly from Levinas. For Simon Critchley, ethical subjectivity is structured according to a primary relationship with alterity that divides it at its core, and he uses this Levinasian position decisively to redirect humour from violent laughter at the butt of a joke, an other, to a paradigm in which the riven subject acknowledges its structural lack of self-coincidence and is able to see itself and its projects as laughable rather than an expression of its power. Using Freud's 1927 reconfiguration of humour in the light of the second topography of ego, superego and id, Critchley follows Freud's suggestion that while jokes are concerned with 'obtain[ing] a yield of pleasure or plac[ing] the yield of pleasure that has been obtained in the service of aggression' (Freud 1927: 162), humour is *'the contribution made to the comic through the agency of the super-ego'* (164). Where jokes offer the possibility of inflating the ego, humour occurs as a function of a narcissistic splitting into ego and superego. Although Freud usually reads the superego as punishing, in humour the superego is given a positive and consolatory function, for Freud realises that, like a parent, the superego can be both punitive and protective (1927: 165). Instead of finding the ego objectionable, the matured, parental superego acknowledges the 'human condition' (in Critchley's terms), its inability, weakness, inauthenticity and finitude, and finds it ridiculous: it says 'Look! here is the world that seems so dangerous. It is nothing but a game for children – just worth making a jest about!' (Freud 1927: 165). And, for Critchley, such humour that recalls us 'to the modesty and limitedness of the human condition, a limitedness that calls not for tragic affirmation but comic *acknowledgement*, not Promethean authenticity but laughable inauthenticity' (Critchley 2002: 102), finds its epitome in Beckett. In Beckett's humour of inability, interruption, weakness and finitude, Critchley indeed finds a subject able to view itself from that position of fracture and acknowledge the ethical demand that divides it, that sunders it primordially, saving it 'from tragic hybris, from the Promethean fantasy of believing [it]self omnipotent' (2002: 105).

So it is comedy that describes the contours of an ethical subject capable of experiencing itself as formed around whorls of inter- and intra-subjective otherness rather than as powerfully self-identical. For Critchley, it is Beckett's comedy that produces a wry smile rather than hearty, triumphant laughter that is the exemplar of this rehabilitated, ethical, newly humanist humour:

> For me, it is this smile – deriding the having and the not having, the pleasure and the pain, the sublimity and suffering of the human situation – that is the essence of humour . . . Yet, this smile does not bring unhappiness, but rather elevation and liberation, the lucidity of consolation. This is why, melancholy animals that we are, human beings are also the most cheerful. We smile and find ourselves ridiculous. Our wretchedness is our greatness. (Critchley 2002: 111)

Although Cohn's and Critchley's readings are separated by forty years and several incommensurable theoretical paradigms, both end up reading Beckett's comedy as an acknowledgement of the melancholy hopelessness of the 'human condition'; as such, both readings regard Beckett's comedy as ultimately consolatory – an elevation, even a liberation. Comedy is thus not simply an unexpected side effect of Beckett's existential and ontological doctoring; rather, it structures and describes his palliative care. To be sure, where Cohn transforms Beckett's comedy into a model for a wearily contingent humanist heroism, Critchley reads the self constructed by and through Beckett's comedy as inauthentic, split and lacking in redemptive coherence; however, this comedy still functions as a means of sublimation. Elsewhere, Critchley indeed names comedy, and Beckett's comedy in particular, as a 'form of minimal sublimation' (2000: 26), although '[o]ur wretchedness is our greatness' sounds like rather more than what might be called, after Beckett, the 'meremost minimum'. For Critchley, Beckett's comedy may be anti-heroic, but it offers a form of sublimation nevertheless.

This book will suggest, however, that Beckett's comic folding of temporality into textuality is far more diversely affective than Critchley's characterisation implies. As we will go on to see, Beckett's comedy does not function simply as a form of consolation and acceptance. Comedy is always impelled by a mastery, even a certain violence, that drives the form forward, although, in Beckett's work, the comedy of superiority also tends to fall forward onto its sword, stumbling beyond any secure laughing victory. Whatever is heroic, then – whether this is the violence of the laughing inflated ego that we see in Hamm in *Endgame*, or that same character's comic fidelity to the awareness that there is nothing to be done – is always interrupted by further and seemingly incompatible moments of comedy (maybe the comedy of violence or the comedy of failure). In what might be characterised as a trembling rhythm, sublimation is mimed in Beckett's work as the transcendence of different kinds of comedy is offered momentarily, but any easy consolation or precipitate appearance of reconciliation is finally refused by a form concerned with using time to materialise resistance in various complex configurations.

If comedy and trembling are both formal and affective, then, they should be thought of as doing far more to time than simply manifesting themselves within it. As affective structures, both comedy and trembling might be said to perform suggestive operations upon lived time. In one sense, both tremor and certain joking or comic forms can be thought of as profoundly annunciatory. The movements of tremor commonly portend the appearance of an event; they are the physical manifestation of a gathering tension that announces the inevitability of its release. One might think of the quivering that precedes the pleasurable release of a sneeze, or the fearful trembling as the body's muscles are pumped with adrenalin in preparation for fight or flight. Joking and comic forms also require the setting up of oxymoronic contradictions and incongruities, and humans are adept at recognising these scene-setting activities as invitations to the release of comic pleasure that these oscillations portend. As an accelerating race towards the instant of a punchline, to the event of pleasure that these tremors announce as impending, joking and certain comic forms seem concerned with condensation as they force words, elements and gestures that might logically be spatially and temporally distant into a comic commerce with one another. If, as Freud has indicated, the quivers of joking and comedy function as short cuts to the production of pleasure, and if, as others have noted, an accelerating form might contract the perception of duration in the quickened passage to pleasure, then time might really seem to fly when one has fun.

But trembling also seems to bear within itself a contradictory logic of distension and delay. Repetitious movements that seem to be treading water or walking on the spot interfere with the quickened passage of time from one moment to the next that could be measured and marked by change. Those comic forms that seem overdetermined or underdetermined, those forms replete with repetitions, deflections and diversions, despite suggesting tendencies towards brevity and acceleration, might also distend and delay the race towards a punchline. The pleating of time through tremor may seem to contract the surface area of duration, but to be stuck within one of these ripples might be to be held within a seemingly endless gathering and distension of lived time.

To argue that the work displays a formal concern with performing and eliciting certain configurations of comic timing is to place Beckett in dialogue with a philosopher central to a modernist tradition in which temporality and form become vitally interlocked. Alongside many other modernists, Beckett was clearly influenced by the intellectual climate produced by the philosopher Henri Bergson who suggested that Enlightenment knowledge, nineteenth-century Positivism and industrial modernity had laid hands on human time. Bergson's famous description of what it means for the human to exist and persist in *Creative Evolution* (1907) affirms that 'we change without ceasing, and that the state itself is nothing but change' (1911a: 2); however, he suggests that modernity has pressed, flattened out and then cut up the world into blocks of temporality divorced from what he often simply refers to as 'life', or the temporal flow of the *élan vital*. As a consequence, time, which is all too often spatialised and abstracted, becomes something available to be exchanged – just one commodity among others. One response from modernist art was to find in its concern with a form that seemed to have something of its own autonomy, in the conscious manipulation of time both within the structure of texts and their inferred and imagined reception, a mode of re-establishing the specificity and singularity of time and its relationship to the human experience.[9] So alongside other modernists, one might say that Beckett's work becomes increasingly fascinated with what it means to take and experience its own time, rather than simply, unconsciously, to allow it to pass.

Unlike Proust or Woolf, however, Beckett's work does not sit easily with Bergsonism. As a young lecturer at Trinity College, Beckett placed much emphasis on Bergson's famous distinction between 'spatial time' and human 'duration',[10] but his long-standing interest in exploring and materialising negativity, the mechanical and multiple modes of repetition seems to maintain a parodic rather than synchronous relationship with Bergson's vitalism. In *Malone Dies*, for example, the prostrate Macmann hardly submits himself intuitively to the flow of a creative evolution; instead he rises only 'when the élan vital or struggle for life began to prod him in the arse again' (*T*: 243). In *Dream of Fair to Middling Women*, the aesthete and scholar Chas can merely throw his thoughts on Bergson from a moving tram, disseminating nothing but misheard confusion about 'sense', 'intuition', 'reason' and the 'absolute' in the listening, repeating students (Beckett 1996: 212).

The fact that references to Bergson appear in parodic form in Beckett's work is perhaps instructive, though, for the influential philosopher of temporality also wrote a major essay theorising laughter and the comic.[11] Surprisingly, in what first seems like another superiority theory of comedy, Bergson offers no account of comic timing in *Laughter* (or indeed elsewhere), although clearly his suggestion that comedy depends on the appearance of '*[s]omething mechanical encrusted on the living*' (1911b: 37) implies a repetitive stutter in the flow of the *élan vital*. Following Bergson, it might be possible to argue that much of Beckett's comedy is funny simply because it indicates a falling away from 'life' in Bergson's terms – from the timeliness of time – into the mechanical world which is policed and corrected through laughter. And yet, Beckett's comic stutters do take time back into the work, raising the singularity of its passage, sometimes painfully, sometimes pleasurably, to the level of consciousness, both in terms of textual form and aesthetic experience. Indeed, this book will argue not only that Beckett's obsessed return to the question of comic timing is part of the work's profound insistence on taking back its own time that resists a certain idea of the temporal experience of modernity; it will also show how Beckett's work makes clear, in a way that productively illuminates an important and surprising counter-narrative within Bergson's own account of the comic, that what might truly be 'living' – what could truly take its own time – is that which has the capacity to experience its own internal temporal contradictions. A truly resistant 'aliveness' might not be the obverse of the mechanical; what is alive might be that which has the capacity to fall away from itself, comically but also consciously, into the automatic, the habitual. What Beckett's persistent, resistant comic timing might reveal then is that 'life' can never simply exist where and as it is in space; it is never simply reducible to itself.

By paying attention to Beckett's comic timing then, by reading the comic within the trembling and interruptive forms that perform themselves as arrhythmias both within the works and in their profoundly uncertain reception, this book traces out the complex and contrary imperatives that structure Beckett's work and their relation to a rigorous yet riskily uncertain questioning of what might matter, and what might even be called ethical, in the production of literary and theatrical form. In so doing, it hopes to offer an account of the comic that is not simply reduced to something transhistorical or unchangingly formal; instead, it strives to describe and illuminate Beckett's comedy's attention to its own time. As Michael North implies, one reason why Bergson's theory of something mechanical encrusted on the living seems to offer so much to readings of twentieth-century comedy (Beckett's included) is precisely because this theory, and the art it seems to illuminate, are both taken up with a truly complex but historically specific confusion of these categories (2009: 22): 'One of the products that industrial society manufactures . . . is comedy, which it makes out of the imbalanced mixture of the unique and the reproduced, the new and the repetitive, the human and the mechanical' (2009: 23). And in each of these binaries, as they are drawn out in twentieth-century modernity, questions of the relationship between the aesthetic and the ethical also find themselves firmly knotted. This book hopes to demonstrate, then, how the comic in Beckett's work adumbrates a historically specific concern with the production of artistic forms that respond to the conditions of modernity while, at the same time, stubbornly refuse to be reduced to them.

Attending, first of all, to the questions of power that insist within all instances of the comic, Chapter 1 analyses Beckett's early critical work. By reading its ironic wit through sadomasochistic oscillations of power and desire, it suggests an alternative narrative to the one that persists in the criticism that Beckett's comedy was inaugurated with a violence the author went on to reject in the 1930s. It argues, instead, that the appearance of a rather unsuccessful comic violence in Beckett's critical work, which is scarred by a sense of anachronism as the young Beckett cannot put himself in time with where he wants or needs to be, is already suggestive of a structure that disarticulates the powerful, laughing subject as much as it confirms it. A link is thus made between the material and formal failure of this early work, alongside the temporal disjunction it evokes, and the formation of the later Beckett's aesthetic ethics of failure, incompetence and asynchronicity. Chapter 2 concerns itself with Beckett's interest in forms of comic gagging strangely literalised within an abjected economy of vomit and shit in the *Trilogy* – an economy that demands that the artwork submit neither to the rule of aesthetic taste nor to the nourishment of a consuming subject. The words that are produced, taken in, vomited or shat forth, only to be reincorporated, are certainly not savoured as delicacies, nor are they welcomed as wholesome fare; instead, like Krapp's delicious circulation of 'the sour cud and the iron stool. Revelled in the word spool. Spooool!' (*CDW*:

222), words are relished, but they are perversely enjoyed as that which is finally inassimilable, that which resists a logic of consumption and incorporation. The chapter argues that it is just this gagging temporal rhythm, shaped by a compulsive obligation both to represent and refuse the world as it is, that constitutes the contours of both the comical and what might be ethical in Beckett. Gagging, here, becomes a way of materialising *how it is* while offering a resistance that opens up a space for seeing *how it ought to be*.

Chapter 3 analyses the play within comic violence in *Endgame*. Structured through paradox, the play as a whole and the comic instants within it demonstrate the necessary interdependence of laughter as an assertion of mastery with the compulsive evacuation of that power. Comedy indeed becomes a site through which *Endgame* enacts a historically determined concern with games that partake of the temporality of play rather than of any final victory. Chapter 4 is concerned with the ways in which the later fiction, and *Ill Seen Ill Said* in particular, manifests a comedy that becomes both an articulation of violence and solicitude. The stuttering form that 'says' and 'missays' suggests an aesthetic imperative that manifests itself as an ethical obligation. Read through Levinas's concepts of the Saying and the Said and the stutters and temporal interruptions that appear there, the text seems both to perform and deform the possibility of an ethical writing. Chapter 5 begins to ask explicitly how these formal oscillations and tremors might be affective. Concentrating on the 'gags' within the late drama that always seem to be going off, this chapter suggests that such gags affectively reproduce their comic timing as a way of passing the time in which the laughing subject begins to fall out of time with itself. In the persistence of a particular failing comedy, the habituated subject thus begins to yield to an otherness within the self at precisely the moment it might have felt most powerfully in control. And it is within a formulation of an ethics of resistance paradoxically constituted as a habit of persisting, of going on, rather than as an articulation of moral principles or value judgements, that the form of Beckett's comic work traces out a historically specific anxiety of modernity – an anxiety that is suspicious of what it would mean to make ethical claims for art, while remaining aware of how it feels to be claimed by that compulsive necessity.

Notes

1. Parenthetical dates for Beckett's works refer, throughout this book, to the years in which texts were written. I have mostly relied on John Pilling's authoritative *A Samuel Beckett Chronology* (2006).

2. See also Kenner (1962), Esslin (1986) and Kern (1970) for existential humanist readings of Beckett's comedy. One of the earliest critical appraisals of Beckett, following the publication of *Molloy*, is Maurice Nadeau's 1951 essay 'Samuel Beckett: Humor and the Void'. Despite its title, however, there is almost no analysis of Beckett's humour, beyond a suggestion that it is *humour noir* (1965: 35).

3. See, for example, Caputo (1993), Connor (1992), Critchley (1997, 1999b); Cornell (1992), Docherty (1996), Eaglestone (1997), Gibson (1999), Kearney and Dooley (1999) and Taylor (1987).

4. See, in particular, Connor (1992: 190–230), Eaglestone (1997), Gibson (1999), Robbins (1999) and Ziarek (1996). Weller analyses, with revealing specificity, Levinas's understanding of literature, particularly the writing of Maurice Blanchot, as a mode that can explore and sometimes even exemplify the ethical relationship to alterity (2006: 10–14).

5. The principle that modifies the primary instinctual impulses was not termed the reality principle until 1911. In the paper on 'Formulations on the Two Principles of Mental Functioning', the reality principle is opposed to the pleasure principle: 'Just as the pleasure-ego can do nothing but *wish*, work for the yield of pleasure, and avoid unpleasure, so the reality-ego need do nothing but strive for what is *useful* and guard itself against damage' (1911: 222).

6. Schopenhauer's joke also finds incongruity in racial difference (1966: 95). Steven Connor notes: 'It is striking how regularly such dynamics of racial or ethnic power and disadvantage creep into those abstract or aestheticised theories of laughter that began to predominate in the later eighteenth century' (1998a: 7).

7. See Lacan's *The Four Fundamental Concepts of Psychoanalysis* (1998: 203–15).

8. See Pfister (2001).

9. See Mary Ann Gillies (1996: 19–23) for an account of Bergson's theories of art and the relationship between British modernism and Bergson's philosophy.

10. Beckett's awareness of Bergson is explored by Uhlmann (2006: 28–30). A detailed knowledge of Bergson is also confirmed in Le Jucz's account of Burrows's student notes of Beckett's lectures on French Literature in 1930–1 (2008: 35).

11. John Pilling suggests that Beckett had read Bergson's book on laughter by stating that the reference to the 'vaudeville de Labiche' in 'Le concentrisme' 'very probably originates in Beckett's reading of Bergson's *Le Rire*' (1997: 239, n. 22).

Chapter 1

Critical Joking: The Early Prose

Even the first line of *Waiting for Godot* can wring from audiences an uncertain, wan smile. 'Nothing to be done' (*CDW*: 11), Estragon states to Vladimir, wearily. For those who have seen the play before it represents the return to familiar territory; they know this is the first utterance of what will become an incessant yet impotent refrain. But even for those coming to the play anew, it represents a beginning that sounds more like an end, and there is a little humour to be squeezed from that. It was Lenin (another Vladimir) who urgently although somewhat parodically demanded '[w]hat is to be done?', and in so doing fashioned a beginning that called for an end – a question to be ineluctably followed by an answer. For this Vladimir, and for Estragon, however, the beginning is already the end; the 'last moment' (12) has already been reached. There is nothing to be done and little to be gained from trying to do even that leastmost thing. And yet because nothing continues to be done, it gradually hardens through the accretion of time into a kind of something that will despoil the pristine immaculacy of any absolute negation. Something can come from a particular kind of nothing, it seems.

Despite sounding more like a philosophical conundrum than a joke, there is, in practice, a wry humour to be wrung from all this. The putative impossibility of continuation that nevertheless continues creates a comic unreasonableness that is absurd, literally 'out of tune', with the recognisable rules of dramatic narratives and common sense. These deadpan repeated phrases that cannot quite decide whether they are part of a running joke or a half-abandoned philosophical dictum produce, as Michael Wood has argued, a comedy of the intellect that becomes a comedy of ignorance: it is 'the sign of striving to know what we don't know – that is, to know the things we don't and perhaps can't know; and in the absence of any detectable success in this direction, to know the rich extent of our lack of knowledge' (1998: 33). As we have seen, such readings distil a certain kind of heroism and dignity from the thickened mire of inescapable suffering. And if this gradual accretion of nothing into something, this uncertain though restricted economy in which less both is and isn't more and less is marked by a humorous effect, comedy and laughter might be thought of as methods through which these insubstantial and temporary gains could be measured.

The comedy that Beckett's readers seem to endure and enjoy is precisely the sort that indulges in these lean and poker-faced quips about the inevitability of inability and suffering – the kind which allows A to say to B in *Rough for Theatre II* (written in French in late 1958), 'Ah Morvan, you'd be the death of me if I were sufficiently alive' (*CDW*: 248). There is, however, another kind of comedy in Beckett's work that, while not absolutely antithetical to this comedy of ignorance, seems rather out of phase with it. And it is marked by a tone that seems significantly less appealing to both professional and amateur readers of Beckett. This comedy is found within the prose works of the late 1920s and 1930s – the fictional works and, more particularly, the academic essays, reviews, letters and the embryonic aesthetic statements. These latter non-fictional works are far less frequently read, save as a useful point of critical leverage on the later fiction and drama, and they are almost totally avoided by critics of Beckett's comedy,[1] even though a consciously wrought wit that can be deft and revealing, although it can also be shrill, mannered and verging on the over-inflated, insists as a rhetorical device throughout these pieces. For this comic Beckett seems out of time not only with his later, more recognisable artistic persona; the comic timing of these early jokes themselves also seems all wrong – tending towards the overwound. This overblown comedy goes with a pedantic bang rather than the familiar fizzle of the later texts; but bangs can resound and rebound in unpredictable ways. Explosions that are meant to destroy targets can easily go off in one's face or back pocket, and if not all destructive impulses need be directed outwards, rhetorical fireworks might also be timed to explode in the hands of their creator.

Superiority, Sarcasm, Scholarship

Although theories of humour have traditionally been split between those of incongruity and superiority, it is the latter compact between humour and power that has been most shrilly insistent. From the start, however, that comedy has found an ambivalent reception. In *Republic*, Plato argues that laughter should be avoided because it is marked by an impulse of irrationality (1997b: 1026); in *Philebus* he asserts that it is characterised by a mixture of pleasure and malice (1997a: 439–40);

and in the *Nicomachean Ethics*, Aristotle worries about the propriety of laughter because of the pain it necessarily causes the butt of the joke (1984a: 1780). Primarily concerned with the laughter of human subjects at others, Bergson's influential twentieth-century theory remains convinced that we laugh when faced with 'a certain *mechanical inelasticity*, just where one would expect to find wide-awake adaptability and the living pliableness of a human being' (1911b: 10). There remains for Bergson a latent aggression in this account of laughter, but he also perceives a necessary lack of sympathy for the humanity of the risible object. Laughter thus becomes, not unproblematically, a 'momentary anesthesia of the heart' (Bergson 1911b: 5).

Beckett was certainly aware of the theoretical relationship between laughter and mastery. He took notes from Alfred Adler's *The Neurotic Constitution* in 1935 that delineates a relationship between neurotic symptoms, pathological laughter and a desired superiority: 'Compulsory laughter often possessed the patient when he was in the presence of a superior person, this compulsion (expressing domination) being erected over weak point of feeling of inferiority' (1934–5: 8/26). But even prior to this, Beckett was exploring the well-rehearsed collocation. His first novel, the archly titled *Dream of Fair to Middling Women* written in Paris in 1931–2, pours witty scorn upon the mannered parting of Belacqua and his beloved Smeraldina-Rima. With onanistic concentration, Belacqua tries to squeeze a little emotion from the scene:

> [Belacqua] sat working himself up to the little gush of tears that would exonerate him . . . [T]he best way to turn the piston was to think of the beret that she had snatched off to wave when the ship began to draw clear . . . It might have been a tuft of grass growing the way she ripped it off her little head and began to wave it with an idiotic clockwork movement of her arm, up and down, not to flutter it like a handkerchief, but grasping it in the middle as though she were doing exercises with a dumb-bell. (Beckett 1996: 4)

And if a reader laughs at this scene, one could imagine part of that response echoing Bergson's laughter at the mechanically repeating human, as both Belacqua and Smeraldina-Rima are revealed to be inelastic, trapped in habit and therefore comic.

Of course, this is not quite the Beckett that readers later came to admire, although the ironic reading of pompous inefficiencies of function can certainly be recognised in the later work. This is the Beckett who is perhaps still too subject to his own mechanical repetitions. '[I]t stinks of Joyce' (*LSB*: 81),[2] he worries almost immediately, although the parodies in *Dream* are not so subtly handled as those in *Ulysses* and the tendency to produce cruel caricatures is more insistent both in terms of form and theme. Later, of course, Beckett was to make a comic virtue out of failure, with *Worstward Ho* (1981–2) raising a necessarily contradictory smirk from its deadpan surroundings: 'All of old. Nothing else ever. Ever tried. Ever failed. No matter. Try again. Fail again. Fail better' (*NO*: 101). But on 13 September 1932, the young Beckett could only desperately write to his friend, the poet Thomas MacGreevy, of his inability to find a publisher for *Dream* in terms of a failure from which the artist of indigence could not squeeze any success: 'nothing seems to come off. I made a desperate attempt to get something started on Gide but failed again' (*LSB*: 121). The voice that deems itself 'failed again', plaintively affirming that nothing can be done, is, of course, anticipating something, with *Waiting for Godot* fashioning a whole ontology and aesthetic and material success in 1949 out of what in 1932 seems like no more nor less than frustration and a personal depression. This later figure was the Beckett able to write to Alan Schneider, who had just directed a poorly reviewed production of *Godot*, a kind and consolatory letter affirming that '[s]uccess and failure on the public level never mattered much to me, in fact I feel more at home with the latter, having breathed deep of its vivifying air all my life up to the last couple of years' (Harmon 1998: 8). It is clear, however, that this represents a benign long view that does not quite march in time with the early Beckett's feelings. In 1956 he seems able to turn past and present failures into the expression of another kind of achievement; without the benefit of hindsight, however, *Dream* represents a sense of incapacity that inisistently resists recuperation.

Dream remains a failure from which seemingly little value could leach out because, in spite of all the young Beckett's hopes, he failed to get it published. David Weisberg suggests that Beckett's famous affirmation that '[t]o be an artist is to fail, as no other dare fail' (Beckett 1999: 125) shadows this overlooked aspect of Beckett's writing life (2000: 10), but why was *Dream* so out of step with what the publishers wanted? The novel was criticised by Edward Garnett, a reader for Jonathan Cape, in terms which imply it was the posturing form and tone that rendered the novel unpublishable: 'I wouldn't touch this with a barge-pole. Beckett is probably a very clever fellow, but here he has elaborated a slavish and rather incoherent imitation of Joyce, most eccentric in language and full of disgustingly affected passages – also *indecent*' (quoted in Knowlson 1996: 163). It is fair to assume that the self-consciously learned wit displayed in *Dream* that verges on arrogance, its caricatures, parodies and coarse joking dressed up in scholarly disguise, are fully implicated in Garnett's dismissive reading.

Even later readers such as Beckett's Irish biographer Anthony Cronin agree that although *Dream* contains humour, it is not one in which most readers can take much pleasure. He emphasises its misogyny, judging its tone to be 'embarrassingly wrong, at once ingratiating, cocky and would-be Olympian' (1996: 170). Beckett revised much of *Dream* into the collection of short stories *More Pricks Than Kicks* (1931–3), but that also bears traces of this same troublesome tone, with a contemporary reviewer calling it a 'farce for highbrows' (quoted in Knowlson 1996: 184). A review in the *Times Literary Supplement* on 26 July 1934 indeed implicitly criticises the whole collection by explicitly criticising its comedy:

> The humour which Mr Beckett extracts from the trivial and vulgar incidents which make up Belacqua's career is largely achieved by bringing to bear on them an elaborate technique of analysis. An implicit effect of satire is obtained by embellishing the commonplace with a wealth of observation and sometime erudition, alternated with a sudden brusqueness . . . It is still a very uneven book; but there is a definite, fresh talent at work in it, though it is a talent not quite sure of itself . . . His humour, with its curious blend of colloquialism, coarseness and sophistication, is unlikely to appeal to a large audience.

By the time Beckett was writing *Watt* (1947–8) and constructing Arsene's oft-quoted taxonomy of laughter, however, the troublesome laughter of implied superiority seems to have been both recognised and tacitly policed. Arsene describes that which, in his opinion, is the lowest form of laughter: 'The bitter laugh laughs at that which is not good, it is the ethical laugh' (Beckett 1976: 47). He implies that laughter becomes more refined the less it has a compact with assertions of superiority that are the results of the application of normative moral, social and cultural values. The lowest of laughs might yet become 'hollow' if it is 'intellectual' and laughs at that 'which is not true' (Beckett 1976: 47); but that laughter might finally achieve the highest status of 'mirthless' or 'dianoetic', the *risus purus*, if it separates itself from those shaky moral structures of the good and the true. '[T]he laugh laughing at the laugh, the beholding, the saluting of the highest joke, in a word the laugh that laughs – silence please – at that which is unhappy' (Beckett 1976: 47), is still, in a rather attenuated sense, a laughter of superiority (it erupts down the snout); but instead of punitively ordering the social, it laughs at the poverty and contingency of those normative categories which attempt to paper over the misery. As these categories become the object towards which humorous derision is directed rather than a comic tool, the highest laughter recognises and salutes the givenness of unhappiness and impotence.

The most common reading of comedy in Beckett's *oeuvre* is one that follows the trajectory suggested by Arsene, constructing a narrative of progression from the early 'ethical' and 'bitter' laughter to the final achievement of the *risus purus*. Topsfield argues that these 'lesser' laughs are mostly in evidence in the early work, but they evolve throughout the plays and the novels until the *risus purus* – 'a philosophical acceptance of existence . . . a release from laughter and tears' – is achieved in *How It Is* (1988: 1). In *On Humour*, Critchley implies a similar progression by making no mention of the earlier work, concentrating instead upon the *risus purus* of the later fiction and drama. In his essay from 1981, Wolfgang Iser also saves the last laugh for the mature author of *Godot* and *Endgame*, describing how 'the dianoetic mockery of unhappiness, that makes the latter transparent . . . allows one to face up to unhappiness' (1993: 173).

In her study of Beckett's comedy, Cohn begins by following the ancient Greek distinction between the liberal and the illiberal jest: '[t]he liberal jest evokes laughter *with*, the illiberal jest *at*' (1962: 8). Conceding that 'Beckett employs both jests, but the illiberal dominate[s] from the start', she goes on to state that Beckett's comedy finally deconstructs such distinctions: '[s]o ambiguous are Beckett's heroes that we scarcely know why we laugh, and whether we laugh *at* or *with*' (Cohn 1962: 8). In the end, though, Cohn confirms the final victory of the last laugh in Beckett's *oeuvre*:

> In Beckett's latest work, Arsene's three laughs are merged; the ethical laugh is aroused by cruelty, the intellectual laugh by ignorance, but cruelty and ignorance dissolve in suffering. Bitter and hollow laughter are drowned in mirthless, dianoetic laughter – the only possible reaction to the impossible human situation, in which we live. (1962: 293)

As an exception which proves something of this rule, only Shane Weller's critique of Critchley's use of Arsene's taxonomy (2006: 122–3) troubles this desire to map the movement towards Beckett's mature and seemingly more ethical work through the putative appearance of the 'last laugh' of the '*risus purus*' (2006: 131–3).

This narrative of progressive refinement is not one I will completely disavow, but I will suggest that it is interrupted and complicated in several important ways, as comedy takes part in unpredictable and reversible economies of violence and pleasure. Perhaps it is clear enough, though, that the 'bitter laugh' is where Beckett's comedy begins, and it is a particularly notable feature of the critical essays and reviews written as he struggled to find publishers and a public who would believe in his work. The most explicit example in Beckett's *oeuvre* of wit as a tool of sarcastic disparagement appears in an unpublished tirade against the ideological restrictions of the Irish state, 'Censorship and the Saorstat' (1935).[3] The essay rails against an Act of censorship that made 'provision for the prohibition of the sale and distribution of unwholesome literature' (*D*: 84), alongside the banning of contraceptives, in the Irish Free State. Beckett himself, who is now writing poetry and literary fiction, had been banned upon the publication of *More Pricks Than Kicks* and he makes reference to his own inclusion among the ranks of censored authors by stating, with a seemingly intentionally overwrought decorum that descends into a tendentious sarcasm: 'My own registered number is 465, number four hundred and sixty five, if I may presume to say so' (88). Larded with a gamey intellectual exhibitionism, the definitions within the Act are described as having been emitted with little more thought than 'as the cuttle squirts ooze from its cod' (84), and the Board of Censors represented as imbecilic and lazy in its pedantic application of 'common sense' and its spurious aesthetic judgement which allows that 'the customer is always right' (85). The Irish people, in turn, are lambasted for their complacent ignorance:

> For the Irish are a characteristic agricultural community in this, that they have something better to do than to read and that they produce a finished type of natural fraudeur having nothing to learn from the nice discriminations of Margaret Sanger and Marie Carmichael Stopes, D. Sc., Ph. D., F. R. S. Litt., etc. (87)

At first glance the comic intention is clear: the critical voice is using comic sarcasm to get one over on the Irish Board of Censors and the philistinism of state-sanctioned Irish culture. There is much to be said in terms of Beckett's uneasy relationship with the Ireland of the 1930s that the voice should define the Irish State as a collection of obnoxious 'cephalopods' (*D*: 87) and the Irish people as pigs who are content to be fed on sugarbeet pulp ('[i]t is all the same to them') (88). The most obvious point to make, however, about the relationship between the widely read artist (as he now considers himself to be) and the Saorstat, is that Beckett refuses to identify with it, even though he is still subject to its authority. Beckett, the artist, also refuses identification with the supposed authentic sentiment of the peasantry that accords with the Romanticism of the Celtic Revival. He suggests instead that the 'pure Gael, drawing his breath from his heels, will never be permitted to defile his mind with even such fairly clean dirt as the *Black Girl in her Search for God* so long as he can glorify his body to the tune of half a dozen byblows [illegitimate offspring]' (87).[4] Both author and the implied reader, in laughing together or at least recognising the sarcastically comic intent of the piece, are interpellated into a position in which those in the Saorstat become derided, illogical, mentally defective and unintentionally laughable breeders: 'Sterilization of the mind and apotheosis of the litter suit well together. Paradise peopled with virgins and the earth with decorticated multiparas, white as pthisis' (87). Skating close to the discourses of eugenics with which many modernist writers were both concerned and enamoured,[5] Beckett is clear that a state that makes a virtue out of rural illiteracy and a fertility unhampered by contraception is incapable of realising that its philistinism cannot partake of the joke; as such, it simply becomes it.

There is a strong implication that this critic, who has already published a defence of Joyce's *Work in Progress* in Eugène Jolas's Parisian avant-gardist magazine *transition*, now situates himself within an international, cosmopolitan and intellectual elite; he is able to make the 'distinction between indecency obiter and ex professo' (*D*: 84) and has read *Ulysses* and the *Decameron*. The Board of Censors are duly admonished for their blinkered complacency, their pompous self-assurance that they have 'better things to do than split hairs, the pubic not excepted' (84), and their logically flawed certainty that the Board need not 'read through' every line of *Ulysses*, a book that has been universally condemned' (85) in order to judge it. It is implied that both critic and reader know enough about literature, or at least about logic, to find this quotation of an unintentionally comic statement humorous. But there is also a Romanticism inherited by certain canonical versions of modernism that resonates across many of Beckett's essays in the implicit separation of the solitary (and most likely financially unsuccessful) artist from the putative philistine pragmatism of bourgeois society. The critical voice of the artist Beckett now considers himself to be indeed distances itself from and bemoans the usurping of questions of aesthetic value by the opinions of the 'common sense man' and the ideology of the marketplace in which 'the customer is always right' (85). By claiming the position of *ressentiment*, formed as a laughing superiority over prudish authorities that ironically sanction prostituted art, Beckett attempts to assert his power over and indifference to both the censoring state authorities and the economies of the market whose bourgeois common-sense tastes had ensured that a mere 500 of the 1,500 published copies of *More Pricks Than Kicks* were sold. And it is this same voice that, when still struggling to find a publisher for *Murphy* in 1937, slips into the comedy of superiority as a well-worn way of putting the rejecting company, Doubleday Doran, in its rightfully abjected marketplace:

Oh Doubleday Doran
Less oxy than moron,
You've a mind like a whore on
A trip to Bundoran.
                    (*LSB*: 570)

In 'Dante ... Bruno . Vico .. Joyce', which appeared in *transition* in 1929, Joyce's revered *Work in Progress* in which 'form *is* content, content *is* form' (*D*: 27) is never the object of humour; instead, it is those readers unable to appreciate this new form of writing that are targeted by Beckett's comic scorn:

> [I]f you don't understand it, Ladies and Gentlemen, it is because you are too decadent to receive it. You are not satisfied unless form is so strictly divorced from content that you can comprehend the one without bothering to read the other. The rapid skimming and absorption of the scant cream of sense is made possible by what I may call a continuous process of copious intellectual salivation. (1983: 26)

This use of somewhat strained humour to defend what was later called *Finnegans Wake* could have easily won Beckett an honorary mention in John Carey's rather partial and partisan account of the oppositional relationship between high modernism and mass culture, *The Intellectuals and the Masses* (1992), although, as with the objects of Carey's critique, it is the bourgeois common sense of the middlebrow that becomes the most common target of the modernist intellectual and aesthetic superiority in which Beckett so thoroughly participates. Nevertheless, it is quite clear that in 1929 Beckett, echoing the subtitle of the *Little Review* in which *Ulysses* was first serialised, is 'Making no Compromise with the Public Taste'.

Even though neither Beckett nor Joyce signed Jolas's 'Proclamation: Revolution of the Word' that also appeared in *transition* 16/17, the bombastic manifesto form and assertions of intellectual superiority find themselves reproduced in the tone of 'Dante ... Bruno . Vico .. Joyce'. In 'The Revolution of the Word', Jolas proclaims:

> 11. THE WRITER EXPRESSES. HE DOES NOT COMMUNICATE.
> 12. THE PLAIN READER BE DAMNED. (1929: 13)

In the 'Dante' essay, Rebecca West, who, as an artist, presumably should have known better than to be such a money-grubbing plain reader, is accused of 'clear[ing] her decks for a sorrowful deprecation of the Narcissistic element in Joyce by the purchase of 3 hats' (*D*: 26). She is skewered alongside all those other slob(berer)s who do not understand what Beckett calls Joyce's 'direct expression': 'one feels that she might very well wear her bib at all her intellectual banquets, or alternatively assert a more noteworthy control over her salivary glands than is possible for Monsieur Pavlov's unfortunate dogs' (26). This grotesquerie, to be picked up again in the 'Censorship' essay, perhaps owes as much to the barks of Surrealist 'black humour' born from the violent and ludic clash of the contradictory as to Jolas's straightly provocative proclamation; nevertheless, the comic tone clearly works to cement both a formal and a thematic identification with the taste of *transition*. As Raymond Williams famously puts it, for modernist writers distanced from their 'national or provincial cultures' and a sense of continuity with the literary traditions of the past, it was necessary to 'found the only community available to them: a community of the medium; of their own practices' (1989: 45). For the Irish Beckett in Paris, then, comic invective becomes a way of registering his community service.

In the essay 'Recent Irish Poetry' (published in a special Irish issue of *The Bookman* in 1934 under the pseudonym of Andrew Belis), the same brittle, intellectually violent, comic intent appears. In 1949, Beckett was to remember it as 'an angry article on modern Irish poets' (quoted in Gunn 2006: 15); it is here, though, that he forges an explicit bond between an intellectual Ireland and the 'community of the medium' of European modernism.[6] Wit remains synonymous with scorn, however, appearing only to chastise those poets or qualities that Belis does not admire. The antiquarians, whom Belis pugnaciously notes are in the majority in contemporary Irish poetry, are enraptured by 'an iridescence of themes – Oisin, Cuchulain, Maeve, Tir-nanog, the Táin Bo Cuailgne, Yoga, the Crone of Beare – segment after segment of cut and dried loveliness' (*D*: 71). The Rev. Monk Gibbon 'is the poet of children ('Chacun Son Goût'), and as such is bound to consider thought a microbe' (73); Mr Higgins 'has accumulated a greater number of "By Gods" than all the other antiquarians put together', though he is still less of the 'glimmering fawn' than Mr Russell and less of the 'lilter and lisper than Mr Coloum' (73).

When a little comedy does creep into the critique of Beckett's friend Denis Devlin, whose work was influenced by Paul Eluard, it simply indicates that particular author's distance from the antiquarians, Romantics and Revivalists, and their enslaving mythic and poetic forms:

> What matters is that [Devlin's poetry] does not proceed from the *Gossoons Wunderhorn* of that Irish Romantic Arnim-Brentano combination, Sir Samuel Ferguson and Standish O'Grady, and that it admits – stupendous innovation – the existence of the author. *Es wandelt niemand ungestraft unter Palmen* [No one wanders under palm trees without being punished][7] is peculiarly

applicable to these islands, where pigeons meet with such encouragements. But it is preferable to dying of mirage. (76)

There is the comic combination of an archaic and arcane learned discourse, exemplified by the use of the rather antiquarian German 'wandeln', with a coy but satisfying exultation in desublimation as Belis warns Devlin to prepare himself for an onslaught of excremental criticism from the bird-brained. In this essay, however, comedy begins to reveal something of its inherent riskiness as a rhetorical strategy. For as a function of this highly wrought humour, the aesthetic surface of the essay becomes brittle to the degree that it becomes unsatisfyingly opaque for the not quite so well-read reader. But one voice in 'Recent Irish Poetry' seems already to have some sense of this and to have fallen out of step with the sarcasm. When the essay implies that critical attack even with abjected material is 'preferable to dying of mirage', there is surely an ironic acknowledgement that the worse fate might be Beckett's own – the failure to be understood and, in the case of 'Censorship' and *Dream*, even to be published at all.

The Loutishness of Learning

The later Beckett was, of course, to dismiss this work, whose youthful bitterness perhaps made it less than palatable to the older, successful writer. The Beckett who had enjoyed the success of *Waiting for Godot* and received a Nobel Prize derided his earlier persona and aesthetic achievements. He spoke of himself as a 'young man with nothing to say and the itch to make' (Harvey 1970: 305), with writing pushed out of the realm of artistic intention into that of bodily compulsion. The Beckett who reread the manuscript in the 1980s considered *Dream* to be so seriously flawed that he judged it 'too awful for him to contemplate it being published' (Knowlson 1996: 830, n. 74), and while he was more forgiving of the early book reviews and critical essays, he was still dismissive enough to suggest to Cohn that they were nothing more than the 'miserable results of financial onus or friendly obligation' (2001: 64). Beckett thus sought to remove this work from the canon of his art, in his strongly modernist understanding of art as autotelic. By the time of the top trumps game of insults in *Godot*, it is indeed Estragon's accusation of 'Crritic!' (Beckett 1990: 70) that beats all the other morons, vermin, abortions, sewer-rats and cretins that are on the table. Here, the bitter comedy of putative superiority in the critical voice of the early work seems to be an absolute anachronism; it becomes the butt of the joke which has been submitted to another, further, perhaps more 'acceptable' form of mastery – a later and a higher form of laughter.

Written shortly after Beckett resigned his academic post at Trinity in 1932 but published in 1934, the short poem 'Gnome' is cited by Lawrence Harvey as evidence of the 'revolt of Beckett the young poet against Beckett the young intellectual' (Harvey 1970: 45):

> Spend the years of learning squandering
> Courage for the years of wandering
> Through a world politely turning
> From the loutishness of learning.
> (Beckett 2002: 7)

For Harvey, the implication is that Beckett has grown weary of the exhibitionism and the early, narcissistic posturing: a new voice of the artist rather than scholar has asserted itself that will produce the later, more creative works, marked perhaps by an increasingly refined, less loutish humour. The trouble with this position is that an aesthetic compulsively bound to the intellect and certain kinds of scholarship does persist in Beckett's work, as far as the meticulously imagined and miniature dimensions of the universe of 'little people' in *The Lost Ones* or the perfected chain of being of tormentor and tormented in *How It Is*. Matthew Feldman's cultural history of Beckett's interwar notes proves decisively that Beckett's self-directed but meticulous study and transcription of writings on art, philosophy and psychology throughout the 1930s were sources to which he persistently returned (2006: 39). And in terms of the reception of his work, as a writer beloved of academia and academics, Beckett can be thought of as always having remained peculiarly emeritus. Even as late as 1981, the Beckett who supposedly so disliked critics wrote *Ohio Impromptu* to be performed during an academic conference at Ohio State University.

It seems hard, then, to enforce a clear distinction between creative expression and scholarly brio, for throughout Beckett's work, intellectual play remains as much the accelerator of aesthetic creativity as its brake. Nevertheless, Knowlson specifically draws attention in his biography to the fact that Beckett's return to Trinity as a lecturer in French in 1930 was disturbed by a new uncertainty about at least the humour of academia, if not necessarily 'learning' as a whole. Knowlson suggests that Beckett began to weary of his former and favourite tutor Thomas Rudmose-Brown and the latter's 'constant anti-clerical, anti-military, anti-Romantic outpourings' (1996: 121), quoting a 1930 letter to MacGreevey where Beckett bemoans his tutor's 'little jokes – the kind that dribble into a subtle smile' (*LSB*: 55). Knowlson states that '[t]o someone listening, as he now was, with a critical ear, scholarly wit and sarcasm sounded all too often like exhibitionism, bitchiness and character assassination' (1996: 121), although he himself concedes that Beckett's disavowal of the scholarly pose and its 'little jokes' was perhaps not totally clear cut.[8] Knowlson nevertheless concentrates upon the seemingly more mature Beckett emerging from the meetings with psychotherapist Wilfred Bion, quoting at length from one of the 'most important' letters to MacGreevy of this period (1935) to indicate Beckett's judgement of his earlier academic persona:

> [At T.C.D. I] lent myself to a crescendo of disparagement of others and myself. But in all that there was nothing that struck me as morbid. The misery & solitude & apathy & the sneers were an index of superiority and guaranteed a feeling of arrogant 'otherness' . . . In short, if the heart [palpitations] had not put the fear of death into me I would still be boozing & sneering & lounging around & feeling I was too good for anything else. (*LSB*: 258–9)

But whether this transformation was successfully effected or remained subject to anxious and unpredictable returns is questionable. For 'sneers', as 'an index of superiority [that] guaranteed a feeling of arrogant "otherness"', continue long after Trinity has been abandoned; indeed, it is as good a description as any of the alternately cynical and furious jokes that appear in the essays and reviews of 1934–5 written at precisely the time Beckett was undergoing therapy for his psychosomatic symptoms.[9]

So the insistence of a conspicuously learned wit that irrupts as occasions of comic violence suggests that Beckett's work of resigning from 'the loutishness of learning' might have been a long and imperfectly effected task. It is, indeed, a narrative subject to interruptions and atavistic returns to a less refined 'intellectual' laughter rather than any 'polite', teleological turn towards a progressively more refined formal and thematic framework. One could smooth out this contradiction, perhaps, by locating the 'turn' from this comedy at the end of the 1930s rather than their beginning, but it might be more instructive to let this contradiction pucker and rend these narratives of progression. It seems obvious that human lives do not follow smooth trajectories but are punctuated by unexpected hiccups, contradictory drives, anachronistic recursions and inassimilable events, but equally, a literary *oeuvre* is not linear or teleological, with the immature, early work necessarily eclipsed in a dialectical movement by the progressively more refined, aesthetically and ethically superior achievements of the greater later works. And if there is a biographical ambivalence to be traced between Beckett's supposed desires, material necessity and certain aesthetic compulsions, there is, equally, a resistance within the *oeuvre* to a putative progression from rebarbative sarcasm to the transcendent thematics of ignorance and impotence that illuminate and salute the 'human condition' in all its untranscendent frailty.

A text such as *First Love* (written in French as *Premier Amour* in 1946 but not translated until 1973) still revels, then, in the unruly persistence of comic violence. There are times when the tone and theme are strangely reminiscent of 'Censorship' or 'Recent Irish Poetry' in the comic representation of a land in thrall to antiquarianism and resistant to contraception:

> What constitutes the charm of our country, apart of course from its scant population, and this without the help of the meanest contraceptive, is that all is derelict, with the sole exception of history's ancient faeces. These are ardently sought after, stuffed and carried in procession. Wherever nauseated time has dropped a nice fat turd you will find our patriots, sniffing it up on all fours, their faces on fire. (*CSP*: 33–4)

But there are even more aggressive moments: 'She began stroking my ankles. I considered kicking her in the cunt' (31). Such verbal violence is never totally divorced from a little frisson of humour, however. The transgression and obviation of sympathy demonstrated here is so incongruous that it does enable a very dark, rather shocked, laughter. And it is Lulu/Anna's pregnancy that offers the most striking expressions of this violently black comedy, this anaesthesia of the heart: 'Look she said, stooping over her breasts, the haloes are darkening already. I summoned up my remaining strength and said, Abort, abort, and they'll blush like new' (44).

Of course, here the narrator's anaesthesia of the heart is not just the tool used to fashion humour; it is also a grotesquely humorous object, to be ranked alongside his useless feet 'beloved of the corn, the cramp, the kibe, the bunion, the hammer toe, the nail ingrown, the fallen arch, the common blain, the club foot, the duck foot, goose foot, pigeon foot, flat foot, trench foot and other curiosities' (*CSP*: 33) in terms of its risibility. There is indeed a strong sense of internal reflexivity and textual critique in *First Love*, an ironic awareness that the narrator's mannered amorousness and superiority are themselves laughable objects rather than simply tools for the laughing subject:

> I thought of Anna then, long long sessions, twenty minutes and even as long as half an hour daily. I obtain these figures by the addition of other, lesser figures. That must have been my way of loving. Are we to infer from this that I loved her with an intellectual love which drew from me such drivel in another place? Somehow I think not. For had my love been of this kind would

I have stooped to inscribe the letters of Anna in time's forgotten cowpats? To divellicate urtica *plenis manibus*? And felt, under my tossing head, her thighs to bounce like so many demon bolsters. Come now! (35)

The hyperactive multiplication of idioms and voices here materialises an ironic and trumping abrasion of differing narrative tones that cannot simply be read as part of a movement away from the loutishness of learning towards a comedy of ignorance. Instead, the precise use and placement of the anachronistic, the inkhorn and the pedantic produces an aesthetic structured paradoxically around both display and the ironically humorous collapse of any putatively singular, sarcastic authority of the intellect.

So perhaps it is inattentive to the material and unnecessary to construct a narrative that suggests a clear move beyond comic mastery to a putatively ethical *risus purus* bound to an aesthetic of inability. Instead, it is more critically revealing both to articulate the persistence of comic violence within the *oeuvre* and to demonstrate the ways in which the contradictory and sadistic exchanges within Beckett's very early comedy can be read as moments that trace the shape of some of those later artistic strategies. Without simply wishing to repeat a critical gesture that rescues from Beckett's self-pariahed early corpus flashes of the 'genius' he was later to become, I want to argue that a very specific form of comic incompetence that emerges in and between these texts begins to be worked with and wrought, rather than transcended, in a way that precisely moulds the contours of the later Beckett's aesthetic of successful incompetence from failure's abjected yet fertile materials.

Diminishing Laughing Returns

Mirroring the insistent return of superiority in theorisations of humour, it would seem that Beckett's work is also never quite able to pass beyond comic aggression. Even the most sadistic of those later works, the horror stories of *How It Is* and *What Where*, are able to squeeze a little humour from the cruelly rational and mathematically perfected reversibility of their systems of torturers and tortured. In *Endgame*, too, a comedy of attempted mastery insists alongside a tantalisingly veiled violence, although, as with all the later work, it becomes increasingly uncertain where or at whom such laughing violence is aimed. I would suggest, however, that the uncertainty of the flow and direction of power in a text such as *Endgame* is not simply a function of a progressive weakening of comic aggression; instead, it should be read as an articulation of the potential and threatening reversal of power that is a structural function of the laughter of superiority. Uncertainty might yet be thought of as something that bleeds into these earlier critical works, not as a usurpation of comic aggression, but as an articulation of the immanent reversibility and incongruity that haunts the laughter of superiority from the start, and with which Beckett's texts begin very seriously to play.

As we have seen, Beckett's scholarly essays and reviews acknowledge and work to cement the critical voice's bond to a community of sympathetic Irish and continental European readers superior to the bourgeois marketplace and the common-sense predilections of the middlebrow, and this at least partially explains their recourse to the sarcastically tendentious joke. For tendentious jokes lead Freud to the discovery that is his truly original contribution to theorisations of humour:

> Generally speaking, a tendentious joke calls for three people: in addition to the one who makes the joke, there must be a second who is taken as the object of the hostility or sexual aggression, and the third in whom the joke's aim of producing pleasure is fulfilled. (1905: 99)

If all jokes are more or less tendentious, for all jokes have an economic purpose of producing pleasure by the lifting of inhibitions, Freud's suspicion that an inter-subjective element is required in tendentious joking can be expanded into a more generalised assertion:

> If one comes across something comic, one can enjoy it by oneself. A joke, on the contrary, *must* be told to someone else . . . I myself cannot laugh at a *joke* that has occurred to me, that I have made, in spite of the unmistakable enjoyment that the joke gives me. It is possible that my need to communicate the joke to someone else is in some way connected with the laughter produced by it, which is denied to me but is manifest in the other person. (1905: 143)

The teller cannot easily laugh at their own joke without the help of an audience because, in bald economic terms, the expenditure of psychical energy on the production of the joke 'is deducted from the yield [of pleasure] resulting from the lifting of the inhibition – an expenditure which is the same as the one the hearer of the joke avoids' (Freud 1905: 149). The laughter of the audience completes the joke for the teller because it offers them 'objective certainty that the joke-work has been successful' (155). It also turns 'the hearer, who was indifferent to begin with, into a co-hater or co-despiser'; it 'creates for the enemy a host of opponents where at first there was only one . . . [and] upsets the critical judgement which otherwise would have examined the dispute' (132). For Beckett, then, the strong attempt of the 'Censorship' essay to mobilise national and international intellectual scorn against the restrictive hypocrisies of the Irish State – that alibi for the 'Catholic Truth Society' (*D*: 86) as the essay has it – uses the weapon of comic scorn as a way of producing a community of co-despisers to bolster a community of artistic practices. Such a tactic necessarily reveals just how subject the young artist still is to certain kinds of discursive authority, but it also enables him to position himself as sufficiently authoritative to demarcate and determine battle lines.

But if the joke demands the interpellation of an audience into a third position that will recognise it and take part in its work, there is always the menacing possibility that the joke might not be received and returned correctly. Freud notes: 'jokes that have a purpose run the risk of meeting with people who do not want to listen to them' (1905: 89); indeed, he goes on to state:

> some degree of benevolence or a kind of neutrality, an absence of any feeling that could provoke feelings opposed to the purpose of the joke, is an indispensable condition if the third person is going to collaborate in completion of the process of making a joke. (144)

In Purdie's account of the comic as a founding moment within discursive exchange, joking enables the confirmation of a joker's ability intentionally to deploy and distort complex discursive constructions. But if the subject's joke is mistakenly or purposefully refused the direction of the flow of power is immediately reversed. The joke that is met with silence disables the teller of the joke to precisely the same extent that it empowered them before. Any claiming of the joking power is submitted to the possibility of refusal or misrecognition as it negotiates a relationship with the other and, by implication, with the unpredictability of an unknown future.

To write as a critic suggests the construction and assumption of a secure position of authority from which that critical voice can speak; it is perfectly possible, however, that Beckett's imagined reader will not offer Freud's benevolent or neutral reception. Even more significantly, it is also quite clearly possible that the reader might interpret the laughing subject, the critical voice, as unconsciously duplicating the very thing it seeks to render laughable. For if one of the main targets of Beckett's 'Censorship' essay is the pompous and pedantic self-assurance that the state knows best, the critical voice's derision and sarcastic debasement of all other ideological positions runs the risk of speaking in sync with that which has already been coded as risible. Freud's rather simplistic reading of irony, which actually sounds more like sarcasm in that it is a form that simply says one thing and means another, nevertheless indicates that such joking is fundamentally susceptible to subsidence: 'Irony can only be employed when the other person is prepared to hear the opposite . . . As a result of this condition, irony is exposed particularly easily to the dangers of being misunderstood' (1905: 173). Laughter might not, in fact, return to consolidate and confirm the critical voice; it might instead render that voice laughable.

Bergson also notes how easily critical laughter can shudder into risibility. For we, as laughers, must be alienated from our objects of derision – we cannot 'put ourselves in tune with a soul which is not in tune with itself' (Bergson 1911b: 141). But in such unsympathetic alienation, the laughing subject with its anaesthetised heart and its unsociable object begin unexpectedly to mirror one another: the 'insensibility in the spectator' (the laugher) begins to parallel the '[u]nsociability in the performer' (or the laughable object) (Bergson 1911b: 145). Humour punishes the inferior, the weak, the putatively inhuman, but such punishment itself can become pompous and mechanically repetitive. Because, in Bergson's terms, the laugher who 'immediately retires within himself, more self-asserted and conceited than ever, and is evidently disposed to look upon another's personality as a marionette of which he pulls the strings' (199) is momentarily incapable of emotion (184), he or she begins to resemble the object of derision – they are unresponsive, contracted into laughing habit, anaesthetised from the unpredictable flux and flow of feeling that is, for Bergson, the locus of the human. And perhaps this is one reason why bitter, scornful laughter is deemed to be 'sardonic'. For sardonic laughter is not joyous or liberating: it is, instead, convulsive and pathological. Sardonic laughter is, after all, etymologically derived from the supposed rictus effect of 'eating a "Sardinian plant" . . . which was said to produce facial convulsions resembling horrible laughter, usually followed by death' (*OED*).

It is revealing, then, that even when writing *Dream* in 1931–2, the sarcastic Beckett demonstrates a burgeoning awareness that an excess of erudition, expressing itself through the 'loutishness of learning', could 'rupture . . . the lines of communication' (1983: 70), as he has it in 'Recent Irish Poetry' (1934). Beckett writes to MacGreevy in 1931, before the main period of writing *Dream*, of the fear that 'I have enough butin verbal [verbal booty] to strangle anything I'm likely to want to say' (*LSB*: 93). Earlier in the year, he declared himself to be 'soiled . . . with the old demon notesnatching' (quoted in Pilling 1999: xiii), suggesting that the myriad of learned quotations from Robert Burton's *An Anatomy of Melancholy* and other sources that appear in the *Dream* Notebook were turning writing into an excremental action. The final text of *Dream* indeed becomes in a letter from 1932 a 'multicuspid stinker' (*LSB*: 135) – a sharply-toothed monstrosity, which, by implication, chews up its material before belching or shitting it out into the world. But it seems significant that strangulation, gagging, belching and shitting, should appear here as marks of artistic incompetence, given the compulsive appearance of a precise and powerful poetics of ingestion and evacuation in the *Trilogy* that forms a recognisably Beckettian and ironically successful aesthetic of failure.[10] So it may be instructive to linger a little on these occasions of verbose intellectual strangulation and soiling in the criticism, rather than passing over them as nothing more than indications of artistic and critical immaturity. For although these 'bad' jokes may well be indicative of a risible stylistic weakness, there is also the beginning of something self-conscious, of an awareness of what a rupturing of the 'lines of communication' might do to a text, and the growth of something intentional from this abjectedly fertile comic ground.

'Schwabenstreich' is Beckett's review of *Mozart on the Way to Prague* by Eduard Mörike – a creative reconstruction of an incident in Mozart's life that supposedly offered to gloss his art. The review appeared in the *Spectator* in 1934, sparking with a truculent sarcasm that suggests even women scorned have little to hold up to unsuccessful young authors. As even the sympathetic Pilling notes, this review is 'witty, terse and waspish', from an author 'unable and unwilling to temper his views from a conventional distance' (1997: 114). But 'waspishness' also throws a spanner in the works of wit, as comedy here marks the creaking, grinding, breakdown of this textual contraption:

> Here is a 'fragment of imaginative composition' short and not at all to the point, but at least short, which is nowadays so rare a quality in a literary work that one cannot refrain from commending this book for having contrived, in 20,000 words instead of 200,000 words, to exhaust the inessential. (D: 61)

Beckett suggests that if you are going to waffle on about a subject and refrain from making any significant observations, it is only good manners to get it over with quickly. Although the tone is comically derisive, the laughing blow does not land altogether firmly, as humour gleaned from the effect of the rigorous putdown is subject to interference by the excess of critical rigour at work in this assertion. '[S]hort and not at all to the point' makes the point perfectly sufficiently, but the addition of 'but at least short' perhaps goes a step too far, implicating the narrator within an economy of excess, as Beckett himself explains the book's critical inefficiencies through a process of long-windedly 'exhaust[ing] the inessential'.[11] The phrase is thus ironic in two senses. Classically, Mörike is being 'blamed' for his weak work by being 'praised' that it does not go on for longer;[12] but secondly, and somewhat unexpectedly, the critic ironically duplicates the lack of concision that he states is the one infelicity that Mörike does not inflict on the reader. The implied distinction between Beckett and Mörike, though, is that Beckett's insistently stuttering rhythm that forces the sentence into a lovingly crafted formal hyperbole is intentional and fashions the appearance of a controlled excess of rigour that is not without critical and comic effect. Pilling notes that 'it adds insult to injury that Beckett can show, in a sentence more than fifty words long, that it is possible to "exhaust the inessential" more economically than Mörike could ever have imagined' (1997: 115). Beckett the critic wins by demonstrating that he can take comic inefficiency and, through a complex parody, render it economically effective. Nevertheless, this is a victory won at a great risk to the sarcastic laughing subject. By ironically mimicking Mörike's faults Beckett succeeds in debasing his object at the expense of the tempered critical impersoanlity the review demands. On at least one level, then, 'Schwabenstreich' fails.

Now whether this is intentional or an irony detectable to the reader but an unintended textual effect is difficult fully to determine, for Beckett's comedy in these early critical essays seems to impale the reader precisely on the horns of a dilemma always immanent within the comic: how stable is the seat of laughing intention? Who or what is finally placed in the position of risibility? To suggest an answer to these questions, however, it is instructive to draw out explicitly the ways in which self-parody begins to function in fictional works from the same period. Given that Rudmose-Brown is taken to be the inspiration for the superior tone and rhetorical force of 'Censorship and the Saorstat', it is useful to press on the fact that he is caricatured in *Dream* and also in 'A Wet Night' (from *More Pricks Than Kicks*) as the Polar Bear. There, the P.B. is lambasted for a learned exhibitionism that is exhilarating but finally revealed to be sententious and ineffective. Never using 'the English word when the foreign pleased him better', the Polar Bear assaults the certainties of Christianity in his discussion with a Jesuit on a bus: the

> Lebensbahn . . . of the Galilean is the tragic-comedy of the solipsism that will not capitulate. The humilities and the retro me's and quaffs of sirreverence are on a par with the hey prestos, arrogance and egoism. He is the first self-contained playboy. (Beckett 1970: 61)

In this rendering of P.B.'s speech, one is perhaps reminded of the arcane and inkhorn comic flourishes of the early essays, such as the portentous use of German in 'Recent Irish Poetry'; but this fictionalised invective is not simply comic in its own terms, even though the P.B. intends it to be received as such. Although the reader may take pleasure in the hypnotic play of language within this atheist pontification, they can also laugh at a tiresome egotism and exhibitionism that the P.B. does not intend to reveal. For it is the Jesuit who gets the last word, leaving the P.B. to pay both bus fares and the reader to get the last laugh. The narrator's framing of the P.B.'s speech with a comically grotesque physical description and an indication of the ineffectiveness of the railing, demonstrates that his failings can become comic in another way for the narrator and the reader.

This technique renders explicit, then, the uncertainty within the reception of the comic that remains implicit within 'Censorship' or 'Schwabenstreich'. It is not just a case of the portentous being revealed to be comic (or a simple interpellation of the first joking position into the second), however, for the P.B.'s rhetoric is not altogether out of tune with the tone and style of the framing narratorial voice. Cohn is absolutely right when she criticises 'A Wet Night' for being a social satire 'suffering from the lack of an implied ideal' (1962: 39). For the framing narrative that should be providing a window onto an 'implied ideal' duplicates (as Bergson fears such a discourse might) that which it is attempting to critique and correct in its comic yet cruel, misogynist caricature of the Frica: 'It was impossible to set aside the awful suspicion that her flattened mammae, in sympathy with the tormented eructation of countenance, had put forth cutwaters and were rowelling her corsage' (Beckett 1970: 66–7). This is pompous, hardly to be distinguished from the P.B.'s rhetoric nor, except in the lack of generosity of its intent, from the Countess of Parambini's markedly overblown comparison of the Frica to the Sistine Chapel. And the reader, having been interpellated into a position where the portentous can be an object for comic scorn, is as likely now to read the narrator's comic flamboyance as bombast as they are to read it as wit. The text in thrall to the laceration of others seems to turn on itself, and indeed a distinctively different register is suddenly heard, as the orotund description is interrupted by a self-defeating metaphor and a frustrated and bathetic comic uncertainty reminiscent of Beckett's later work: 'This may be premature. We have set it down too soon, perhaps. Still, let it bloody well stand' (67). This third position is one from which laughably turgid rhetoric can be read as an intentionally produced parody of the overblown. It thus suggests that the previous rhetoric of egotistical comic superiority was an ironic representation of the very risibility readers might have suspected the narrator of unwittingly producing, or at least that the textual failure has been marked and policed. But by forcing these different voices and registers into an uncertain dialogue with one another, textual comic sadism never remains just that; instead, the text begins to shudder into the dehiscing contortions of self-parody. As such, the flagellation of a seemingly comically empowered self, at a signalled moment of textual failure, begins to announce an artistic strategy of ironic success.

Art vs. Book-Keeping

If Beckett's fictional texts are staging an economy of intentional failure as early as 1932, it is suggestive that Beckett began his writing career in a genre in which he could only fail, according to his own strictures. In 1929, Beckett famously begins 'Dante . . . Bruno . Vico . . Joyce' with an assertion that the 'danger is in the neatness of identifications' (*D*: 19). He bemoans the tendency of criticism to force philosophy and philology into a necessarily distorting mirroring of one another, alongside its strategic temptation to 'wring the neck of a certain system in order to stuff it into a contemporary pigeon-hole, or modify the dimensions of that pigeon-hole for the satisfaction of the analogymongers': 'Literary criticism is not book-keeping', Beckett opines (19). Clearly Beckett's own literary criticism is nothing like the marketplace symmetries of book-keeping or the slow measure of the ledger. From the start, it lurches untidily from impersonal exposition, through expressions of a personal reluctance to partake in criticism – 'And now here am I, with my handful of abstractions', writes Beckett, just after having criticised the gesture of forcing 'philosophical abstraction and empirical illustration' into a violently tendentious collocation (1983: 19) – into a sarcastically superior attack on those 'Ladies and Gentlemen' unable to recognise Mr Joyce's achievements. Pilling reads the essay as part of Beckett's attempt as an artist to create his own form of 'direct expression' (1997: 16), but the very lack of measure such 'direct expression' (*D*: 26) requires turns the text into something of a critical failure. For good criticism (in its early twentieth-century modernist manifestation) does have a fair amount of book-keeping in it – a measured and even construction, a certain impersonality in the exposition of its argument. It is instead Beckett's particular construction of art that refuses the strictures of book-keeping, and it is this idea of art that finds itself ironically mirrored in his somewhat unsuccessful criticism.

In Beckett's 1936 review of *The Amaranthers* by Jack B. Yeats, the true artist is explicitly opposed to those who work like critics: 'The chartered recountants take the thing to pieces and put it back together again. They enjoy it. The artist takes it to pieces and makes a new thing . . . *The Amaranthers* is art, not horology' (*D*: 89). In this formulation, art does not partake of the world of bourgeois work from which the biographical Beckett was still struggling to hold himself distinct: 'There is no allegory, that glorious double-entry, with every credit in the said account a debit in the meant, and inversely; but the single series of imaginative transactions' (90) that cannot be reduced to good economics. In art there is always an excess that cannot be neatly recuperated. Of course, for Beckett himself, the review loudly fails to achieve the status of art. Clearly torn between an idea of the artist he was trying at that point to be and a sense of the requirements of the genre into which he was miserably coerced by either the 'financial onus or friendly obligation', Beckett can only anxiously speak to MacGreevy of this piece as hack work – a 'tortuous puff' (*LSB*: 486). At the same time, though, the refusal to create 'order out of disorder' (Henning 1988: 15) that characterises art for Beckett does appear in the excessive comic form of his criticism, just as it does in his essays' propositions. As such and ironically, because it can neither be tidied up into book-keeping, chartered recountancy nor horology, this is criticism that, like art itself, refuses to 'work'.

So it is important to note that towards the end of 'Recent Irish Poetry' there is a clear moment where it defines itself as a failure, refusing to offer up 'segment after segment of cut and dried loveliness' (*D*: 71) that makes for fine criticism but certainly bad art, according to Belis's schema. In an explicit and somewhat humorous moment of (feigned?) incompetence, the insistently know-it-all Belis undercuts his previous critical and comic complacency to assert that, in fact, things don't work in this essay: he knows 'nothing at all' (76) of the poetry of Niall Sheridan, Donagh MacDonagh, Irene Haugh and Niall Montgomery. But the unmeasured comedy and polyvocal excess of this piece, which forces it into a particular kind of critical failure, begins to suggest the possibility of another kind of success. Sinéad Mooney is right to notice that, on close reading, an essay like 'Recent Irish Poetry' 'dissolves . . . into a curiously clotted affair of coinages, misquotations and segments of bravura sarcasm' (2005: 36), with Beckett's '"narrative," such as it is . . . full of gaps, slits, "dislocations" that serve as part of the text's metaphorics of rupture' (2005: 40). For, as she suggests, it is precisely in these dislocations, in the formal refusal of complacency and correctness of the Celtic scene in 'Recent Irish Poetry', that there begins to emerge an uncanny, seemingly proleptic, sense of Beckett's later writing and his 'ethics of incompetence' (40).

Tyrus Miller claims that Beckett's criticism espouses a high modernist position on the role of the artist and the production of autonomous, unified art because of his critique of Irish cultural conservatism (1999: 176), but he suggests that Beckett's fiction of the same period effects a specific sabotaging of a high modernist aesthetic. 'Perhaps at first defensively and only later as a "positive" strategy, Beckett would turn to parody and self-ridicule to call into question a number of modernist authorship's basic assumptions' (177), or to a late modernism, in Miller's terms. This argument is dependent, however, on Miller's ignoring one of the most obvious aspects of Beckett's 'lateness' – his smarting self-consciousness of being delayed as an artist written on the body of the early critical texts and letters in a stigmata of snorting, sardonic, superiority. It is also dependent on a rather straight reading of Beckett's criticism, which pays little attention to its potential and indeed sometime propensity for ironic parody and self-ridicule. And by ignoring the less than totally successful comic forms in Beckett's critical writing a significant moment in the evolution of an aesthetic of failure fades from view.

It is true that on at least one level Beckett's critical joking suggests the intention to forge an identification with particular versions of high modernism that heroically preserve themselves from an inchoate modernity and a bourgeois marketplace. As we have seen, though, a joke that binds teller and audience securely and successfully into a strong and mutually confirming identification needs to have a legible, clearly intentional, comic form. Good jokes are witty, if one follows Schlegel's account of wit as chemical – a rapid unification of disparate elements bound together and recognised under a higher principle of congruity (Schlegel 1991: 355). A good joke binds its excesses into the joking intention and is necessarily free from outbursts of spleen or personal gripes that display themselves too keenly or in an untransformed fashion. The witty joke uses the libidinal and instinctual drives of teller and audience in order to effect a pleasurable release, but it displaces and disguises the 'personality' of these elements. The good joke might thus, surprisingly, be thought of as having some kind of kinship with the modernist version of artistic impersonality that T. S. Eliot espouses in 'Tradition and the Individual Talent' (1919). Here, the poet's mind, already figured as a 'catalyst', transmutes experience to produce the artwork, but leaves no excess or residue of itself in the final product. Later in the essay, Eliot refigures the poet's mind as 'a receptacle for seizing and storing up numberless feelings, phrases, images, which remain there until all the particles which can unite to form a new compound are present together' (1920: 13). The poet's mind and the artwork produced are thus chemically synthetic, with no space given over to messy precipitates. For Eliot, the successful modernist artwork, like the successful joke, requires a binding of excessive detail beneath the pattern of a more global form.

But alongside the critical Beckett who does, at least partially, identify with the aesthetic mastery of certain versions of high modernism, there is a Beckett whose work begins to pull against conceptual and aesthetic synthesis and those forms of double-entry book-keeping necessary for the production of securely witty comedy, literary criticism and, indeed, particular versions of modernist art. Beckett's suspicions of such technical mastery in fact emerge very early. Even during the writing of his study of Proust in July 1930, Beckett told MacGreevy that the French author 'is so absolutely the master of his own form that he becomes its slave as often as not', while his own efforts at criticism shift the discourse from mastery and domination to the abjection of the anal and the production of waste rather than an easily exchangeable object: 'And to think that I have to contemplate him at stool for 16 volumes' (quoted in Knowlson 1996: 726), he groans. As much as the comedy of the criticism moves towards a centripetal effect that consolidates author and reader into positions of mastery, then, it also functions as a centrifugal force that pulls with an untidy insistence against the high modernist enthrallment to synthesis and system.[13]

In his influential essay from 1945, 'Spatial Form and Modern Literature', Joseph Frank both describes and expresses a high modernist attachment to an idea that the work of Pound, Eliot, Proust and Joyce, among others, represents a carving of the disparate, untidy material of experience, and the temporality of the medium of language, into a stable, unified and controlled spatial form. Joyce is read, not unproblematically, as an artist whose 'unbelievably laborious fragmentation of narrative structure, proceeded on the assumption that a unified spatial apprehension of his work would ultimately be possible' (Frank 1991: 21). Beckett, though, remembered a rather different Joyce – a Joyce who wondered in 1937 whether he had 'oversystematized *Ulysses*' (Ellman 1983: 650). And certainly by 15 January 1937, the Beckett now writing in his 'German Diary' offers a clear sense that any straightforward mastery of form has been relinquished:

> I am not interested in a 'unification' of the historical chaos any more than I am in the 'clarification' of the individual chaos, and still less in the anthropomorphisation of the inhuman necessities that provoke the chaos. What I want is the straws, flotsam, etc., names, dates, births and deaths, because that is all I can know. Pas [l'ordre/l'onde?], mais les bouchons . . . Rationalism is the last form of animism. Whereas the pure incoherence of times and men and places is at least amusing. (Quoted in Knowlson 1996: 244)[14]

It is significant that Beckett remembers that this transcription of excess 'is at least amusing', and perhaps, by implication, that an excessive comedy can produce 'incoherence', for it seems as though it is precisely within the overreaching comedy of his early work, in those moments of insecure joking where comic mastery begins to shift into the convulsions of irony, even into self-parody, that an art of failure begins to shape its densely polyvocal form.

S/M: Scholarship and Mimicry

To read the writing of the early Samuel Beckett, especially to read his published pieces alongside the 'grey canon' of his letters and notes, is to come across a young man who feels strikingly out of time with himself, or at least out of step. For the reader well versed in the self-effacements of the later Beckett, he sometimes seems to be getting embarrassingly ahead of things. In 1931, Beckett had just given up a seemingly promising career as a lecturer at Trinity and was struggling to get his work published, yet the self-penned biographical note written to accompany the four poems included in *The European Caravan* tells the reader, with a straight-faced intentness, that

> Samuel Beckett is the most interesting of the younger Irish writers. He is a graduate of Trinity College, Dublin, and has lectured at the École Normale Supérieure in Paris. He has a great knowledge of Romance literature, is a friend of Rudmose-Brown and of Joyce, and has adapted the Joyce method to his poetry with original results. His impulse is lyric, but has been deepened through the influence of Proust and the historic method. (Putnam 1931: 475)

As accurate as this assessment would later turn out to be, at this moment the self-defined superiority seems unwarranted, suggesting a rather anxious striving in its assertion of a position of mastery. And Beckett's letters show that he found himself all too easily falling out of phase with that overweening pose. In a letter of 3 September 1932 he seems to have lost his confidence; there is indeed an implication that it may never have been all that secure: 'I felt more than ever that all the early [poems] – all the Caravan ones – were fake and that nothing could be done with them' (*LSB*: 123). At this point, then, Beckett seems misaligned with where he wants or needs to be as he finds inner doubt suddenly speaking in chorus with the seemingly indifferent outside world.

In *Krapp's Last Tape* (1958) Beckett was famously to turn a sense of being out of phase with the perceptions and projections of a former self – a barely recognisable other – and with a world that could bestow material success, into an ontological exploration of the impossibility of self-coincidence. Something gets translated from biography into art, though, in the fact that the ironic expression of anachronism centres on hearing the thirty-nine year old Krapp's almost confident assertion that he is, 'I have every reason now to suspect at the . . . [*hesitates*] . . . crest of a wave' (*CDW*: 217) in terms of his publications. Of course, this is interpreted by the sixty-nine year old as laughable: 'Just been listening to that stupid bastard I took myself for thirty years ago, hard to believe I was ever as bad as that' (222). For here, the 'crest of a wave' re-emerges, with savage irony, as a form of storm-tossed and forced literary emigration: 'Seventeen copies sold, of which eleven at trade price to free circulating libraries beyond the seas. Getting known' (222). But it is important to note that even this thirty-nine year old Krapp, turgid with seeming self-confidence, nevertheless feels himself to be out of time with an even younger self of about twenty-seven. That arch tyro can now be judged as brittle and artificial as he '[s]neers at what he calls his youth and thanks to God that it's over [*Pause.*] False ring there. [Pause.] Shadows of the opus . . . magnum. Closing with a – [*brief laugh*] – yelp to Providence. [*Prolonged laugh at which* KRAPP *joins*.]' (218). Although doubling or mistaken identity is one of the great recurrent comic themes, it is precisely the attempt at a resounding laughter of superiority, both at the young Krapp and at the one on the brink of middle age, that fails here and articulates the impossibility of an assertion of risibility fixed in the fullness of time.

In his letter to Nuala Costello of 1934 (not quite thirty years before *Krapp*), the young Beckett feels nothing more than artistically disabled by his inability to be at one with himself and the exterior world. He yearns to produce something, either in life or art, that ploughs a straight furrow forwards rather than surges ahead and then lags behind: 'It's a great handicap to me in all my anabases [military advances] and stases that I can't express myself in a straightforward manner, and that I cannot behave in a way that has the most tenuous propriety of relationship to circumstance' (*LSB*: 184–5). As that anonymous reviewer of *More Pricks Than Kicks* from the *TLS* sagely notes, the 'uneven' tone produced by Beckett's comedy is indeed an indication of 'a talent not quite sure of itself' – a talent persistently overreaching or falling behind. It becomes particularly clear in the letters from the 1930s that Beckett's scornful and bleakly comic laughter at those publishers who refused to recognise him as 'the most interesting of the younger Irish writers' is not the articulation of any simple form of 'sudden glory'. In a letter to George Reavey of 8 October 1932, the desire to write a 'stinger' to the publishers who were delaying making their decision on *Dream* that Beckett was savvy enough to hold on to emerges in a sardonic humour with an emphasis on the lavatorial typical of the letters of late 1920s and early to mid-1930s:

> The novel doesn't go. Shatton & Windup [Chatto and Windus] thought it
> was wonderful but they couldn't they simply could not. The Hogarth Private
> Lunatic Asylum [Leonard Woolf] rejected it the way Punch would. [Jonathan]
> Cape was écoeuré [disgusted] in pipe and cardigan and his Aberdeen terrier
> agreed with him. Grayson has lost or cleaned himself with it. (*LSB*: 125)

Beckett clearly feels himself to be the butt of the joke in various respects,
and as such the aggression of the joke begins to turn inwards. He is the
one who has been '[s]hatton', the producer of work that has been used
as toilet paper; he is the one who has been abjected and who cannot find
himself in the right place at the right time or with a book that suits the
current mood.

When Beckett writes with bitter comedy to Mary Manning in 1936
of his difficulties in finding a publisher for *Murphy* and an editor's suggestion that he cut it by a third, there is again an imagined confluence
of writing and toilet paper suited to the reader's sense of the work as
shit-stained:

> My next work shall be on rice paper wound about a spool, with a perforated
> line every six inches and on sale in Boots. The length of each chapter will be
> carefully calculated to suit with the average free motion. And with every copy
> a free sample of some laxative to promote sales. The Beckett Bowel Books.
> Jesus in farto. Issued in imperishable tissue. Thistledown end papers. All
> edges disinfected. 1000 wipes of clean fun. Also in Braille for anal pruritics.
> (*LSB*: 383)

This scatological comedy is complicated, however, and turned away
from any simple mastery by the fact that Beckett, as we have seen,
associates his own work with an excremental action – with the same
disgusted and angry expulsion that he senses from the publishers. He
tells Reavey in 1932 that he will 'excavate for a poem for you one of
these dies diarrhoeae' (*LSB* 2009: 124–5), with the *dies irae* (the days
of wrath) comically aligned here with an angry anality. In a letter
to MacGreevy from August 1930, the poems sent to *The European
Caravan* are similarly described by this 'most interesting of the younger
Irish Writers' as 'three turds from my central lavatory' (*LSB*: 42), while
his monograph is expelled in a letter to Samuel Putnam from 1931 as
neither more nor less than 'my Proust turd' (*LSB*: 86).

So Beckett's comic aggression in these letters is obviously a response
to disappointment, but it is both turned outwards in the direction of a
hostile and putatively philistine world and inwards towards a scored and
lacerated internal landscape. Humour indeed invokes a sadistic violence
explicitly aligned with the anal that takes the materially failing author
and his works as both laughing comic master and risible comic object at

almost the same moment. At times Beckett could clearly place himself at a sufficient tangent to his scorn to see himself in the position of abject object, describing the just published *Proust* in 1931 as 'very grey & disgustingly juvenile – pompous almost – angry at best' (*LSB*: 65). The abrasion of the subjects and objects of aggression that appears between and within the letters marks Beckett's frustrated and perhaps rather adolescent insistence that he is not yet where he needs or deserves to be – something he comically rails against at one moment and sardonically accepts as inevitable confirmation at another. So for the young Beckett, the sense of being out of time with the self of the successful artist he hopes he can be indeed precipitates comedy, but it remains ambivalently caught between the idea that it is the world that is risibly out of step and the notion that it is Beckett himself who is rigidly stuck in an anal phase of being able to offer the world no more than faecal gifts. The letters reveal, then, Beckett's manifest failure to be on place, all at once to assume the position from which 'sudden glory' can be declared. There is, however, a sense that Beckett's work in the 1930s might be drawing to itself, from what it is learning about comedy, the raw materials for another aesthetic strategy that uses rather than transcends anachronism, ambivalence and uncertainty.

As Rachel Burrows's notes on Beckett's 1930 lectures on French literature reveal, Beckett admired writing that worked to express multiplicity and incoherence rather than unification under an ordered technical surface. Naturalists were duly criticised for their 'forced unification (Zola, etc.)' (Burrows, quoted in Le Juez 2008: 31). Dostoyevsky, however, was admired for his faithfulness to the inexpressible and the incoherent – to the 'abnégation qui permet dans l'âme de Dostoïevski les sentiments contraires [sacrifice which makes it possible for two contradictory feelings to exist in Dostoevsky's soul]' (37). Beckett also underlined the importance of Gide's '*polylogue* technique' (59) – the expression of different and potentially incompatible voices – and there is a suggestive resonance between Beckett's ideas of what he thought and hoped literature might be and an influential twentieth-century account of the novel that draws its force from an idea of comedy.

Mikhail Bakhtin argues in his essay from the 1930s 'From the Prehistory of Novelistic Discourse' that the novel, as a genre, is internally dialogised; it represents a *polyglossic* multiplicity of voices and ideological positions that never submit to an ultimate synthesis under a totalising authorial discourse. The novel is, however, only repeating a resistance to 'monologic' discourse inherent within an earlier tradition of parody and satire in which there is always dialogue between incompatible registers and world-views. Bakhtin describes how, in parody, one must recognise the form that is to be imperfectly repeated, its ideologies and ways of seeing, before submitting it to a dialogue with another discourse that might then render it laughable. It is through such discursive splitting, however, that parody offers the novel a new method of seeing and representing, the possibility of looking 'at language from the outside, with another's eyes, from the point of view of a potentially different language or style' (1981: 60). In contradistinction to a 'mono-logic' discourse that 'deals only with a subject whose praises he sings, or represents, or expresses . . . in his own language that is perceived as the sole and fully adequate tool for realizing the word's direct, objectiv-ized meaning' (61), the creation of parody requires, by its very nature, a form of discourse that is doubled and split, as two languages 'are crossed with each other' (75) – the language being parodied and the lan-guage that parodies. As such, 'every parody is an intentional dialogized hybrid. Within it, languages and styles actively and mutually illuminate one another' (76). Parody thus becomes a moment of resistance to the power of a monologic discourse that would seek to hold all meaning in its thrall; it is marked by the irruptive and interruptive return of another discourse that both produces the incongruities of comedy but also submits the laughter that appears to a radical evacuation of any absolute or uni-directional power.

Mooney has suggested that 'Recent Irish Poetry' is a 'dialogic text' (2005: 41) that consciously exhibits its untidiness as a way of critiquing the strident clarity of a nationalist aesthetic, but the entangled ques-tions of intention, reception and the dialogical, alongside the relations between criticism and aesthetic practice, are perhaps even more tightly knotted into a text from 1930 entitled 'Le concentrisme'. Written after Beckett's first forays into academic writing but before the journalistic reviews, 'Le concentrisme' is the text of a lecture given in French to Trinity's Modern Language Society on a fictitious French poet and founder of a literary movement – Jean du Chas. Consisting of a fake letter from Toulouse that recounts a meeting with Chas and indicates where the remains of his writing have been deposited, alongside a schol-arly examination of the poet's slender biography and uncertain aesthetic principles, the lecture was a hoax and meant to be recognised as such – an elaborate parody in the manner fashionable at the École Normale Supérieure from which Beckett had just returned. On one level it is an 'academic prank' (Cohn 2001: 21) that mimics in order to parody both the earnest academic exhilaration of unearthing new primary material and punctilious assessment of a writer's work, and what Beckett referred to in the same year as the 'grotesque comedy of lecturing' (*LSB*: 53). But 'Le concentrisme' is also a tensely uncertain, dialogical articulation of the contradictory desires and obligations that writing, reading and criticism in particular demand.

'Le concentrisme' is a comedy of pseudonyms, false origins, forgery and intentional misrecognition. The biographical Beckett delivered the lecture, but the text bears within itself a cacophony of dialogically intertwined voices. There is the writer of the letter, cited at the beginning of the work, who is supposedly responsible for placing the textual remains of Chas in a library. There is the lecturer who is delivering the lecture at the Modern Language Society, presumably visibly indistinguishable from Beckett. There is also Chas himself, whom it is hard surgically to separate from the biographical Beckett in that he happens to share Beckett's birthday, his supposed indolence, his resistance to academia and his knowledge of Descartes, Racine and Proust (Knowlson 1996: 121). The 'concentrisme' of the title seemingly refers to the Chasien aesthetic creed of 'Buddhistic Cartesianism' (Henning 1988: 12) that recommends a movement inwards, a retreat into asceticism, self-contemplation and then perhaps suicide; however, the image of a series of concentric circles also describes the structural *mise-en-abîme* of the piece and its ironically intertwined voices and sources.

There is clearly something intentionally comic in the bad-tempered tone of the opening letter. Chas is described by this anonymous and unknown writer as an 'imbécile', an 'idiot' (D: 35–6); his death is an 'incommodité' and the author of the letter only hopes that the work Chas left with him might be lost forever. He is bored, aggressive and rendered a little laughable to an audience or readership of academics for being totally unmoved by the part he has played in what appears to be a great literary detective story. But it soon becomes clear that academics are as much a target of laughter as they are laughing subjects. Indeed, as it turns out, the reader or lecture audience might not find the anonymous letter writer's posture so risibly out of step with his or her own position. After the lecturer's somewhat deadpan and rather unrevealing account of Chas's life and aesthetic creed, and with a growing sense of a somewhat strained spoof, one might well concur that the whole thing is just a waste of time. For the final page of Chas's journal is simply comically opaque: his is 'une de ces vies horizontals, sans sommet . . . inauguré, par l'accident d'une naissance, terminé, sans être conclu' (38) – the antithesis of a life that culminates in revelation. Of course, the lecturer undercuts his project, telling us that Chas transcends the sphere of the biographical with its boring, discreet conventions within which he and the audience have just been implicated: 'amour, amitié, gloire et le reste, que tout cela n'était qu'une dimension, ou l'attribut d'une dimension, inévitable, comme la friction, une condition de son adhésion à la surface de la terre' (38). Even the lecturer's conclusions concerning the project of explicating Chas's work become self-defeating, stating, as they do, that both Chas's work and life are and should remain inexplicable and detached from the orbit of academic criticism: 'Rien que l'idée d'une apologie, de la réduction de sa substance en hoquets universitaires – ce qu'il appelle: *reductio ad obscenum* – lui crispe et enchevêtre de nerfs' (*D*: 41).

Crucially, though, the lecturer of 'Le concentrisme' is walking in step with the critique of art and criticism that Beckett mounts in the essays of the late 1920s and restates throughout his critical work of the 1930s. For Chas's art is described as 'parfaitement intelligible et parfaitement inexplicable' (*D*: 42) – the very phrase Beckett uses admiringly to describe Proust's work (Beckett 1999: 92). In his review of '*Intercessions* by Denis Devlin' in 1937, Beckett will still deride those who demand that 'the creative act should burke its own conditions for the sake of clarity' (*D*: 94), and it is a savage yet strained comedy that is brought to bear on the critic in 'Le concentrisme' who cannot resist the temptations of interpretation. Criticism is staged as a rape that initiates the audience into those somewhat Sadeian pleasures of observing and enjoying violations by the powerful. The lecturer indeed bemoans the absence of the Supreme Highness of Monaco as he prepares himself to 'violer ce sujet', for he knows 'avec quelle violence les coeurs nobles sont actives par une matière intacte' (*D*: 36). 'Le concentrisme' shows how the 'con'/'cunt' of Chas's art is being forcibly, comically, pentratrated by the critic as con artist.

Despite this, the position outside of academia exemplified by the letter writer and artist is not uncritically lauded. The letter is bored, sulky: 'Vous êtes le premier à vous intéresser à cet imbecile. Voici tout ce que j'en sais . . . à cette époque, j'avais l'excellente habitude d'aller me soûler deux fois par semaine' (*D*: 35). Of course, the anonymous letter writer's scorn does not separate him from Chas the arist, nor from the critic who receives his letter, despite his obvious desire to place both in the position of risibility. Indeed, it is his stupidity, his 'connerie', as the French might have it, that cements Chas's identification with him: '"Vous avez l'air" me dit-il "suffisament idiot pour inspirer une confiance extreme . . . "Je vous embrasse, mon frère!"' (35). He is bored, but Chas, whose aesthetic maxim is taken to be '*va t'embêter ailleurs*' (38),[15] embraces the anonymous author as his ideal reader, just as Baudelaire, in the first poem of *Les Fleurs du Mal*, brings his reader within the orbit of that famous Symbolist 'Ennui' of '[l]a sottise, l'erreur, la péché, la lésine' (1975: 5). 'Hypocrite lecteur', he cries in recognition, 'mon semblable – mon frère' (Baudelaire 1975: 6). But concentrism cannot become a manifesto for a retreat inwards or out of the world – a call to go and 'be bored elsewhere'. Instead, each centre, each narrative voice with which the reader might rest in comic identification – including ideas Beckett held seriously – ends up being 'con': stupid. So although Chas is, ironically, the author of *Discours de la Sortie*, a parodically Cartesian title of *Discourse on the Way-Out*, for the reader/audience, the difficult and obstructed way inwards through Chas (the eye of a needle) offers neither the hope of a final penetration of the meaning of his art – for Chas's art is a non-existent hoax and the 'best' art is 'inexplicable' anyway – nor does it offer the listener/reader the possibility of refraining from the movement of implication. Each position that the reader/audience assumes has already been ventriloquised and rendered laughable by the text in an ironic, spiralling concentrism. Hypocrisy, boredom and the inviolable nature of art all become the tools for this rather aggressive prank that perhaps, in the end, has both too much sixth-form self-satisfaction and too much self-loathing about it really to succeed in straightforward comic terms. From the start, then, Beckett's comic aggression seems to be turning in on itself, chasing the tail of the comedy of superiority that ends up as a gnawing irony.

In 'The Rhetoric of Temporality', Paul de Man rehabilitates irony from its implication in the classical suspicion of comedy as aggressive self-confirmation by precisely drawing out a circling reflexivity found in Baudelaire's 1855 essay 'Of the Essence of Laughter'. Baudelaire suggests that anyone can laugh at an other, at a man who falls down in the street, but it is only the man who has acquired, 'by the force of habit, the power of getting outside himself quickly and watching, as a disinterested spectator, the phenomenon of his own ego' (1972: 148), who can laugh at himself. It is only a man who is perhaps a philosopher or an artist – the reflective human being rather than the one caught in everyday concerns – who can find himself amusing, interpellate himself into the second position within the joke and even, having recognised the new placement of a risible object, ventriloquise the third.

Using this notion of *dédoublement* or self-multiplication, De Man draws out Baudelaire's distinction between an intersubjective comedy that is oriented towards others – 'the comedy of superiority and inferiority, of master and slave' – and *'le comique absolu'*, which, at other moments in Baudelaire's work, is called irony (De Man 1983: 212). Within the realm of intersubjectivity, De Man claims that one speaks of 'difference in terms of the superiority of the one subject over another, with all the implications of will to power, of violence, and possession which come into play when a person is laughing at someone else' (1983: 212). This is the laughter of superiority that functions as a social corrective. But 'le comique absolu' is not intersubjective: it is self-conscious; it is intrasubjective. In Baudelaire's terms it displays the human 'capacity of being both himself and someone else at one and the same time' (1972: 160). The 'reflective disjunction' that occurs in certain self-conscious philosophical or aesthetic modes of language is coterminous with comic irony because each uses the potential of the human to stand at a distance from its experience and to take itself rather than the other as an object. De Man asserts, however, that the

> ironic, twofold self that the writer or philosopher constitutes by his language seems able to come into being only at the expense of his empirical self . . . The ironic language splits the subject into an empirical self that exists only in the form of a language that asserts the knowledge of this inauthenticity. (De Man 1983: 214)

So the ironic, doubled self is constituted at a cost to the lucid and self-identical subject, for despite all that has been said concerning the will to mastery in humour, the dehiscence and doubling in irony cannot finally be a reassuring movement: 'to know inauthenticity is not the same as to be authentic' (214). As De Man puts it, '[i]rony is unrelieved *vertige*, dizziness to the point of madness' (215), and irony's pathos is vertigo because of the sudden teetering suspension of omnipotence's imagined heights.

As we have seen, in the ventriloquies of 'Le concentrisme' laughing superiority clashes comically with other registers and narrative voices, leading to the bathos and irony of a complex self-reflective critique. It remains clear, though, that laughing superiority is neither simply transcended nor finally achieved; instead, the positions of laughing subject and risible 'butt' are passed, with ludic enthusiasm, around these different narrative voices. By interpellating incommensurable positions within the space of the comic text, violence still insists, though, for these incongruous registers clash rather than sit amiably with one another; they jostle for power. So despite the fact that De Man's irony does not offer a position of self-mastery (even the mastery of understanding oneself as split), neither does it pass beyond violence; irony instead seems to turn violence inwards. The aggression within laughter is withdrawn from the other and is instead applied to the self as other.

Now it is clear that Beckett is concerned throughout his *oeuvre* with both the pleasures and aesthetics of self-torment. There are, for example, a number of quotations in his *Dream* notebook from the pseudonymous William M. Cooper's 1887 *Flagellation and Flagellants* (Pilling 1999: 47), alongside a careful noting down of the phrase 'Masoch-Sade'. Although the desire to explore figures that are both tormentors and tormented never really goes away, persisting across the *oeuvre*,[16] Beckett had encountered Sade perhaps as early as 1931 through reading and taking notes on Mario Praz's *The Romantic Agony*. He told MacGreevy that he had been reading Sade directly in 1934 (Weller 2008: 108–9), and in 1938 Beckett considered and finally accepted a commission to translate *Les 120 Jours de Sodome*, claiming it to be 'one of the capital works of the 18th century' (quoted in Knowlson 1996: 293). He feared, though, that the project might come back to bite him. 'I don't want to be spiked as a writer' (*LSB*: 604), he confided to Reavey, seeming to find that particular version of masochism unappealing. Nevertheless, the letters from the 1930s clearly reveal Beckett's insistent association of writing with passive self-torment, for amid the desire to write 'stingers' to others, he confides to MacGreevy in 1931, '[y]ou know I can't write at all. The simplest sentence is torture' (*LSB*: 62). Consequently, even the very early 'Le concentrisme' might be thought of as being part of a peculiarly Beckettian tradition that describes and worries away at the uneasy power struggles between author/editor/narrator and readers by means of a comic form in which textual sadism and masochism inhabit the same space.

There is a way of understanding the reversal of joking sadism into ironic masochism in Beckett's early work through the economies of psychoanalysis, and in 1934 Beckett encountered Freud's 'Instincts and Their Vicissitudes' (1915) as he read Ernest Jones's *Papers on Psychoanalysis* from which he was taking notes in what appears to be an attempt at self-diagnosis. He transcribes how the development of sexual instinct may proceed through 'a change in instinct from active to passive (sadism into masochism, scoptophilia into exhibitionism, love into being loved), or as a reversal of content (love into hate)' (Beckett 1934–5: 8/5 6). Freud describes instinct as an innate biological drive to action whose aim is to achieve satisfaction by removing the state of stimulation at the source of the instinct, thus discharging or reducing it to the lowest possible level. At first, Freud asserts a distinction between the ego or self-preservative instincts and the sexual instincts. He then goes on to suggest, however, that these instincts, both of which are in thrall to the pleasure principle, are not so neatly distinguishable; they possess instead 'the capacity to act vicariously for one another to a wide extent' and to 'change their objects readily' (Freud 1915: 125) – their objects being the things through which the instinct can achieve its aim. Freud thus determines that although the ultimate aim of each instinct is unchangeable, there are many paths that can lead to it. Instinct can suddenly seem to twist and invert into its opposite: voyeurism can become exhibitionism; sadism can twist into masochism; love can become hate.

This possibility of the reversal of sadism into masochism tells us a good deal about the shifting of positions that takes place within joking and irony. If the laughter of superiority can be taken to be sadistic (defined by Freud as 'the exercise of violence or power upon some other person as object' (1915: 126)), then irony can be read as a form of self-torture as the 'object is given up and replaced by the subject's self' (126). As Freud puts it, '[t]he desire to torture has turned into self-torture and self-punishment . . . The active voice has changed, not into the passive, but into the reflexive, middle voice' (127).[17] For a tendentious joke to work, in Freud's terms, it must be directed outwards; it must indicate a social process in which the joke is aimed at an object, an other (in the second position), and shared with an audience (in the third position). And in terms of 'proper' joking, the appearance of an other person in the third position who tortures the self by refusing to recognise or respond to the joke can spell the end of joking pleasure. The third position has the power to confirm the joke and takes a central role in the production of its pleasures, but, as such, it renders the first position powerfully subject to the benevolence of the third. It is this structural demand for a third that is the weakness of power within all jokes.

Although irony is not always onanistic – it will sometimes let others in on the joke – it does, however, seem to represent something of a refusal to share or be subjected to the other's estimate, as its process of splitting enables the self to become a laughing subject, its own object and its audience. As such, it is a properly sadomasochistic form. Within the ironic text, comic sadism is directed from the textual self towards an object, but that object, which is also the textual self, experiences this deflection in masochistic terms. The receiver of the joke is also the self who may sadistically confirm the risibility of the second position, but it might place that primary sadistic subject into the second position under the dominance of its own lacerating authority; the receiver of the joke may well, in turn, be subject to a masochistic reversal of power as its judgements, too, are turned into the object of the joke. And so there remains much comic aggression within the sparring and incompatible voices of 'Le concentrisme': the sarcastic debunking of the academic industry and its desperate search for new heroes and movements to violate; the caricaturing of a sneeringly superior figure who considers himself outside of the academy and the artistic world; the stereotypical rendering of the posturing poet who retreats inwards into 'folie' and away from rationality or interpretation; the lambasting of the academic who tries to have his cake and eat it by adhering to the cult of the supreme, inviolable purity of the artwork, but gorges himself on the deciphering of such artworks anyway. There are certainly moments of mastery, even of momentary laughing superiority. But these are only temporary, passing possibilities of stability, for each position, once assumed, is then rendered risible as laughing superiority stages its persistence and its power, alongside its immanent instability. 'Le concentrisme' is thus a text traversed by a temporal comic rhythm of mastery and loss, the bolstering of the laughing self and the immanent splitting of the empowered subject, in which the potentially secure communal laughter of shared joking is radically undercut. In such irony laughter does not disappear, but it does become very uncertain. As Beckett puts it in his only critical discussion of irony, perhaps the 'face remains grave, but the mind has smiled' (*D*: 89).

Critical Timing

In a 1934 review of 'Windfalls' by Sean O'Casey, Beckett describes how comedy can function as a disintegrative force. He states that 'Mr O'Casey is a master of knockabout in this very serious and honourable sense – that he discerns the principle of disintegration in even the most complacent solidities and activates it to their explosion' (*D*: 82). He describes O'Casey's admired method as a form of 'dramatic dehiscence [in which] mind and world come asunder in irreparable dissociation' (82), confirming the ways in which comedy, as method, resists the creation of an art that is neatly explicable.[18] As we have seen, however, Beckett's comic method becomes a way of constructing a powerful authority over the material under analysis, even if that power reveals itself to be partial or occasionally even illegitimate, as it is placed into dialogue with other suspicious and self-defeating voices. The dialogical comedy of these early texts thus enacts a reversible drama in which positions are both consolidated and split. Rather than an immutable spatial positioning of subject over object, this dialogical comedy dramatises a continuously changing temporal movement in which there is no final victory: there is none of what the critical voice in *Proust* dismissively calls the 'vulgarity of a plausible concatenation' (Beckett 1999: 81–2) or the review of *The Amaranthers* calls the use of 'the rule of three' (*D*: 90) – thesis, antithesis, synthesis. Beckett's comedy describes itself instead through the temporal rhythms of unresolved contradiction – rhythms that trace out an oscillation rather than a *telos*.

In a letter of 1938, despite (or perhaps because of) his own critical works, Beckett remains scornful of the ordering ambitions of literary critics who 'in a phrase from Bergson can't be happy till they have "solidified the flowing"' (*LSB*: 599). By this time, Beckett had found in his rather particular irony a method that unpicked the stitches of neat critical identifications, that mimed critical failure, but permitted 'the flowing' in its shuttling between agonistic discourses that appeared over, through and as time. Of course, if Beckett uses irony to enact a critical failure, his criticism also fails to produce good, witty jokes that mask their movements through time by effecting sudden and speedy unifications or combinations of the seemingly heterogeneous. In Schlegel's terms: 'Many witty ideas are like the sudden meeting of two friendly thoughts after a long separation' (1991: 37); wit is thus a moment of synthesis that is only later subject to the vicissitudes latent within the temporal moment of exchange. So, Critchley suggests, if wit is 'synthetic, the chemical mixing of disparate elements, then irony is diaeretic, the separation or division of those elements' (1997: 114). Where wit binds, irony unbinds; where wit creates new links and relationships, irony loosens previously established positions. De Man similarly emphasises the temporal structure of irony – a structure that does not progress towards the achievement of a totality: 'irony engenders a temporal sequence of acts of consciousness which is endless . . . irony is not temporary but repetitive, the recurrence of a self-escalating act of consciousness' (1983: 220). Irony indeed works through a spiralling structure rather than through any teleological movement, for, as De Man puts it, the time of irony is not Hegelian time: irony 'can know inauthenticity but can never overcome it' (1983: 222); it is never 'a preliminary movement toward a recovered unity' (219).

So Beckett's ironic joking narratives are structures that refuse the shape of neat identifications. As Freud implies through his use of multiple examples of joke work, joking has no essence, only the framework of social exchange and the interchangeability of its structural elements. Joking is an economy, then, a nexus of exchanges rather than a spatially determinable, secure and neat form in which the unpredictability of reception, of the future, is implicated into its structure from the very beginning. As Steven Connor puts it, economic activity is necessarily oriented towards a goal, but 'every transaction (symbolic or otherwise) can go wrong, not only as a matter of accident, but as a structural principle' (1992: 91). And because '[e]conomic activity takes place hazardously over time' (Connor 1992: 92), the risk of misrecognition and the necessity for uncertainty is built into its economies from the start. One can always be deceived and cheated in an exchange and, as Norman Knox implies, irony has 'form' for this: the definition of irony throughout the centuries never strays too far from the tendency to deceive and dissimulate (1961: 38–43).

By sensing and staging the necessary immanence of modes of failure within joking economies, then, Beckett's very early texts begin to produce a method that folds the uncertainty of temporality and social exchange, of intercourses between selves and others and the self as other, into the very form and fabric of the writing. Beckett's early writing is thus shaped by its compulsive, uncertain assertions of comedy into its own rhetoric of temporality, with humour marking what can only ever be a contingent, temporary authority. What Frank influentially described in 1945 as the high modernist enthrallment to a spatial form and aesthetic mastery finds itself coming undone. Beckett's late modernism instead uses a technique inherited from the vicissitudes of the comic and the savage deformations it perpetrates upon texts and writing subjects to produce a new aesthetic: an aesthetic dominated by the disintegrations, dislocations and the uncertain economics of temporality – an aesthetic determined by anachronism and an emphasis on a timing which, more often than not, is comic.

Notes

1. Both full-length studies by Cohn and Topsfield of Beckett's comedy and humour refer only in passing to the critical essays. Topsfield (1988) reads them as statements that illuminate Beckett's intent in the fictional and dramatic works while Cohn offers only a very brief analysis of the critical essays (1962: 16–17).
2. Beckett is referring to the short story 'Sedendo and Quiescendo' which was excerpted from the unpublished *Dream*.
3. Written in 1935, this piece was commissioned by *The Bookman*. Beckett took such a long time writing the essay that by the time it was completed *The Bookman* had ceased publication. Although it was offered to Eugène and Maria Jolas's *transition*, they were not interested in a contribution of this sort, believing they had solicited a 'prose sketch' (see Fehsenfeld and Overbeck 2009: 333). Beckett's response to the rejection was furious (Fehsenfeld and Overbeck 2009: 340).
4. Beckett refers here to George Bernard Shaw's short story 'The Black Girl in Her Search of God', published in 1932. It is the story of an African woman who seeks God by questioning a number of Judeo-Christian, Muslim and scientific figures, whom she then sees off through argumentation and the use of her knobkerry (an African club). The black girl finally marries an Irishman, with whom she has children, resuming her search for God when they have left home. The suggestion of inter-racial marriage may have enraged the censors, even as it makes the black girl's children legitimate. Beckett seems to be pointing out the irony that the production of children within wedlock is being censored here by the religious state.
5. A thorough and historically nuanced account of eugenicist ideas and their impact on the public statements and private concerns of Yeats, Woolf and Eliot is developed by Childs (2001).

6. Coughlan reads the whole essay as 'an Irish modernist manifesto' (1995: 178).
7. I am grateful to Eckart Voigts-Virchow for the translation and suggestions.
8. Knowlson reminds us that 'Censorship in the Saorstat' demonstrates the clear and persisting influence of Rudmose-Brown, 'who tried to set Beckett against all orthodoxies, whether religious, philosophical or ethical' (1996: 51).
9. Knowlson is quite right, however, to note an increasing uncertainty and suspicion of the 'crescendo of disparagement' in this period – an uncertainty to which we will return.
10. These tropes will be considered in detail in Chapter 2.
11. As Pilling notes, readers might 'have already felt Beckett's opening sentence to be "overlong"' (1997: 115).
12. Norman Knox suggests one definition of irony as 'blame-by-praise and praise-by-blame' (1961: 4).
13. Henning usefully notes the tension between centripetal and centrifugal elements in Beckett's early work (1988: 32).
14. I am grateful to Mark Nixon for adding details to this entry omitted in Knowlson's transcription.
15. Cohn states that Beckett translated this Chasien motto in a personal letter as 'feck off' (1983: 169). In *A Beckett Canon*, she translates it as 'go be bored elsewhere' (2001: 21).
16. See Sheehan (2008: 97–9), Weller (2008: 109–12).
17. Stéphanie Ravez describes the construction of a tortured space in *Malone Dies* through the trope of *autontimorumenos* (literally, 'I torment myself') (2002: 144).
18. Beckett learns the word 'dehiscence', which he notes down in the *Dream* notebook, from a context explicitly concerned with the libidinal: Pierre Garnier's *Onanisme seul et à deux sous toutes leurs formes et leurs conséquences* (Pilling 1999: 64).

Chapter 2

Gagging in the *Trilogy*

'My life, my life, now I speak of it as something over, now as of a joke which still goes on, and it is neither, for at the same time it is over and it goes on, and is there any tense for that?' (*T*: 36). So muses Molloy, bound to that sometimes boggy, sometimes shiftingly stony hinterland between being fully present to his own life and being able to rest on the still bedrock of death imagined as a final, merciful extinction. Unable to find a 'tense' to materialise this push and pull, the *Trilogy* evokes instead its extraordinary capacity for retarded goings on in the tension between these desired yet refused poles – a tension that, in turn, produces one of the essential rhythms of the texts. As we will see, particularly in *Malone Dies* (written in French in 1948) and *The Unnamable* (written in French in 1949), the longed-for achievement of self-presence perversely offers to enact consummation as extinction in a coincidence of contraries. Malone looks to make an end for himself; as such, he is on his guard against 'throes' (*T*: 179), the agonised labour of childbirth that sits as an uneasy mirror image of his own death struggles. But the stories that might serve as a distraction from himself and thus hasten his end, of course, produce tensions and take their time, leading to further throes – becoming the very thing which makes an ending impossible. As Malone's stories are delivered into the world according to an irresistible 'sense of dilation' (235) that marks the peculiarly Beckettian association of birth with anality (Hill 1990: 101), there is the beginning of a sense that the bodily motions imagined to materialise the unthinkable 'tense' of being caught in this space, this time, might produce matter that only magnifies the subject's spatial occupation in the world rather than enacts any wasting away.[1] '[M]y arse, for example, which can hardly be accused of being the end of anything', writes Malone, is of such potential expanse and power that it could achieve an intercontinental incontinence: 'if [it] suddenly started to shit at the present moment, which God forbid, I firmly believe the lumps would fall out in Australia'

(235). Malone encircles himself with words, but as that linguistic matter tightens around the mouth of the textual subject, narration is in the end more strongly in thrall to the gag reflex than to the pleasures of either suffocation or starvation; matter pushed down the gullet is thrown up in and as a throe of its own – '[c]hoke, go down, come up, suppose, deny, affirm, drown' (210).

Words are matter here, and they offer sustenance; indeed they offer the only sort of 'nourishing murk' (*T*: 193) a fictional character can ever really have. But words can also be a choking hazard: irreducible matter that resists absorption and is coughed up in gobbets only to be swallowed again as a bare subsistence diet. There is, of course, no chance of Malone simply giving up on words. Even to articulate the desire to give up on expression enacts a paradox by which words become both the method and means of force-feeding: 'when they cannot swallow any more someone rams a tube down their gullet, or up their rectum, and fills them full of vitaminised pap, so as not to be accused of murder' (253–4). The subjects, including Malone himself, are nourished by words because not just any death will do; there is a requirement that each die after its own fashion, replete and 'glutted', 'of old age pure and simple' (254), rather than in a silence in which pen or book is simply put down. In *The Unnamable*, where birth rather than death is the chief concern, the desire to labour and bring a subject into the world that could speak of itself alone rather than its avatars is similarly interfered with by a gagging mechanism that interrupts the clean birth as much as the quick death. Here, words contaminate the body into which they are violently forced, infecting the subject so that it brings up a monstrosity that is never the longed-for thing itself but always some kind of regurgitated other: 'It's a poor trick that consists of ramming a set of words down your gullet on the principle that you can't bring them up without being branded as belonging to their breed' (327). The Unnamable's only hope is the alimentary dysfunction perhaps caused by the constant application of emetics, its 'inability to absorb, [its] genius for forgetting'. Knowing it has 'never understood a word of it in any case, not a word of the stories it spews, like gobbets in a vomit' (327), means perhaps it will know enough to sense that these force-fed words, this matter, are not completely at one with it.

Gagging For It

It is clear that across Beckett's *oeuvre* gags are associated with the torturous violence of forced expression. In *Rough for Radio II* (1976), Fox is gagged, blindfolded, ears plugged and hooded. When the play is 'in session' constraints are removed and Fox is forced to articulate, even though all previous words have been unacceptable. The gag prevents words from slipping out unheard, in a space free from obligation, but the ligature forced round and into the mouth also ensures that Fox cannot enjoy the peace of simple and silent expiration. As in Malone's imaginings, Fox is subject to the 'rigid enforcement of the tube-feed, be it per buccam or be it on the other hand per rectum' (276), that will keep him alive to utter. By the time *Catastrophe* (written in French in 1982) has been reached, the gag seems so obviously to call forth tortures associated with artistic expression, whether that be the totalitarian attempt to stop up the artist's mouth or the compulsion to articulate words that always risk being those of others, it seems like an ironic acknowledgement of what has become a familiar Beckettian prop. 'What about a little . . . a little . . . gag?', asks the assistant, only for the director to bark, 'For God's sake! This craze for explication! Every i dotted to death! Little gag! For's God's sake!' (*CDW*: 459).

Although literal gags are associated with torture and forced expression in Beckett's theatre, there is, however, another tradition of gagging into which the *Trilogy* insinuates itself. For the logic of linguistic peristalsis and compulsive expression that displaces the Unnamable's repeated attempt to give birth to its voice alone is not simply torturous, there is also something painfully funny, even enlivening, about it. The ineluctable sinus rhythm of these spasms, whose interruptive force works at the level of narrative but shudders down to the aporetic syntactical refusals of individual sentences, produces gagging in that more conventional theatrical sense. And there is more than a fortuitous link between structures of interruption, deferral and the comic, as revealed by the etymology of the theatrical 'gag'. In the nineteenth century, 'gag' was used to denote an interruption within a written piece by some extempore play, with it only later applying more specifically to a deliberately staged joke. Defined as '[e]xpressions, remarks, etc. not occurring in the written piece but interpolated or substituted by the actor' (*OED*), 'gag' perhaps evolved from a mining term for a piece of wood that could be used to stay a collapse. In one sense, then, the maundering of the *Trilogy* is nothing but a series of gags, of interpolations, of jokes which still go on, that never give way to the main story.

In this defeat of a certain narrative expectation, it is possible to see why such theatrical gags are now commonly associated with a particular kind of deliberately staged joke. In the *Trilogy* interruption and interpolation certainly work within a recognisable climate of comic incongruity as expectation is derailed by clownish failure and pointless persistence. Moran never finds Molloy (apart from within himself perhaps) yet he continues; Malone doesn't die but continues to throw up 'throes'; despite all that effort the Unnamable never articulates words that are its alone but gags on the lexicon of others. At the level of narrative episode, interruption is similarly and persistently the cause of comic effect; Malone diverts his story of Macmann and Moll in the asylum, which is, in itself, a detour in his drive towards the longed-for destination of death, to note, comically, that he is picking up: 'I pause to record that I feel in extraordinary form. Delirium perhaps' (*T*: 258). Even in the construction of individual sentences, this sense that syntactical trajectories are comically derailed is clearly everywhere to be found. Critchley indeed notes that what Beckett famously termed his 'syntax of weakness' (Harvey 1970: 249) is an inherently comic form which stages 'sequences of antithetical inabilities: unable to go on, unable not to go on' (Critchley 1997: 23).[2] It functions as 'a paradoxical form of speech which defeats our expectations, producing laughter with its unexpected verbal inversions, contortions and explosions' (Critchley 1997: 159).

There is, however, something particular about Beckett's comedy that borrows from the vaudeville or burlesque gag but draws out and exorbitantly extends a significant part of the latent form of such performances. Leo Bersani and Ulysse Dutoit have noted Beckett's theatrical interest in the side-show, pointing out, however, that the side-show usually retires in favour of the main act for which it functions as a warm-up. But Vladimir and Estragon in *Godot* 'have to do their number for far longer than they had planned, indeed are condemned never to make way for the big number' (Bersani and Dutoit 1993: 32). In *The Unnamable*, too, the torturously repeated attempts to bring a voice into existence, the hiccups in narration as the story gags and commences again, are duly imaged as the staging of a 'compulsory show', a form of forced entertainment. '[Y]ou hear a voice, perhaps it's a recitation, that's the show, someone reciting, selected passages, old favourites', it states; but both narrator and reader come to realise that we're still watching the gags and not the main event at all: 'he's only preluding, clearing his throat', but 'that's the show, waiting for the show, to the sound of a murmur' (*T*: 385).

Now in one sense this persistence, of continuing in the face of the mutely malign object world that will not submit to the subject's projects, is the very essence of clowning. But narration that hopelessly keeps on keeping on enacts something of a defection from standard forms of comic writing. Although it is obvious that Beckett's 'syntax of weakness' is amusing, the verbal comedy of the *Trilogy* is also not what one might call securely witty. Instead, the comic moments are more like Murphy's 'jokes that had once been good jokes', but are perhaps no longer quite so, than those that 'had never been good jokes' (Beckett 1993: 41). One reason why it is so hard to extract quotable comic matter from the *Trilogy* is not because of its lack; it is more that comic incongruities are everywhere, but they never give up on going on. Malone ponders on a phial he once had: 'Laxatives? Sedatives? I forget. To turn to them for calm and obtain diarrhoea, my, that would be annoying' (*T*: 256). But he immediately and irresistibly expels an excess of matter, a smear of verbal diarrhoea, into the scene that substitutes a languid fading out for the concussive crack and slap of comic disjunction: 'In any case the question does not arise I am calm, insufficiently, I still lack a little calm. But enough about me' (256). So although this clearly produces comic effects, it also causes the end of the joke to become increasingly hard to detect, as the synthesis of the punchline towards which a comic instance races is overshot in a logic that does not simply make a masterful joke of clownish failure. This joking is instead brought into commerce with a particular, although not total, failure of comic writing, with the comic gag partaking of the violent evacuations of a gagging reflex which brings up and reconsumes the same old words, the same old jokes – jokes that are winding down but are never finally wound up.

Maybe, though, it is precisely in the comic timing of this textual gagging, played out according to the rhythms of a body, that Beckett finds the impossible 'tense' able to evoke what is 'over and still goes on' (*T*: 36). For the Unnamable imagines an end for itself in a laugh, a form of final word: 'I'll laugh, that's how it will end, in a chuckle' (*T*: 412), but that chuckle sputters on, moving the orality of laughter down towards the other end of the peristaltic system: 'chuck chuck, ow, ha, pa, I'll practise, nyum, hoo, plop, psss, nothing but emotion, bing bang, that's blows, ugh, pooh, what else, oooh, aaah, that's love, enough, it's tiring, hee hee, that's the Abderite,[3] no, the other' (412). Although the Unnamable hopes for an end, a 'real silence, not the one where I macerate up to the mouth' (412), it becomes clear as the narration gurgles on and the peristaltic system chugs into a retching reverse that nothing sufficiently new that it could make a real end is ever really taken into the system – only words which are the expectorant matter both of the self and of others. Instead of invention, then, what is offered up is narration as incontinence or an emetic compulsion, to be followed by a reconsumption of the body's undigested discharges. The stories are indeed ironically nourished by that which resists either being smoothly incorporated into a curve towards a denouement, or passed through the body of the text according to the unconscious muscular spasms of peristalsis that deliver matter downwards from mouth to anus. Purging is not cathartic, here; instead, matter is endlessly churned, expressed and reincorporated into a narrative system figured as a derailed digestive system: 'They chew, swallow, then after a short pause effortlessly bring up the next mouthful. A neck muscle stirs and the jaws begin to grind again' (9).[4]

Partial Incorporation

This sense that narrative in the *Trilogy* is compelled by modes of regurgitation and partial incorporation is suggestively echoed within the extra-textual lives of these works. First written in French and relatively quickly translated, the French texts of the *Trilogy* and their English afterlives, which mark the beginning of Beckett's lifelong determination to translate his own work, indeed play out a churned and compulsive game of sameness and difference through 'rewritings' that sometimes appear as faithful ventriloquies of a seemingly 'original' text, but always fold disturbance and dislocation into their fabric. As Leslie Hill rightly points out, in the *Trilogy* translation 'becomes an exercise in disruption rather than transposition' (1990: 46), for, as enacted thematically in these texts, there is neither a completely faithful repetition nor a sense of revision towards a more perfected whole.[5] The French text seems already to know that it has a fraternal rather than identical twin waiting to be born; indeed, in the case of *Molloy* (written in French in 1947) and its complicated birth, Beckett's English translation of part of the text was actually published before its French 'original'.[6]

It is a truism of writing about comedy that joking forms, with their keen attention to idiom and rhythm, are notoriously resistant to translation. It is significant, then, that in Beckett's work tropes of partial repetition, compulsive recommencement and the refusal of the absolute innovation or uniqueness that would enable, for example, the Unnamable's 'true' voice to be articulated, constellate around the comic. For if comedy is a locus of untranslatability in any text, it becomes for Beckett a site where the impossibility of producing a faithful singular voice might find itself being most powerfully staged.[7] There is indeed a sense that the 'gagging' which so directs both form and theme of the particular novels within the *Trilogy* is also echoed in their extra-textual existence. Lived out under the dominating sign of disruptive revision and partial incorporation and bound to a metaphorics of incomplete digestion, the forced returns of translation produce and intensify through comedy those morbidly aspirant modes of going on with which this work remains fundamentally concerned.

A writer with even greater facility for multilingualism than Beckett, Vladimir Nabokov, once criticised the Irish writer by noting that

'Beckett's French is a schoolmaster's French, a preserved French, but in English you feel the moisture of verbal association and of the spreading live roots of his prose' (1990: 172). The limpid liveliness and loveliness of the organic lines of beauty in Nabokov's own divergences from his mother tongue and his sense of the 'private tragedy' of having to abandon his 'infinitely rich and docile Russian' (15) are, of course, hardly part of a recognisably Beckettian aesthetic. Perhaps the artist who insisted that he was anxious about writing in English 'because you couldn't help writing poetry in it' (Coe 1962: 14) would not have been too disturbed by being accused of the foreign speaker's lack of naturalisation. But it is certainly true that the English text is alive with a comic use of idiom in a way that the French is not. Contra Nabokov, however, the disruption of the French text produces an anxious vividness rather than any comforting organicism or return to a motherland, a mother tongue. For despite the intensifications of the comic in English, humour never appears there without advertising the disturbances within the abrasions of idiom that emerge precisely from the inevitable 'failure' of complete translation – the failure of total incorporation of one text into another.

An example. When Molloy begins a new narrative episode – the tale of his stiffening legs – the French text hiccups and stutters, inaugurating a mode of narration that becomes central to the *Trilogy* as a whole: 'Quelle histoire, pourvu que je ne me foute pas dedans' (Beckett 1952: 103). A straight translation might be 'What a story, provided I don't muck it up'. But in Beckett's Anglo-Irish, 'pourvu que' (provided that) is intensified, concentrating the sense of jagging and gagging already present in the French into '[w]hat a story, God send I don't make a balls of it' (*T*: 77). The abrasion of divinity against 'low' corporeality and the determination that the story of this failing body is sufficiently important that it requires God's protection – a godsend that the reader likely assumes will never materialise – allows Hiberno-English to improve on the gag. 'God send' indeed seems like an Irishism, but it is also disruptive and odd. Beckett does not choose the more recognisable 'God forbid' or 'please God'. 'God send' seems instead like a half-remembered archaism, intensifying the reader's sense of Molloy's estrangement from both his topographical and textual landscape.

Now this structural narrative aside, which hitches up the forward movement of the narration but forces comic intensifications in the English *Molloy*, becomes the fundamental narrative method of *Malone Dies*. And in the first few pages of that novel, Beckett indeed roots out a fine and rhythmic idiomatic rhyme in his metamorphosis of a faintly vaudevillian image of '[m]aintenant j'ai besoin d'un bossu, il en arrivait un aussitôt, fier de la belle bosse qui allait faire son numéro' (Beckett

1951b: 9) into '[n]ow I need a hunchback, immediately one came running, proud as punch of his fine hunch that was going to perform' (*T*: 180). The invocation of comic type in a Mr Punch with his trademark hunch certainly increases a sense of knockabout, but here the point is that the comic vividness of this hunchback isn't what Malone says he wants. He wants to 'die tepid, without enthusiasm' (180), without making a song and dance of it. In fact he wants both to be still and to play, to have company and to be alone, to continue and to have done. Indeed, when the French text suggests that if he is left alone he will nevertheless 'jouerai[t] tout seul' (10), the English rewriting works up a masturbation joke: 'I shall play with myself. To be able to conceive such a plan is encouraging' (181), with the juxtaposition of onanism and conception, and the intensified sense of the addition of something new into the text – a plan, a joke – contributing to a sense of the resistant aliveness of Malone's comic impotence. Marking a similar mode, the description of Sapo's body stumbling on, just as the text does, 'tottering for a moment, then suddenly was off again, in a new direction . . . drifting, as though tossed by the earth' (196), is tailed by an addition in the English that is simply absent in the French. The English text interjects an ironic reminder of the contingency and intermittency of this textual incarnation. For Sapo, like Malone himself, is just one among many, subject to an endless and interruptive reworking. 'There is a choice of images' (196), intones the English text.

Malone's uncertainty as to whether all this business of adding and inventing is a form of 'losing time or gaining it' (*T*: 182) is crucial. The comedy certainly facilitates the passing of time, but Malone becomes clear that such textual liveliness does not hasten the longed-for approach of the 'tepidity' of death. Beckett concurs somewhat with Nabokov's determination that his French is 'school-masterly' by telling Alan Schneider in a letter of 1958 that in *L'Innomable* he had 'felt the old tug to write in French again, where control is easier for me' (Harmon 1998: 37). But Beckett does not leave Schneider with an image of self-satisfaction, adding and admitting that such linguistic control is 'probably excessive' (Harmon 1998: 37). Beckett seems forced again into the old difficulty of a facing a highly controlled set of circumstances that nevertheless seem always to be leaking towards moments of incontinence and excess. His complaint to Israel Shenker of a 'lack of brakes' (1956: 2.3) intrinsic to his idea of English thus accords with a sense that the uncontrolled addition of 'gagging' material in an English idiom that seems at times to run away with itself presents a textual risk. Malone states this explicitly, remarking, with a certain comedy, that something is 'funny, I have made a joke'. But he then overwrites this with '[n]o matter' (*T*: 184). In the

English, there is a little comedy to be found in learning that making a joke in this text obsessed with the emergence of textual matter doesn't matter a jot; it produces 'no matter' at a point where it is clear from the alteration to the French '[c]'est bien, c'est bien' that something that 'matters' – that signifies and has a presence – has indeed emerged. But the flatness of '[n]o matter', the sense that its addition is excessive, also causes humour to diminish. Consequently, the comedy of the text fades in and out, is produced by textual additions both in the French and then to an even greater degree in the English reworking, and then is rhythmically written out or over. The additions, the breaths of life taken in as hiccups into the textual body, thus produce a comic gagging from incongruity, but they disable any easy humorous satisfaction by the insertion of an excessive out of placeness. The textual rhythm of assertion and retreat ('the fiasco, the solace, the repose, I began again' (195)) instead both intensifies and disrupts the text's comic timing.

These temporal hiccups introduce air and thus life into the text, producing something that seems as marked by the reflexive and the automatic as by the intentional, aligning the textual body with the human body's insistent subjection to rhythms and temporalities that press it beyond or beside itself. In *Play* (1962–3), Beckett makes explicit the relationship between the comic gag and corporeal interruption. The adulterous man, gabbling on and interred in an urn, still has body enough to produce a hiccup that is both a tiny temporal deflection in the fluency of his speech mechanism and an unexpected gag capable of producing audience laughter: 'We were not long together when she smelled the rat. Give up that whore, she said, or I'll cut my throat – [*Hiccup*] pardon – so help me God' (*CDW*: 308). But if *Play* materialises comic interruption in a spasm of an actor's corporeality, in the *Trilogy*, as Hill points out, Beckett creates what might be thought of as a particular kind of body language:

> the body in Beckett's trilogy finally dissolves into a writing, a writing that functions as a body, as a rhythm ... This body, like the fictional text it becomes, is not unchanging or static, but exists as a continual process of assertion and negation, affirmation and difference. (1990: 120)

What appears most insistently, however, in Beckett's gagging, in his use of the reflexive and compulsive elements of the peristaltic system to figure incomplete incorporation and unfinished expulsion, is the production of a textual body that is not the peaceable servant of intention. Shadowing the determinedly disruptive movement traced out by the comic life of the *Trilogy*, textual and corporeal matter becomes compelled by the temporal rhythms of reflexes rather than a smooth or static container for a subjective interiority that accords only with the life of the mind.

An Obligation to Express

In 1934, Beckett transcribed in his psychology notebook sections from Ernest Jones's *Papers on Psychoanalysis*, with significant parts of the chapter entitled 'Anal-Erotic Character Traits' making their way into his jottings. Matthew Feldman has shown that specific psychoanalytic terms migrate from this notebook into particular moments within the *Trilogy* (2006: 109), but there is also a way of reading the *Trilogy* as a whole as peculiarly stained with tropes and rhythms that bear suggestive comparison with Jones's account of anal eroticism. In 1932, Beckett had already imagined in the poem 'Sanies I' '[a]ll heaven in the sphincter' (Beckett 1977: 17), but in reading Jones he was to learn how the anally fixated neurotic presents as a bundle of specific symptoms. Bound to furious, hate-filled and ambivalently pleasurable attempts at compulsive control, retention and refusal, Jones writes:

> Such people are very given to procrastination; they delay and postpone what they might have to do until the eleventh or even the twelfth hour. Then they plunge into work with a desperate and almost a ferocious energy which nothing is allowed to thwart ... Such people are often notorious bores. They are equally hard to move to a given course of action as to bring from it once they have started on it ... [T]here is no breaking off from it until they have gone up hill and down dale in saying all they want to about it, and in the meantime no one else is allowed to interrupt or get a in word in on the matter. (1923: 683)

Procrastination, ferocious energy, tediousness, interminability: these are the symptoms manifested, in various configurations, by Molloy/Moran, Malone and the Unnamable's 'vice-existers'. But psychoanalysis is not straightforwardly absorbed, for these characters also possess a synecdochic relation to the form of the text, as the refusal either to make progress or to stop, the urge to retain and to expel which enacts the famous oscillation between 'you must go on, I can't go on, I'll go on' (*T*: 418), become symptoms that infect the whole of the textual body.[8]

In formal terms, what Jones refers to as 'the tendency to keep back and postpone production and to produce feverishly' (1923: 680) within the anal neurotic is perhaps most obviously present in the stuttering temporality of the *Trilogy*'s comic gags. These moments of repetition and recursion, where the narrative seems to be walking on the spot, such as

Molloy's six-page account of the distribution of his sucking stones (*T*: 69–75) or his farting, bear a strong formal resemblance to the theatrical gag not simply because they are comic, although, of course, they are. Molloy states of his farting:

> I can't help it, gas escapes from my fundament on the least pretext, it's hard not to mention it now and then, however great my distaste. One day I counted them. Three hundred and fifteen farts in nineteen hours, or an average of over sixteen farts an hour. After all it's not excessive. Four farts every fifteen minutes. It's nothing. Not even one fart every four minutes. It's unbelievable. Damn it, I hardly fart at all, I should never have mentioned it. Extraordinary how mathematics help you to know yourself. (30)

As we have seen, this partakes of the humour of incongruity as the effort of calculation seems misaligned with the 'low' subject matter. Mathematics as self-knowledge or abstract illumination is reframed as a literally fundamental waste of time, as farting becomes Molloy's most essential temporal measure, although also his most useless one. But the incessant calculation (a literalising pun on calculus in the case of the sucking stones), which stands in for description here, is also significant because it seems to hold back the story's forward progression. This 'exhaustive enumeration', found earlier in Murphy's account of his biscuits or in the tireless linguistic permutations of *Watt* in which signification is written to its material limit, pushed and pulled like a stone on an abacus, are strongly reminiscent of the circus or vaudeville gags, such as the famous hat swapping routine that appears in *Godot*, of which the theatrical Beckett seemed fond. As the elements of the scene in *Molloy* are mechanically circulated, conventional narrative progress is interrupted or held up by seemingly extempore play; linguistic matter is retarded and accumulated as the text seems to gag on itself, momentarily reversing the peristaltic motion that seems as though it ought to be moving the subject matter of the text forwards through time towards the fundament or a narrative denouement.

Read alongside the model that Beckett notes from Jones, these moments of narrative rumination bring the orality of language and the anal into a queasy contiguity. Jones indeed theorises a link in the mind of the anal neurotic between gathering matter together, speech, writing and faeces. Beckett transcribed into his psychology notebook the idea that gathering objects such as stones (like Molloy's pebbles) or words (like those that Molloy, Moran and Malone scrawl onto paper), can be related to the child's desire to recapture its primal sense of omnipotence by controlling its bowel movements and hoarding its products.[9] Beckett's longest and most complete transcription from this chapter, following Jones's description of the anal-erotic associations between speech, thought and farting,[10] concerns a man who was 'habitually reticent in speech', or perhaps verbally constipated, and whose anal symptom consisted of the accumulation and retention of words which were then emitted in the form of a controlled explosion:

> [He] cherished the ambition, largely carried out, of being so able to construct his clauses, on a very German model, as to expel all he might have to say in one massive but superbly finished sentence that could be flung out and the whole matter done with. (1934–5: 8/19)

This 'reculer pour mieux sauter' routine is, of course, cherished within the form of the *Trilogy*, although here modes of drawing back are given as much narrative power as the ambition towards absolute expulsion.

Now a style based upon the desire to gather and control 'fundamental sounds' sufficiently that the subject could build up enough force to offer a complete description is visible in the patterns of permutation within Molloy's episode with his sucking stones:

> [I]t is clear that after the next series, of sucks and transfers, I shall be back where I started, that is to say with the first six stones back in my supply pocket, the next five in the right pocket of my stinking old trousers and finally with the last five in left pocket of same, and my sixteen stones will have been sucked once at least in impeccable succession, not one sucked twice, not one left unsucked. (*T*: 72–3)

But this mode, clearly to be glimpsed in the earlier parts of the *Trilogy* within the linguistically recursive gags, has taken over centre stage in *The Unnamable*, as the furies of retention and expulsion become central to the narration. For, inevitably, the desire of the Unnamable to achieve and produce a small, round full stop produces an incomplete act of voiding, as it is interrupted by what Jones observes in his patient as a stuttered or 'habitual reticen[ce]'. Despite the desire to '[t]hrow up for good', as *Worstward Ho* has it (*NO*: 102), the comma splice that becomes the signature of the later sections of *The Unnamable* reverses the direction of the peristaltic narrative system, forcing the sentence and the matter of the system relentlessly back on itself.

So by the time *The Unnamable* is reached, narration and excretion have explicitly become part of the same embodied motion that proceeds compulsively to incarnate that which is not yet the thing itself, but the matter of the world that is held in the alimentary system and then evacuated: 'For if I am Mahood, I am Worm too, plop. Or if I am not yet Worm, I shall be when I cease to be Mahood, plop. On now to serious matters, no not yet' (*T*: 340). Malone asserts that '[w]hat matters is to eat and excrete. Dish and pot, dish and pot, those are the poles' (185), and in *The Unnamable*, anal excretion similarly becomes an analogue for the birth of subject and artwork: 'I'll let down my trousers and shit stories on them, stories, photographs, records, sites, lights, gods and fellow-creatures. Be born, dear friends, be born, enter my arse, you'll just love my colic pains, it won't take long, I've the bloody flux' (383–4). But to be born is to breathe, and to be materialised causes a further gagging. To breathe 'air is to make you choke' (368) on words that are never yours but clichés of Romantic inspiration as self-expression: 'ah misery, will I never stop wanting a life for myself . . . I've tried, lashed to the stake, blindfold, gagged to the gullet, you take the air, under the elms in se, murmuring Shelley' (396).

So what is forced down the throat of the Unnamable's momentarily materialised selves, taking on the character of a reflexive or neurotic compulsion, is bound from the beginning to an obligation to express itself in a way that that could have done with all expressing:[11]

> Strange task, which consists of speaking of oneself. Strange hope, turned towards silence and peace. Possessed of nothing but my voice, the voice, it may seem natural, once the idea of obligation has been swallowed, that I should interpret it as an obligation to say something. (*T*: 313)

Obligation – etymologically linked to the notion of being bound to something through the Latin *ligare* – once swallowed, does not stay in the space of 'interpretation' for long; instead, it is brought back up as an embodied compulsion to express and figured according to the model of anality that is, for Jones, characterised by 'features of compulsion and doubt' (1923: 540). Jones describes how anal neurotics may seemingly sublimate their primary concerns into an excessive interest in what is moral or just (687), but what remains is a more fundamental pulsion in which the 'person has an overwhelming sense of "mustness"' (684) that is driven by the force of the unconscious.[12] Indeed, in *Treatment of the Neuroses*, that Beckett also read, Jones glosses that primary symptom of obsessional neurosis, the 'feeling of compulsion' (*Zwang*), as precisely this 'feeling of "mustness"' (1920: 191). Such compulsion, Jones argues, strips back the subject's capacity for intentional thought: 'The patient oscillates between the two conditions of not being able to act or think (when he wants to) and being obliged to act and think (when he doesn't want to)' (1920: 195).

Of course, it is hard to see how obligations figured as irruptions of unconscious desire or the reflexive processes of the body could be ethical in the normative sense in which a subject is bound to an oath or law within the terms of which it stages its acts. But then even the famous

Beckettian 'obligation to express', which appears in *Three Dialogues* with Georges Duthuit (begun the same month as *L'Innommable*), suggests an artistic obligation loosened from the realm of what could be rationally chosen.[13] For if there is 'nothing to express, nothing with which to express, nothing from which to express, no power to express, no desire to express, together with the obligation to express' (Beckett 1999: 103), then artistic expression becomes an obligation that is not bound by and through the reason of an autonomous or self-determined subject. As Beckett wrote to Duthuit in 1949, the obligation to express is precisely a need, a compulsive drive; indeed, it remains 'innocent' because beyond choice or intention: 'If you ask me why the canvas doesn't remain blank, I can only invoke this clear need, forever innocent, to fuck it with color, if need be through vomiting one's being' (Beckett 2006: 20).

In 1932 Beckett wrote to MacGreevy about the failure of most of his poetry:

> I'm not ashamed to stutter like this with you who are used to my way of failing to say what I imagine I want to say and who understand that until the gag is chewed fit to swallow or spit out the mouth must stutter or rest. And it needs a more stoical mind than mine to rest. (*LSB*: 134)

In 1932 Beckett seems uncertain whether the gag that prevents the expressive flow of language, causing it to stutter, could be successfully masticated, incorporated, expectorated. The 'until' suggests the gag might be overcome, although it is clear that neither mouth nor mind are inclined to rest. Later in the letter, however, Beckett begins to laud an art born of the involuntary, the reflexive – language that is compulsively produced rather than 'facultatif [optional]' (*LSB*: 133):

> I'm in mourning for the integrity of a pendu's [hanged man's] emission of semen, what I find in Homer & Dante & Racine & sometimes Rimbaud, the integrity of the eyelids coming down before the brain knows of grit in the wind. (*LSB*: 134–5)

If the idea of language as spontaneous bodily emission is born in the early 1930s, it is, however, in the *Trilogy* that the negative theology of the obligation of artistic expression finally finds its textual aesthetic. For the alibis of artistic expression invoked here insist on a compulsive, embodied quality; language is spewed, vomited, dribbled, shat and belched. Beckett is certainly not miming an automatic writing, and neither are the invoked motions completely unconscious, for all can be retarded or interfered with by intention, or, more strictly, trained, according to habit that inscribes intention into the automatic processes of the body. Such is the anal-erotic's site of power. Nevertheless, such motions remain expressions of the body that will in the end admit no cognitive denial.

So what is so often represented in Beckett studies as the ethical obligation to express is here figured as a compulsion that binds textual subjects within a space of linguistic assault, neurotic drive and embodied reflex below the threshold of what might conventionally be considered ethical choice or action made in relation to a priori principles of abstract universality – a moral law that could be binding upon practical reason in Kantian terms. Beckett's texts clearly do not stage such ethical questions or possibilities. Reason is a sufficiently rare achievement that any ethical framework bound and authorised by the autonomous willed commitments of the rational subject would flare up only intermittently and would, thus, be fatally denuded of its universal quality. An ethics based upon shared moral sentiments or passions would similarly be hard to sustain when the characters of the *Trilogy* find normative affects sufficiently puzzling that they can only be performed rather than felt or comprehended. Such passions are rarely more than transitory affects that flicker on the surface of the skin or are passed through a subject in such a way that it becomes, in the end, little more than an agglutination of those drives, desires and sensations – insufficiently coherent even really to allow it to qualify as a subject, never mind the lodestone of a moral theory.

Tiring Desire

Alain Badiou, writing specifically of Beckett's drama, has forged a link between the comic, and indeed the stubbornness and fury in the work, and his particular conception of a politicised ethics:

> Beckett must be played with the most intense humour, taking advantage of the enduring variety of inherited theatrical types. It is only then that the true destination of the comical emerges: neither a symbol nor a metaphysics in disguise, and even less a derision, but rather a powerful love for human obstinacy, for tireless desire, for humanity reduced to its stubbornness and malice. (2003: 75)

For Badiou, Beckett's characters represent in and through their comedy a tireless desire that is ethical. In *Ethics*, Badiou returns persistently to the maxim 'Keep Going!' which finds its epitome in the oft-quoted final lines of *The Unnamable*, 'you must go on, I can't go on, I'll go on'. This heroic decision to continue that is the foundation of Badiou's ethics cuts specifically across an ethics of alterity, however. Where Levinas privileges an ethics of difference and distance as sacred, Badiou counters that infinite alterity isn't ethical, it is simply banal: '[i]nfinite alterity is quite simply *what there is*' (2001: 25). Sameness, however, is what '*comes to be*', what is faithfully worked for and affirmed in the face of the differences which are the terrain of exclusion and ground for the injustice of the relationships between people. Sameness offers the possibility of something universal, of a truth (or, more properly, truths) '*indifferent to differences* . . .; a truth is *the same for all*' (2001: 27). An ethics of the same is concrete and situated in the world; its demand for fidelity, which Andrew Gibson has described as 'the determination to think the world according to the principle of what has come to change it, to make it new' (Gibson 2006: 98), is the demand to face the as yet unknown. Badiou borrows Lacan's formulation of the ethics of psychoanalysis which orientates itself towards unconscious desire as a maxim for an ethic of truth that exceeds the present state of the human who has not yet become a subject: '"do not give up on your desire" . . . "do not give up on that part of yourself that you do not know" . . .: "Do all you can to persevere in that which exceeds your perseverance. Persevere in the interruption. Seize in your being that which has seized and broken you"' (2001: 47).

Badiou suggests, rather rashly, that 'all of Beckett's genius tends towards affirmation' (2003: 41); consequently, the clownish refusal to give up on failed action in *The Unnamable*, or to submit to given orders of reason, knowledge or sense – the refusal to give up on that which currently exceeds it – is an articulation of ethics. Critchley rightly objects, however, that the most characteristic feature of Beckett's writing, and particularly his comedy, 'is not just the decision to continue, but also the acknowledgement that I cannot continue' (Critchley 2000: 26). After all, Molloy refers to his testicles as '*decaying* circus clowns' (*T*: 36, ital. mine), residues of vitality squeezed of their purpose, and lumps of matter in a joke of a life in which they can play no meaningful part. Critchley explicitly forces Badiou's conception of heroism to face the weakness and inability that is the contrary imperative of Beckett's work: the imperative that articulates Critchley's own conception of Beckett's comedy as one of weakness, inauthenticity and the acknowledgement of finitude. Critchley might justifiably argue that Badiou's maxim of continuation isn't really comic at all, or only becomes comic in its commerce with the failure and inability that persistently retards its progression. One might note, however, that Badiou himself complicates matters: he writes that it is through '[i]nterruption, or the maxims of comedy' that 'Beckett's writing attempts, at one and the same time, to speak unrepentantly of the stony ingratitude of the Earth and to isolate, according to its proper density, that which exceeds it' (2003: 44). Although comic interruption is that which breaks with the given world and is thus on the side of continuation in relation to what will come to change it, it is also implicit that the defeat of expectation in the comic only appears in a world in which this change is still to come. Because comedy marks the 'stony ingratitude of the Earth' alongside 'that which exceeds it', it may represent an orientation towards the event, but it necessarily pre-exists it.

In his reading of Beckett alongside Badiou, Gibson takes issue with the ways Badiou's rather teleological version of Beckett's writing career risks occluding the persistent sense that the work functions according to more general pulsions of intermittence and oscillation, 'disunity and complicating incoherence' (2006: 132), that poststructuralist Beckett criticism has relentlessly illuminated and invoked. And Gibson offers a brilliant supplement to Badiou's account of Beckett because, instead of swerving away from the inertia in Beckett's work towards those moments that assert affirmation more clearly, he reads this sense of intermittency as part of a pathos of modernity which feels that banal difference is everywhere and that truth and event are rare, although not non-existent. Modernist art such as Beckett's registers this ironic truth, or perhaps the rareness of truth, which speaks itself in irony.

For Gibson, the inability of the characters in *The Unnamable*, for example, to subtract themselves sufficiently from the given world interrogates that world, but ensures that they have no means to express other than the words of others; they gag on and compulsively bring up the language that 'a whole college of tyrants' (*T*: 312) forces down their throats: 'It is they who dictate this torrent of balls, they who stuffed me full of these groans that choke me' (338). In Gibson's terms this plight is 'quintessentially comic' (2006: 191); nevertheless, irony is not everywhere: affirmation supersedes inability in the end. There is progression, of sorts, for stories shat out or vomited forth are not as easy to take back into the system as if they had never been born. Gibson thus suggests that *The Unnamable* takes us to the threshold of an event, of something new being born which is not just another shape broken from the same mould as what has gone before. But if the 'pathos of intermittency' marks the limit of the given world and is melancholic, it nevertheless affirms an orientation towards what comes to render things anew. If comedy could also be thought of as the sign of a materialisation of the paucity of that world alongside a raging against it – a gagging in disgust – then Gibson's reading of *The Unnamable* as 'intense, aggressive, furious, even violent' (2006: 191) makes sense of the necessary will to mastery, the drive to transform, that impels and compels the comic gagging in the texts. Taking at least some impetus from satire, the *Trilogy* never flinches from representing the torture of 'tyrants', nor of materialising such torture for textual and reading subjects in submitting them to fading comic forms bound only to 'on' rather than the enjoyments of the finale. Nevertheless, these comic forms oscillate between a sense of having to bear it and refusing to bear it – of bearing it in a paradoxically furious yet etiolated fashion that refuses to give up on the desire to materialise change. Beckett's gagging becomes a way of reproducing *how it is* while opening up a space for *how it ought to be*.[14]

As we have seen, Critchley finds something different in Beckett – a comic paradigm structured by a consoling acknowledgement of the weakness and inability of the human. He uses the late Freud's model of humour in which the superego gently mocks and protects the ego in its fragile finitude and the man who is being led to the gallows is able to look up at the sky and say, 'Well, the week's beginning nicely' (Freud 1927: 160). But while Critchley emphasises the acknowledgement of finitude, Freud, as Weller rightly points out, is willing to entertain that such humour is also a function of narcissistic omnipotence – a 'rebellious denial of the real' (Weller 2006: 108). Freud himself is clear that this humour represents 'the triumph of narcissism, the victorious assertion of the ego's invulnerability. The ego refuses to be distressed by the provocations of reality' (161). For the gallows are dangerous. This humour offers a sublimation, but it is also a lie in relation to death. Ethics may well be not giving up on one's desire;[15] nevertheless, as Beckett's texts intuit with both hope and fear, desire will one day give up on us.

It is strange that Critchley refuses what Weller identifies as the duplication of a fairly standard self–other relation in this account of the superego's gentle mockery of the ego, alongside the implication of a cognitive supremacy of one over the other, that occurs in Freud's model of humour (2006: 109). In an instructively analogous occlusion, Critchley persistently resists the rage and desperate desire for mastery so clearly visible in Beckett's sardonic early work, but that also resounds within the *Trilogy*. If joking always has certain sensations of mastery implicated within it, what makes something funny is not just an awareness of finitude; it is the cognitive recognition of incongruity – the capacity to dissolve finitude sufficiently to see it as a finitude registered from the very moment of its temporary supersession. Critchley's model accepts and delineates precisely this doubleness, this eccentricity at the heart of the human that ensures 'not only *are* we our bodies, we also *have* our bodies' (2002: 42), but it brushes aside the degree to which humour uses recognition and acknowledgement as a form of mastery that, at least momentarily, allows a subject to march in time with an idea that it might exceed its finitude, be more than itself.

But if there is no comedy to be found in absolute finitude, it would be equally hard to imagine jokes in a realm of just sameness, and this perhaps is the reason why Badiou has little sustained interest in Beckett's comedy except as a clownish orientation towards persistence. Badiou reads the *Trilogy* as a work of radical subtraction from the world as given – a vomited forth realm of banal difference – which offers to clear the way for an event. Gibson suggests that the Unnamable's labours leave it at the 'threshold of what, for Badiou, is historical time, the time of a truth-sequence that begins with the event'; however, in his careful fidelity to Beckett, Gibson insists that 'it is not Beckett's concern to take us across that threshold' (2006: 196). In Badiou's reading, *how it is* is persistently ceded to *how it ought to be* because he is articulating a politics: and politics does not come to interpret the world but to change it. But the comedy of the *Trilogy* seems more like a marker of how things are in a world perceived according to an impossibly binding finitude that the subject can neither fully encompass nor exceed. Gibson, who reads Beckett from the space of subtraction rather than from what it portends, sees the vagaries of the enraged, sometimes manic refusal to give up on 'on', as part of its refusal of 'the world dished up' (2006: 189), a violent and angry pitting of text and subject against a powerful inertia. And this is one reason why a comedy of mastery and indeed of violence does inhere in the text (in spite of Critchley's very proper hopes for an ethical Beckett); the rage of the text to lift itself out of its world always risks the production of 'a great crackle of laughter, at the sight of his terror and distress . . . To see him flooded with light, then suddenly plunged back in darkness, must strike them as irresistibly funny' (*T*: 358). Yet there is also a powerful motivation here, for if the Unnamable 'has no apparent hope of becoming a subject, it also resists objecthood' (2006: 197), Gibson claims. It both exceeds the given world through thought and remains nailed to it. For Gibson, the pathos of this structure is melancholy and irony, but it is also the basal condition for Beckett's failing gags, always being played out according to a logic of the punchline, even if the end of the joke, the transcendent 'topper' gag (the one that surpasses all the previous material in a vaudeville act), never arrives. The profound difference between the *Trilogy* and Badiou's ethics, however, is that the each version of the Unnamable knows that even though this is all just 'preluding, clearing the throat' before a journey driven by the desire to be itself, nevertheless, 'you can't leave, you're afraid to leave, it might be worse elsewhere' (385). Where Badiou believes he knows what an event looks like and can recognise in it the glimmer of a new world, the Unnamable's incarnations always fear that the main act might be nothing other than a violent punchline, a tortured mastery from which no further incongruity could ever wrest itself.

Toilet Training, Resistant Material

The comedy of the *Trilogy* represents a materialisation and acknowledgement of the 'world dished up', then, or the world repeatedly thrown up, but it also ensures that the text is bound for critique. And this world of seemingly banal differentiation, of subjects that are never the things themselves but always the regurgitations of others, is the given world of late modernity in one clear sense. Molloy knows to what his habits of narration will lead: '[i]f I go on long enough calling that my life I'll end up believing it. It's the principle of advertising' (*T*: 53); and the discourse of repetition, consumption and circulation in the *Trilogy* could similarly be read as a parodic mirroring of the fantasies of a world of commodification and late capitalist exchange. In these texts, the repetitions of regurgitation that mark out body and writing seem to hope to become perfected systems of infinite circulation in which matter could be incorporated, expelled or excreted, then reincorporated, in a parody of a smoothly self-sustaining machine. But if capitalism imagines the possibility of absolute exchangeability, unfettered by the material or by use-value, it nevertheless has, as its final aim, the desire to hold up the system of exchange sufficiently to extract some surplus value from it. Here, however, the force-fed body resists becoming toilet-trained and docile, resists the retention that would allow the smooth incorporation of the matter of the world into its digestive system to produce fuel and waste. The textual bodies of the *Trilogy* have instead become habituated and trained by the application of textual emetics to gag on gobbets of inassimilable matter, bringing them up or excreting them in a fundamentally comic movement that is both a reproduction of the given world and its fantasies of consumption, and an embodied refusal of the ways in which that given world believes the material can always be possessed and transformed.

On 5 January 1938, Beckett wrote to MacGreevy that he was hoping to see Charlie Chaplin's *Modern Times* with the Joyces later in the day (*LSB*: 580). I'd like to imagine he went, given that Chaplin, of whom Beckett seemed enduringly fond, uses this film to literalise an intersection of comic gagging, violent force-feeding and the interruption of the machines of capitalism, that bears suggestive comparison with the modes of resistant incorporation and expulsion within the *Trilogy*. The opening sections of *Modern Times* (1936) function as a parody of the institutionalisation of Frederick W. Taylor's processes of 'scientific management' in factories in the early decades of the twentieth century. 'Scientific management' observed skilled workers, decided on the exact series of fundamental operations that constituted their work and then selected the quickest series. Each fundamental operation was then assessed with a stop-watch to find minimum 'unit times' and jobs were subsequently reconstituted with new composite times set as standard. Henry Ford's factories, infamous for their Taylorism, introduced the first moving assembly line in 1913, enabling the use of unskilled labour for singular, repetitive tasks.

In *Modern Times*, the unnamed 'steel worker' (Charlie) is strapped into position on his production line and subjected to a new technology brought in to assist efficiency in the factory. The 'Bellows Feeding Machine' offers to 'eliminate the lunch hour, increase your production and decrease your overhead', by feeding workers at their station, but, of course, as Charlie's slowness on the production line has already demonstrated, body and machine are not necessarily easily habituated to one another. As Charlie is force-fed at increasing rates of rapidity and unpredictability, he ceases to be able to consume smoothly and begins to spit out what can no longer be incorporated by a mouth filled according to the strangely unpredictable, highly artificial time of a machine. This classic gag indeed demonstrates the unruly resistance of human materiality, as digestive system and systems of production refuse to be smoothly aligned. In the next scene Charlie again disrupts factory time, although here it is a sneeze that throws the line off kilter and causes his body to be taken by conveyor belt into the workings of the plant. In both gags the obdurate materiality of the little man also introduces a small hiccup into the conventional, if noticeably slight and sidelined, narrative progression of the film. And as Charlie clogs the cogs and forces the peristalsis of the machine into reverse (just as the film is literally reversed at this moment), this little piece of human matter is regurgitated in a gagging that momentarily rewinds the linear time of capitalist production, just as the comic gag interrupts the story and the onward roll of the film with something that partakes of another time, some extempore play.

Tim Armstrong writes that in *Modern Times*, an early gag about the gleaming but exposed and panoptical facilities in Henry Ford's factories, designed to make loitering at the toilet less likely, demonstrates capitalist modernity's equal concern with excretion and ingestion (1998: 65). For it is here that Taylorism and the desire to turn all the waste time of production into leisure time – the time of commodity consumption that characterises Fordism – breaks down in the face of the body's own will and necessity to eat and excrete and an enteric nervous system under weak conscious control. As Jean Walton has illuminated in her reading of the peristaltic subject of modernity, twentieth-century neurology reveals the enteric nervous system running from mouth to anus to be a 'second brain', an independent site of neural integration and processing that can function without conscious directives of the 'first brain' processed through the central nervous system (2010: 247): it is therefore devoid of mind (in a straightforward sense). Walton emphasises, however, that this system is susceptible to influence from the natural and cultural environment. And because it will submit to being trained according to certain intentions, she reads the peristaltic system and its engagements with the world as an anxious site of disciplinary control. In one sense, as Walton suggests, capitalist modernity's will to rationalise, to train, the potentially unruly enteric nervous system through enforcing certain kinds of habituation creates disciplined and docile consuming and producing subjects. The fact that peristalsis cannot be controlled simply according to intention, however, means that its forces and demands, played out on the border of the economy of work and leisure, are always liable to make a disruptive return.

Now the Unnamable's creatures may be under what Beckett would have read in Jones as the 'lasting influence of the infant's ambition to achieve *control* of his sphincters' (1923: 690), but this hate-filled resistance does not make them compliant subjects within late capitalist modernity. Unlike Jones's anal-erotics, who can harness their interests in retention and expulsion sufficiently to slog away at their chosen work, within the scene of these texts there is a persistent refusal of such useful habits and the sublimation that would produce anything beyond their own gagging and paradoxically autotelic 'wordshit', as it is called in the *Texts for Nothing*. Although the Unnamable's incarnations are sardonically represented as not yet totally beyond the ministrations of the given world – 'The organs of digestion and evacuation, though sluggish, are not wholly inactive, as is shown by the attentions I receive. It's encouraging. While there's life there's hope' (*T*: 336) – it is clear that one would neither give Beckett's characters jobs in a factory nor invite them round for polite after-dinner conversation. For their imperfectly controlled gagging and shitting is held and repossessed according to pleasures that remain comically perverse, and perhaps perversely comic, rather than more straightforwardly productive.

It is perhaps significant that the longest variant passage in the holograph manuscript of the French *Molloy* explicitly concerns itself with these same relations of faecal circulation. Moran proposes to review everything he knows about Molloy and his country before setting out to find him, and his scatologically comical account of the wealth and lush agricultural productivity of the region of Ballyba, which stems from the use of the population's excrement as fertiliser, comprises some 2,400 words excised from the published text. For the inhabitants of Ballyba, the manuscript tells us, the production of shit is a duty, an 'obligation' in fact. This 'obligation' is determined according to a quota system rigorously administered by 'l'O.M. (Organisation Maraichère)', with the townspeople's faeces used as fertiliser for growing fruit and vegetables that they both consume and sell. Shit is a matter of civic pride: it is collected in gleaming silver bins and highly prized diplomas are awarded to the most productive citizens. Nothing, not even time, is wasted here; trips away from Ballyba, and the consequent loss of faecal input into the economy, all need to be compensated for, and the redistribution of this civic duty is organised by Obidil, a high-ranking official of l'O.M. Now Obidil does appear in the published version of *Molloy*, but briefly, and without any real explanation: 'Obidil . . . I never saw him' (*T*: 162), Moran notes. The fact that Obidil, whose name is an anagram of libido, should be associated with anal production seems to confirm *Molloy*'s concern with the collocation of the anal and the erotic, however. And it is indeed significant, in terms of the resistant peristaltic obsessions of the *Trilogy* as a whole, that this parody of a perfectly ordered petit-bourgeois social world and a smoothly functioning capitalist economy based on the uninterrupted passage of consumption and excretion is disrupted by 'quelques ~~enragés~~ ano-érotiques . . . tranquilles garde-colle de l'exil' (Beckett 1948: 136). These quietly resistant people will not submit to the economic circulation of shit. They refuse to stay at home producing faecal matter like docile citizens; instead, they exclude themselves, and their motions, which are perversely pleasurable rather than obviously productive, from the capitalist economy.

We have seen that a fantasy of pure circulation is clearly absorbed into the *Trilogy*, just as anal eroticism, which holds up the possibility of a resistance to such productive modes of capitalism, obtains both thematically and within the characterisation; as such, it is hard to know precisely why Beckett chose to place this economy of shit in textual exile. It is quite possible that the publisher found material such as the discussion of the particular properties of stools from certain social groups – perhaps, in particular, the especially fertile qualities of the faeces of the clergy attributed to 'la presence, dans le bol, d'élémements ~~sexuel~~ séminaux' – unsuited to their or to the public taste (Beckett 1948: 132). But perhaps the expulsion can be analysed more tellingly according to the furious oscillation between incorporation, retention and expulsion that persists as a textual symptom throughout the *Trilogy*. For none of the main characters that remain in the *Trilogy* insert themselves into economies of exchange willingly. Like the 'enragés ano-érotiques' of Ballyba, they produce (excessively or insufficiently) inassimilable material; they thus resist being digested by the system. So in the published French version of *Molloy*, instead of following 'D'où tirait donc Ballyba ses richesses? Je vais vous dire' (132) with an account of the smooth functioning of an economy of shit, Moran simply enacts a refusal: 'D'où Ballyba tirait-il donc son opulence. Je vais vous le dire. Non, je ne dirai rien. Rien' (Beckett 1951: 183). Moran, like those 'anal-erotics' who cause hiccups in the uninterrupted peristalsis of the faecal economy of Ballyba, furiously resists delivering up his 'wordshit' in a form that would allow its smooth incorporation into an economy of textual exchange and production.

What remains in the *Trilogy*, then, are minds and bodies that cannot be habituated to the temporality of early to mid-century capitalist production nor to the linearity of its favoured mode – the nineteenth-century bourgeois novel or the classic Hollywood narrative film that races towards the production of a denouement. There just isn't enough to nourish the *Bildung* of the *Bildungsroman*; instead, words produce little for the Unnamable other than their own resistant materiality and a failed textual incorporation that enacts a temporal looping rather than liberates time for work or leisure. But it is also clear that the figures in the *Trilogy* are creatures of habit, although they are collections of bad habits, according to normative social models. And of all the habits articulated within the text and materialised in the characters, the most insistent is one of simple persistence, of resistance. In *The Unnamable*, bodies and minds are constantly force-fed in ways that ironically habituate them into refusing to absorb the words rammed down their throats, and this orientates the text towards a defending itself against what is served up: 'I never understood a word of it in any case, not a word of the stories it spews, like gobbets in a vomit ... Dear incomprehension, it's thanks to you I'll be myself, in the end' (*T*: 327). In these texts, then, where the gagging side show increasingly has taken centre stage, textual matter is produced in a way that materialises a choking resistance to the ideas of discipline and transformation that subtend given social modes of production.

Now Theodor Adorno, although famously an admirer of Beckett, was less than convinced of the potential for radical critique in Chaplin's gags. Writing to Walter Benjamin in 1936, he opined that audience laughter at Chaplin's films is 'anything but good and revolutionary; instead, it is full of the worst bourgeois sadism' (1980b: 123). As is well known, however, Beckett's texts became exemplary for Adorno of those

artworks that could somehow both instantiate the world of late capitalism and occupy a space of potential critique. And importantly for the
argument advanced here, Adorno's hope for Beckett's art lies in its form
of resistance, its material particularity, which seems to hold back from a
reconciliation with the world of late capitalist modernity.

Adorno's philosophy, like Beckett's work, is clearly driven by concerns that might broadly be described as ethical, but cannot quite be
reconciled with moral philosophy or more normative ethics. 'Wrong life
cannot be lived rightly', Adorno determines (1974: 39). Nevertheless, he
produces a sustained critique of what becomes known as identity thinking – that logic which, according to David Cunningham, is to be found
within 'metaphysical idealism, instrumental rationality and the fetishis-
tic character of the commodity form' that functions as 'a repetition of
the "ever-always-the-same"' (2002: 127). For Adorno, philosophical
thought and human understanding, formed by a society in which an
exchange principle persistently demands an equivalence (a reduction to
exchange value) of what is always inherently non-equivalent (the particular use value of the material world), works by compulsively subsum-
ing diversity and difference, the otherness of the object world, into itself.
As he puts it with Max Horkheimer in *The Dialectic of Enlightenment*
(1944), 'the levelling domination of abstraction ... makes everything
in nature repeatable' (1997: 13), as material particularity is turned
into idea, enabling the technical and conceptual mastery of the world.
Although Adorno recognises that the minimum conditions for encoun-
tering otherness involve perceptual and sensible models of awareness,
the identity of a subject or thought system seems always to be determined according to categories such as subject and object, universal and
particular, which remain on the side of the conceptual. Subsumed under
a general concept heading, the quality of the thing itself, its materiality, thus shears away. In *Negative Dialectics* (1966), Adorno precisely
critiques what he perceives to be the affirmative character of the dialectic in Hegel's work that attempts always to unify or synthesise under
identity the relation between subject and object. A negative dialectic
offers something else, however; it offers to enact a critical consciousness that could perceive rather than ingest and incorporate the asymmetrical relationship between material object and its concept. A negative
dialectic can assess the non-identical relationship between the sets of
properties implied by the concept and the object's concrete particularity. For Adorno, then, a negative dialectic becomes the articulation of a
non-identical relationship between identity and non-identity.

Such a resistance to identity-thinking is also be found in Adorno's
belief in an autonomous art that refuses to be thought under the concept

of a universal aesthetics but asserts instead its material, historical, non-conceptual character. Adorno argues in *Aesthetic Theory* (1970), which was to be dedicated to Beckett, that art has autonomy because it claims to possess something that cannot be reduced to price, to exchange value. For Adorno, the possibility that something might be sufficiently alienated from the world to become an end in itself is a direct result of the capitalist dissociation of objects from their immediate function. But while commodities are articulations of surplus labour – production divorced from need – the autonomous artwork differs from such commodities because it does not pretend to satisfy need or to have a use-value. The artwork as 'absolute commodity' has the possibility of presenting itself as 'a social product that has rejected every semblance of existing for society, a semblance to which commodities otherwise urgently cling' (Adorno 2002: 236). Art is therefore fundamentally determined by the social world, but in expressing the illusory nature of its autonomy rather than occluding the perception of that truth, it paradoxically achieves autonomy in relation to empirical reality by self-consciously rounding on and revealing its own determined character. Although determined by a particular historical, social situation, works of art such as those by Beckett do not simply represent reality in a way that achieves identity or becomes reconciled with it. Beckett's is not the 'committed' art of Sartre or Brecht that illustrates the absurd alienations of late modernity. Autonomous art functions instead as 'the social antithesis of society' (Adorno 2002: 8) because it is determined by the social world, even though, in its resistant autonomy, it paradoxically functions as that world's 'determinate negation'.

It is significant that in the 1967 essay 'Is Art Lighthearted?', Adorno considers that there may be something within Beckett's comic work that articulates the possibilities of an autonomous art. Of course, Beckett's is not an art that is deceptively pleasurable, that passes over the real material and historical exigencies of the world with 'a joke [that] has become the smirking caricature of advertising pure and simple' (Adorno 1992b: 250); Beckett's comedy is not a kind of leisure time to be prescribed to 'tired businesspeople as a shot in the arm' (Adorno 1992b: 248), which was perhaps how he imagined *Modern Times*. For Adorno there is something in the formal quality of Beckett's work that aligns it with the 'lightheartedness' that inheres within all art and indicates its potential for autonomy. Art is lighthearted not simply because it might be funny, then; art is lighthearted because there is something about its purposelessness that refuses to be brought into the economy of exchange. By repeating the seemingly inexhaustible fungibility that is the 'brute seriousness that reality imposes upon human beings' (1992b: 248), but in reflecting on it self-consciously, the work of art materialises a space in which there is a minimal difference between its own determined quality and the formal freedom that can see and register this determination. Art thus 'opens out over the reality to whose violence it bears witness at the same time' (Adorno 1992b: 248). With the knowledge that this repetition is experienced and experiences itself as a repetition with difference rather than simply a perpetuation of the same, the non-identity of the artwork appears in all its material specificity and indigestible autonomy. As Adorno suggests in his notes on *The Unnamable*, modern art such as this is the manifestation of 'a disenchanted world, the illusionless, *"comment c'est"*' (2010: 177); at the same time, however, precisely by reflecting on how it is, autonomous artworks offer 'instructions for the praxis they refrain from: the production of life lived as it ought to be' (Adorno 1992a: 93).

Now it seems to me that a significant part of the difficult autonomy of the *Trilogy* lies in its gagging. This gagging savagely and angrily materialises, in all its queasy inevitability, words that are, in one sense, only exchangeable, only the words of others that are circulated but inadequately digested. This formal enactment draws force from the commodity character of art, its fundamental uselessness and abstract insubstantiality – its existence as nothing but words to be exchanged – to which the *Trilogy* reflexively bears witness. So the matter that circulates in the *Trilogy* remains tirelessly nailed to the world of exchange; nevertheless, it furiously reveals that world's paucity and insufficiency and thus adumbrates the minimal conditions according to which it might be different, offering, as Adorno suggests in *Minima Moralia* (1946–7), '[p]erspectives . . . that displace and estrange the world, reveal it to be, with its rifts and crevices, as indigent and distorted as it will appear one day in the messianic light' (1974: 247). These stubbornly material words of the *Trilogy* refuse, in the end, to be sublated into the realm of idea, or to be absorbed and made identical with a subject. For although the Unnamable's 'vice-existers' have never properly been born, ironically it is because they have a surfeit of substance rather than a lack: 'Ah if they could only begin, and do what they want with me, and succeed at last . . . I'm tired of being matter, matter, pawed and pummelled endlessly in vain' (*T*: 350). Although 'even Worm . . . [is] an idea they have, a word they use, when speaking about them' (369–70), these figures maintain a resistant materiality, even if just as words, that finally pulls away from that portion of textual desire that mimes the possibility of simply circulating them as linguistic ideas: 'It is true one forgets everything. And yet it is greatly to be feared that Mahood will never let himself be completely resorbed . . . It's not clear, tut tut, it's not clear at all' (376–7).

By turning words into matter that is refused easy passage, by forcing language which imagines itself to be solely cognition and idea to face its commerce with embodied reflex, compulsion and the irreducibly material quality of the written sign, the *Trilogy* refuses to accede to what it experiences as the violence of a social world which always believes that matter is awaiting transformation and circulation.

Nihil in Intellectu

Suggestively, the *Trilogy*'s gagging language, obsessed with the materialisation of words imaged according to the processes of peristalsis, seems to follow through and use an unexpected peculiarity of the construction of the body. The body, it turns out, is not an object smoothly enclosed in space, because the linings of all the exocrine glands, including the digestive glands, are continuous with its surface. Anything taken into the lumen remains, in a strict sense, exterior to the body (Gershon 1998: 84). Representing words as matter in the gut allows them to be imaged as both inside and outside the subject, then, and this matter that is on the threshold of becoming part of the body but stalls before it is fully absorbed offers the *Trilogy* a way of representing language, so often imagined as simply a synecdoche of the interiority of an intending mind, as something that might prove resistant to clean transformation. Held on the inside/outside of the body, Beckett's language is forced into commerce with resistance and negation, with embodied waste and untransformable excess that both produces and is produced by a formal gag reflex within the artwork itself.

In the *Trilogy*, then, words can neither be taken in as air, for they are too material, producing the coughing textual equivalent of something having gone down the wrong way, nor can they be incorporated as nourishment, for they are stonily resistant to the absorption that would feed the textual subject. There is no conceptual Heimlich manoeuvre performed within the text that could clear the windpipe sufficiently that matter could then go down smoothly and be assimilated; instead, words become misplaced matter – vomit and shit – that is indigent and *unheimlich*. Becoming part of the signature of the final part of the *Trilogy*, these indigestibly material words offer a form of recursive autonomy, derailing both narrative progression and even a certain productive logic in the comic gag itself. For the joking synthesis of elements within a witty denouement or punchline is overwritten, in the end, by a gagging form that produces excessive textual matter that cannot be turned to any easily assimilable profit.

In *Malone Dies*, Jackson's pink and grey parrot perhaps stages most clearly the uneasy relationship between a language proper to the intending mind and a material language pressed out and then absorbed (or not) according to reflex. The parrot repeatedly utters the scholastic dictum *nihil in intellectu*, but is unable to get as far as what Malone calls the 'the celebrated restriction'; that 'was too much for it, all you heard was a series of squawks' (*T*: 218). The joke is that the parrot is only able to utter that there is nothing in the mind at all, without the usual qualifier, *quod non prius fuerat in sensu*. If it is true that there is nothing in the mind that has not first been in the senses, the parrot cannot articulate it; it remains nailed to reproductions that are, in the end, nothing but matter, that have never securely been in the mind. Beckett noted down the dictum from Wilhelm Windelband's *A History of Philosophy* in his 'Whoroscope Notebook' (1932–7), but included Leibniz's response to Locke's empiricism: *nisi ipse intellectus* (Beckett 1930s: 62) – except the mind itself (Windelband 1931: 464). Of course, philosophy from the tongue of a parrot can hardly assert the singularity of the mind and its linguistic productions. Words are instead threateningly automatic; they are mindless, at least in terms of the human conception of mind, as avian matter speaks according to habituation rather than recognisable linguistic intention. For the slightly more human subjects of *The Unnamable*, there is also a sense in which words, rendered as bodily discharge, are somehow stuck in the senses and figured according to the non sequiturs of mind and body that form the material for so much comedy. 'Better still, arrogate to me a mind', one of the Unnamable's incarnations indeed muses, sardonically, as it vaguely hopes to '[s]peak of a world of my own, sometimes referred to as the inner, without choking' (394). Here, though, notions are more like motions than anything else, all sweat and spasm, and the idea of a mind ever neatly separable from the body is nothing but a joke, a retching interruption of the omnipotent fantasies of cognition. Imagined as held in that inside/outside of the guts, the linguistic matter of the world figured as vomit and shit presents a fundamental resistance to being lifted up into the realm of textual idea or absorbed by a coherent subject. So rather than a subject, it's a 'parrot, that's what they're up against, a parrot' (338).

The other word used to describe the language towards which the *Trilogy* seems to be heading is 'drivel' – a word which resounds across the *oeuvre*, appearing in *Rough for Theatre II* as the maundering on which precisely postpones the achievement of the communication of sense: 'Hold on till I find the verb and to hell with all this drivel in the middle' (*CDW*: 243). As drivel, language maintains its orality; however, it is reduced to an excessive, misplaced and therefore abjected secretion of saliva. Drivel as a collocation of saliva, slobber and 'letting silly non-sense drop from the lips' (*OED*), in one sense accords with Beckett's familiar articulation of language at odds with securely intentional capacity. But what is more significant is that slobbering in *The Unnamable* becomes a longed-for state in which the 'speech-parched voice at rest would fill with spittle' (*T*: 312). The Unnamable speaks of having 'a pensum to discharge, before I can be free, free to dribble, free to speak no more, listen no more' (312), and evokes the image of a slavering mouth as a way of imagining a bodily expression that has denuded words of their intentional, straightforwardly expressive capacity:

> Evoke at painful junctures, when discouragement threatens to raise its head, the image of a vast cretinous mouth, red, blubber and slobbering, in solitary confinement, extruding indefatigably, with a noise of wet kisses and washing in a tub, the words that obstruct it. Set aside once and for all, at the same time as the analogy with orthodox damnation, all idea of beginning and end. Overcome, that goes without saying, the fatal leaning towards expressiveness. (394)

Here, at rest in the body in a way that seems to offer both hope and resistance, language becomes reflexive rather than an expression of consciousness.

It is strange that in 1929 Beckett clearly believed that salivation and writing should be kept apart. He writes dismissively of the 'process of copious intellectual salivation' employed by readers of Joyce's *Work in Progress* who hope merely to skim off a 'scant cream of sense' (*D*: 26) – its rational content. As we have seen, Rebecca West, who criticised the work, is accused of having no more 'control over her salivary glands than is possible for Monsieur Pavlov's unfortunate dogs' (26), with the satirically disgusted reference to Ivan Pavlov suggesting that reading and writing have been reduced to a mere conditioned reflex – a habit. In the 1930s, however, Beckett was perhaps to become more attracted to the non-dualist idea of the senses' strong relationship to the mind.[16] In his psychology notebook Beckett transcribed from R. S. Woodworth's *Contemporary Schools of Psychology* detailed accounts of the psychology of behaviourism whose development was, by this account, greatly assisted by the work of Pavlov. Woodworth describes Pavlov's famous experiment with the 'secretory reflexes' of dogs, observing how they began to salivate not just at the taste of food, but 'at the sight of the dish containing the food, or even at the approach of the attendant who customarily brought the food, or even at the sound of the attendant's footsteps' (Woodworth 1931: 64). Beckett accordingly notes: 'All learned behaviour is a matter of conditioned reflexes and a function

of the cerebrum . . . Pavlov is not a psychologist, but a brain physiolo-
gist' (1934–5: 7/8). He then goes on to transcribe how J. B. Watson's
experimental psychology, based on Pavlov's brain physiology, allowed
him to apply 'the conditioned reflex concept to all human habit formation' (Beckett 1934–5: 7/8) – formations that according to Woodworth
could include 'all learning' (Woodworth 1931: 69). Although Beckett
notes that this extrapolation from physiology towards psychology led
to behaviourism being derided '"muscle twitch psychology"', he repro-
duces carefully Watson's idea that '[t]hinking is implicit speech reac-
tions, sub-vocal talking, an implicit sensorimotor performance', while
'[e]motion is changes in visceral and glandular systems' (1934–5: 7/9).[17]
According to the behaviourism that clearly intrigued Beckett, then,
various forms of experimental psychology gave a scientific grounding
to the Aristotelian idea that there is indeed nothing in the mind – no
subjective state – that has not first been in the senses.

At about the same period as he was reading Woodworth, Beckett
wrote to MacGreevy of his inability to produce a writing with which
he felt happy. He affirmed that it was not 'a question of being "tongue-
tied", but of being afflicted with a stammer . . . I said on my card de
mes nouvelles n'on peut dire, et c'est bien ça. Nothing in the mind but
spittle' (Beckett: 1932).[18] Later, though, Beckett was to make a virtue
of this necessary failure to incorporate language fully into the realm of
cognitive intention – language stammered out as spittle. Indeed, language in the *Trilogy* precisely becomes slobber, vomit and shit in the
guts – resistant, reflex driven, matter that is mercifully held to offer
some release from the intending *cogito*. In 1972, Beckett affirmed that
Mouth's speech in *Not I* 'is a purely buccal phenomenon without mental
control or understanding, only half heard. Function running away with
organ' (Harmon 1998: 283). Mouth indeed experiences herself as subjected to the jags, gags, glitches, fastforwards and rewinds of the automatic: 'the machine . . . so disconnected . . . never got the message . . . or
powerless to respond' (*CDW*: 378). But it is vital to recall that she also
has memory, sensation and an experience of trauma that she expresses
through language. As indeed becomes clear in the television play of
Not I (broadcast 1977), Billie Whitelaw's mouth, spitting and leaking
words and saliva, is something that seems precisely held in an anxious
hinterland between voluntary and involuntary expression. It is true that
slobber may be produced automatically, as with M. Pavolv's unfortunate dogs; as saliva collects and has contact with sensitive mucous mem-
branes it can indeed be swallowed reflexively or dribbled out. But saliva
can also be consciously withheld or intentionally spat into the world;
both saliva and mouth can be used as a tool of the intending mind.

Of course, Beckett was concerned with both ends of the peristaltic system. And just as saliva can be at least partially controlled at the point where it comes into contact with exteriority, Walton has shown that although defecation is neither cognitive nor a site of mind and intention, it is not simply an 'impulse urge' either (2010: 252). It is this, I think, that might, at least in part, explain Beckett's obsession with it. For the trained human subject, defecation is a physiological impulse more or less effectively modified and controlled according to habit. But habit itself is neither securely within the realm of intention and cognition, nor is it simply the operation of physiological or automatic processes. As Pavlov proved, habits are learned rather than instinctive behaviours, but they are enacted without specific cognitive intentions. As William James influentially put it in *Principles of Psychology* (1890), 'a strictly voluntary act has to be guided by idea, perception, and volition, throughout its whole course. In a habitual action, mere sensation is a sufficient guide, and the upper regions of brain and mind are set comparatively free' (1890: 115–16). Nevertheless and significantly, habits can be altered by the action of will, by the intentional laying down of new grooves in the plastic material of the nervous system; indeed, there is often a degree of intention at the beginning or end of a habitual action. James perceives the resemblance between the action of habit and the process of digestion:

> [i]n habitual action . . . the only impulse which the centres of idea or perception need send down is the initial impulse, the command to *start* . . . [N]o sooner has the conscious thought or volition instigated movement *A*, than *A*, through the sensation *a* of its own occurrence, awakens *B* reflexly; *B* then excites *C* through *B*, and so on till the chain is ended when the intellect generally takes cognizance of the final result. The process, in fact, resembles the passage of a wave of 'peristaltic' motion down the bowels. (1890: 116–17)

So not only is peristalsis habitual, habit itself is peristaltic – a site on the border of cognitive intention and reflex.

As we have seen, in the *Trilogy* gagging textual matter and bodies refuse to submit to socially acceptable habits of behaviour. In *Molloy*, Moran's son Jacques remains constipated, despite the father's desire to inculcate the child's body into the habits of the petit-bourgeoisie, just as the voices of the Unnamable are unable to produce words fit for the purpose of incarnating and nourishing a subject. But the perpetual and intentional force-feeding of words in these texts creates something else, something which is not simply an idea, but more like a habit of going on, or of continuation in the world as it is, even though the engine of the force-feeding machine is driven by the hope of a glimpse of something different – a world in which things might truly be able to be for themselves. As Adorno puts it, '[t]he legacy of action in it [Beckett's work] is a carrying-on which seems stoical but is full of inaudible cries that things should be different' (1990: 381). As an acquired habit, held in the hinterland between mind and body, the intentional and the reflexive, the conceptual and the material, this going on acknowledges the world as it is and the thought that subtends it, but it also carves out a space, both within and using the material resistance of the world, that cannot be violently lifted up and simultaneously abolished within the conceptual.

In Beckett's critical essay *Proust*, written in 1930, habit is most clearly an agent of dullness, exiling immediate, sensuous perception. Looked at in this way, habituation is likely to function as a tool of what Adorno would call identity-thinking, and Beckett describes how '[t]he creature of habit turns aside from the object that cannot be made to correspond with one or other of his intellectual prejudices, that resists the propositions of his team of syntheses, organised by Habit on labour-saving principles' (Beckett 1999: 23). Here, habit subtends the logic of capitalist production in its 'labour-saving principles' and desire to synthesise all under its own pre-existing conceptual categories; habit thus becomes a realm of unconscious submission to the way things are. So for the early Beckett it is precisely Proust's 'inefficient habit' (1999: 29) that makes him an artist rather than a compliant subject within modernity. He sardonically notes that '[h]abit is the ballast that chains the dog to its vomit. Breathing is habit. Life is habit' (19). Beckett seems clear here that habit is dullness and regurgitation that works against the aesthetic experience instantiated by modernist art. And any call to acquire particular habits imbued with a moral authority is simply playing for the other team:

> An automatic adjustment of the human organism to the conditions of its existence has as little moral significance as casting of a clout when May is in or out; and the exhortation to cultivate a habit as little sense as an exhortation to cultivate a coryza. (20)

By the time of the *Trilogy*, however, neither boredom nor habit is opposed to the creation of art, nor perhaps even to the production of certain minimised ethical possibilities. Here, the artistic habit the texts reproduce is a parodic repetition on an inexhaustible going on, a fantasy of absolute exchangeability within the realm of capitalist production in which shit and vomit might become a recycled sustenance. In the end, though, it is laughable, in the *Trilogy* as elsewhere, to imagine that all – body, thought, system – will go on automatically as before. The comic precisely preserves something in these texts that remains indigestible to the habits of the system and an idea of infinite exchangeability that projects itself into the future and believes that things will be preserved in their given form. The future, writes Beckett in *Proust*, '[l]azily considered in anticipation and in the haze of our smug will to live, of our pernicious and uncurable optimism . . . seems exempt from the bitterness and fatality: in store for us, not in store in us' (1999: 15). But that ultimate future of death – the untransformable materiality of human finitude – remains an absolute anachronism inassimilable to the projects of the individual and social world: '[d]eath has not required us to keep a day free' (Beckett 1999: 17). Finitude does not need to wait for a narrative denouement from which to do its final reckoning. Death isn't waiting for a window in the diary in which to score itself in darkest pencil, and the efforts to institute docile habits of production and consumption, to control the future laid down according to the smug repetitions of advertising, are, in one sense, simply attempts to keep us 'regular', in the cosy belief that the future will remain as it is. 'The art of publicity has been revolutionised by a similar consideration. Thus I am exhorted, not merely to try the aperient [laxative] of the Shepherd, but to try it at seven o'clock' (Beckett 1999: 17), Beckett notes.

So the gagging of the *Trilogy* parodies fantasies of the given world of habit, desire, consumption, reproduction as laughable because things don't come anywhere close to being 'regular' here – there is a materiality that cannot be transformed into the subject's projects, despite repetition. This gagging on the material, this incessant warm-up for a main act that never shows up, may reveal something of the unhomely indigence of how things are, but it also institutes another kind of habit, a habit of persistence, that takes its furious drive from an orientation towards a future that could render such banal circulations finally absurd once and for all. By placing the matter of word and world in the lumen, however, in a system habituated to resist complete digestion, the texts hold back from achieving that towards which they find themselves driven. Such gagging thus becomes finally a resistance to being lifted up into both the world of commodified habit and circulation and the realm of truth that Badiou sees and Adorno merely glimpses; it causes the texts to remain, to use a word from *The Unnamable*, 'ephectic' – held back from judgement. 'Can one be ephectic otherwise than unawares?' (*T*: 293), the Unnamable asks. Taking the matter of word and world into the habituated body certainly removes from the text a sense of obligation and ethical action to be experienced cognitively by the subject, but the resistance of the material, its grudging refusal to be more than it is for either the world of commodification or for philosophy, is nevertheless held against a compulsive sense that things should be different. Unawareness is rounded on by a persistent awareness in a movement that is the very root of the comic. The *Trilogy* remains humorous, then, because it furiously spits out its given world. But a changed future is only ever a triangulation point on a map that allows the terrain to be measured rather than a summit that is reached. Like Clov at the end of *Endgame*, the texts are packed and ready for the road, even though we know Clov will probably never leave, although clearly neither can he stay. '[L]et's drive on now to the end of the joke, we must be nearly there' (363), says the Unnamable. We're probably not nearly there, but we're carrying some indigestible sustenance, some 'nourishing murk', for the journey.

Notes

1. See also Banfield's account of the relationship between birth, shit and language in Beckett's work (2003: 9).
2. See also Ricks (1995: 83).
3. The Abderite is Democritus, the so-called laughing philosopher.
4. Daniela Caselli notes a similar mode in *How It Is*: 'endless repetition/ repetitiveness is . . . part of the "top to bottom" digestive circularity of the text, in which shit and vomit are food and nourishment' (2005: 169).
5. See also Mooney (2010: 197).
6. Shane Weller describes how a section of the English translation of *Molloy* was published in Georges Duthuit's *Transition Fifty*, no. 6, '[s]ix months *before* the appearance of the French edition in March 1951' (2009: x).
7. Hill notes that sometimes the English texts revel in an overly literal Gallicism (1990: 47), while at others they intensify comic affect by pressing English idiom to its absurdly (il)logical terminus (46). Ricks also suggests that such 'failures' in translation act as opportunities for an intensification of textual humour as he finds Beckett squeezing an extra comic life out of minimal adjustments to clichés and dead metaphors in English that the French cannot quite muster for itself (1995: 62–78).
8. Ackerley and Gontarski note that 'the Unnamable, considering various forms he might take (339), includes Jones' (2004: 284), only to reject it in another moment of partial incorporation that ironically mirrors the anal-erotic desire both to ingest and to refuse the power of textual objects drawn from the external world.
9. Jones also writes of the 'transference of interest from the original substance [faeces] to a similar one, which, however, is odourless – *i.e.*, mud-pies; from this to one that is dehydrated – *i.e.*, sand; from this to one of a harder consistence – *i.e.*, pebbles' (1923: 694). Jones notes that '[b]ooks and other printed matter are a curious symbol of faeces, presumably through the association of paper with the idea of pressing (smearing, imprinting)' (1923: 692).
10. Jones notes that 'both the ideas of speech and of thinking are equivalent in the unconscious with that of passing flatus, which they frequently symbolise in consciousness' (1923: 559)

11. Sheehan notes that the obligation to express is figured as an inhuman and mechanical compulsion in the *Trilogy* (2002: 170–4).
12. Beckett transcribed from Jones: 'Obsessional neurosis (Zwangneurose): feeling of mustness. Symptoms: 1) Motor: Ewangshandlungen (avoiding cracks in pavement, etc) (2) Sensory: (3) Ideational: Zwangsvorstellungen. (4) Affective (obsessive emotions). Also tics (habit spasms). The Zwang may appear as paralysis of will, e.g. paralysis at the most trifling dilemma' (1934–5: 8/23).
13. It is revealing to note that one of Beckett's first references to 'obligation' appears in the description of a cyst he developed on the perineum when in Germany in 1937. It left him bed-bound, describing, in terms that will emerge in the *Trilogy* in relation to writing, 'intervals of obligations discharged in sweat & torture' (*LSB*: 422).
14. I owe the formulation of 'how it ought to be' to Peter Boxall.
15. Critchley also uses Lacan's articulation of the ethics of psychoanalysis in his theory of humour, but in relation to the infinite demand of the ethical relationship to otherness (2007: 69–87).
16. See Maude (2012).
17. Beckett does not, however, transcribe Woodworth's critique of behaviourism (1931: 76).
18. I am grateful to Ulrika Maude for alerting me to this quotation.

Chapter 3

Power Playing in *Endgame*

Endgame – end game: said slowly, over time, it suggests a paradox. To speak of an end indicates a desire and implies a menacing necessity. Clov's first words express the typically anxious Beckettian need to have done: 'Finished, it's finished, nearly finished, it must be nearly finished' (*CDW*: 93). But the addition of the concept of gaming threatens the purity of this longed-for consummation, with Hamm's inaugural utterance 'Me – to play' (93) placing Clov's compulsion to finish under threat, undermining its very possibility. Bound in what seems like a master– slave dialectic of violent hatred and mutual dependence, Clov cannot have done while Hamm persists in playing, as the end is woven only to be unravelled by the necessity of the continuing game between them.

'Enough, it's time it ended, in the refuge too. And yet I hesitate to, I hesitate to ... to end. Yes, there it is, it's time it ended and yet I hesitate to – to end ... [*He whistles*]' (*CDW*: 93). Hamm wishes to wrap up his existence, perhaps even time itself, but his resolve wavers. He whistles for Clov, who enters immediately, and thus the elaborate game of mastery and domination that becomes an assertion of power and a symbolic revenge against the recalcitrant other disallows that moment of closure before which he hesitates. This hesitation thus assumes the form of a stammer, with the desire to 'have done' becoming an infernal repetition in which the anxious need to get to the end of the sentence paradoxically forces the speaker to articulate more. Hamm's attempt to pronounce a sentence of death only defers such a terminal moment. The sentence is commuted as it is represented and he is given life. Even in the dying moments of the play, then, the desire to 'play and lose and have done with losing' (132) is overwritten by Hamm's fractured discourse and its traumatic renewal of the present tense. As such, the end of the performance attains a troubling ambivalence: 'Clov! No? Good. Since that's the way we're playing it ... let's play it that way ... and speak no more about it ... speak no more ... Old stancher! You ... remain'

(133–4). Hamm's articulated desire to 'speak no more' is characteristically stuttered, repeated, deferred, to become a stammered assertion of endless gaming: 'Since that's the way we're playing it . . . let's play it that way' (133).

So even when *Endgame* seems to have reached its termination, Clov remains, waiting perhaps for the moment when Hamm will call him (into being) again. If humanity might start again from a flea or a crab-louse, in fact from any perceiving 'rational being' (*CDW*: 108) (perhaps another audience on another day?), it seems clear that the play/game has merely ossified into a tableau, a frozen moment which indicates, meta-theatrically, the end of one night's play rather than final closure. Of course, just as the performance stops, games can be finished. But in such instances closure becomes the disavowal of play. The terminal moments of *Endgame* represent not an end to gaming, however; they trace instead the elusive possibility of making a game of ending, for as Beckett affirmed to Alan Schneider, Hamm's invocation of a gradually gathering heap of grain intimates

> the impossibility logically, i.e. eristically, of the 'thing' ever coming to an end. 'The end is the beginning and yet we go on'. In other words the impossibility of catastrophe. Ended at its inception, and at every subsequent instant, it continues, ergo can never end. Don't mention any of this to your actors! (Harmon 1998: 23)

Because ending is everywhere multiplied, the play continues.

So the movement of assertion and retreat, coming and going, which figures the whole work is created by an accumulation of self-deconstructing moments where the end can become a site of fear and pain, as when Hamm, thinking he has been left alone states: 'You prayed – You CRIED for night; it comes – It FALLS: now cry in darkness' (133). But it can simultaneously exist as a comfort and pleasure, as Clov grimly reminds us: 'If I could kill him I'd die happy' (105). Clov's statement 'The end is terrific!' (115) captures such a semantic doubling. Clov wants to put an end to it all in the traumatic awareness that a game without end is horrifying, stating, 'imploringly', '[l]et's stop playing' (130). But the end is that which he knows will never come:

> CLOV: Will it not soon be the end?
> HAMM: I'm afraid it will.
> CLOV: Pah! You'll make up another [story].
> (123)

Of course Clov also clings to the hope of the life's continuation, of the persistence of deadly playing. 'I feel too old, and too far, to form new

habits. Good, it'll never end, I'll never go' (132), he states, even though
to finish would simultaneously make him 'weep for happiness' (132).
For the characters, and perhaps for the audience too, pleasure is col-
located with pain as each can be affixed to either side of this endgame
paradox.

Perhaps

This pairing of ending and gaming is only one of a number of binary
oppositions that form and deform the action, thematics and aesthetic
structure of *Endgame*. Gabriele Schwab defines the essential movement
to be between the poles of closure and openness (1992: 87–99), while
Paul Lawley states that the most insistent binaries of onstage/offstage,
inside/outside determine all those other oppositions – past/present, land/
sea, nature/non-nature, light/darkness – with which the text is concerned (1992: 124). What Lawley describes as this 'habit of polarisa-
tion' (124) offers the promise of a little order which, after all, is Clov's
dream (*CDW*: 120), but these binaries become subject to a threatening,
if somewhat comic, collapse. Although Hamm confidently intones '[o]
utside of here it's death' (96, 124), the possibility of a small boy out
there (130–1) interferes with the stability of the system that seemed to
have life on the inside, on stage, and death without. Similarly, as Clov
peers into the outside world with his telescope, to Hamm's surprise it is
neither night nor day, it is 'GRREY!' (107). Clov attempts to bring this
interstitial state back into a secure structure of impermeable oppositions
by stating that the grey is '[l]ight black. From pole to pole' (107). But,
of course, 'light black' only serves to indicate the porousness of these
seeming antitheses. For all is not quite black and white here; binaries are
proposed only later to refuse to remain distinct. This is not to say that
these structures are fully interconvertible: inside is not the same thing as
outside, black as white, life as death. Staying is not quite the same thing
as going, although the effects of living with and through these antitheses
are strangely fluctuant and unpredictable; instead, antitheses are established as distinct and then subjected to a form of rigorous collapse.

In 1961, a few years after *Endgame* was written, Beckett explained to
Tom Driver the necessary presence of uncertain oppositions in his work:

> If life and death did not both present themselves to us, there would be no
> inscrutability. If there were only darkness, all would be clear. It is because
> there is not only darkness but also light that our situation becomes inexpli-
> cable . . . The question would also be removed if we believed in the contrary

– total salvation. But where we have both light and dark we have also the inexplicable. The key word of my plays is 'perhaps'. (Driver 1979: 220)

In this statement, which is as much a statement of formal as thematic intent, it is the strained relationship between these antitheses, not the static structure of the antitheses themselves, which is dramatically significant. Light and dark, life and death, salvation and damnation exist in a form of vibrant tension where one term never seems to transcend the other. Beckett asks Driver: 'Take Augustine's doctrine of grace given and grace withheld: have you pondered the dramatic qualities in this theology? Two thieves are crucified, one is saved and the other damned. How can we make sense of this division?' (220). Of course, 'perhaps' also has 'dramatic qualities' in its expression of contrary pulsions: it is 'a word qualifying a statement to express possibility with uncertainty' (*OED*). 'Perhaps' is the glimmer of possibility and persistence when there is 'nothing to be done' (*CDW*: 11); it is the Unnamable's momentary belief that it has defined a tremulous way of proceeding 'by aporia pure and simple' or by 'affirmations and negations invalidated as uttered' (*T*: 293). For there is a way forward in *The Unnamable*: '[t]here must be other shifts. Otherwise it would be quite hopeless' (293). But 'perhaps' is simultaneously the low murmur that undoes solid certainty; for 'it is quite hopeless . . . I say aporia without knowing what it means' (293). 'Perhaps' is the niggle of weakness in an expression of power, but it is also the insistence of strength when all potential has seemingly leached away.

As Beckett himself intuited, there is something potentially off-balance, both over- and under-reaching, about the shape of *Endgame*. He wrote to Schneider complaining that *Fin de Partie* (later to be translated as *Endgame*) was not proving easy to finish: '[i]t has turned out a three-legged giraffe, to mention only the architectonics, and leaves me in doubt whether to take a leg off or add one on' (Harmon 1998: 10). Strangely reminiscent of Hamm's three-legged stuffed dog that cannot have its ribbon put on because, as Clov barks, 'he isn't finished, I tell you! First you finish your dog and then you put on his ribbon' (*CDW*: 111), Beckett's flickeringly comic metaphor suggests that he cannot complete the play because he cannot decide whether to give it the ability to stand or to render it completely prone. Given that Beckett did proceed with it, perhaps, in the end, he felt able to make a virtue of this precariously unbalanced balance – to abandon what Molloy might have called the 'principle of trim' (*T*: 71) by refusing to side with either the sedentary Hamm or the stiffly upright Clov. Placing the desire to end alongside its persistent impossibility, the insistent urge to keep on gaming or playing held against the sense that all is winding down or perhaps finally '[w]inding up' (*CDW*: 127), creates a structural tremor in which neither aim achieves its consummation, but neither is willing to give up on its desire. Within this dramatic structure, then, binaries are not secure; instead, they make deforming contact with one another.

As Steven Connor suggests in his discussion of shaking and trembling, '[t]remor makes out a mobile firmament in which strength and weakness can communicate' (2000: 4). The desire to make an end, Clov's urge to 'clear everything away' (*CDW*: 120), fails in the face of the strength of the compulsion to keep on playing that causes life to shudder on. But the game is, in turn, too weak to overwrite the desire to stop once and for all, or 'for good', as the later Beckett might have it. Of course, it is difficult to know whether this weakened oscillation is the excessively prolonged aftershock of an original dilemma or contradiction that first set everything in motion but will eventually lose its tension in the increasing disorganisation of entropy, or whether it is a sign of an immanent, gathering force that will finally shake the whole world of the play apart, causing Clov either to leave or to give up the idea of leaving once and for all. Within the time of the play, the clash between gaming and ending, staying and going, is never resolved; instead, it insists and persists as a dramatic tremor that describes the moment where possibility and impossibility are forced into a tense, irresolvable compact.

Seemingly unacceptable to the logic of non-contradiction, the paradox of the endgame, like many physiological tremors, is clearly wearyingly uncomfortable, even painful, for both characters and audience. But the bringing together of the incongruous that occurs in a paradox can also be amusing, comic, pleasurable (maybe like the quivers that announce the imminent release of a sneeze), as much as it is logically infuriating and troubling. Admittedly, pleasure becomes difficult and uncertain here; but it is useful to remember that Beckett said of *Endgame*, supposedly his favourite play: 'Let's get as many laughs as we can out of this horrible mess' (Cohn 1973: 151–2). This work, which has so often been cited as bleak, difficult and resistant to the consoling exigencies of interpretation should, according to Beckett's own suggestion, precipitate some laughter.

It is Freud who offers a psychological explanation for why the absurd, the self-contradictory and the nonsensical all offer pleasures. The paradoxical works like a 'short circuit', bringing together two circles of ideas and concepts that would otherwise remain distinct. Freud argues that pleasure appears due to a saving of psychic expenditure on the repressive processes of critical reason that would seek to order the mind rather than indulge in childish free play (1905: 124–5); as such, the payoff of pleasure gained from the short-circuiting of repression allows the mind to tolerate contradiction, at least temporarily. As Beckett himself notes down from Jones's *Papers on Psychoanalysis*, wit, the comic and humour all produce a saving on expenditure of psychical energy on repression and the pleasure produced carries us back into a state that precedes the rule of the law: 'All three transport us into a state of childhood "in which we did not know the comic, were not capable of wit and did not need humour to make us happy"' (Beckett 1934–5: 8/3). Although this psychoanalytic account is primarily concerned with repression and the production of pleasure, such a model also implies that by mortgaging itself to pleasure, comedy might buy a space for the exploration of logical paradox and aporia – a space into which what Freud was later to be call the reality principle's desire to repossess the mind, to solve contradiction and impose the rule of law on the 'horrible mess', does not, at least momentarily, intrude. So if comedy enables an exploration of 'perhaps' because, temporarily, it can stave off the resolution of paradox sufficiently for an examination of the conflictual, the illogical, the irreconcilable, to occur, it is possible to read the humour of *Endgame* as no longer simply a side effect or symptom precipitated by a more essential structural uncertainty. Instead, humour is a textual effect fundamentally bound into the demand to produce the structural formation of a paradox that could persist in and as itself, without being converted into logical resolution.

Now some of the comedy within *Endgame* clearly resides in the macrocosmic, in the way in which the whole form of the play is structured around these paradoxically antithetical abilities and inabilities. But, as in the *Trilogy*, much humour also emerges through the strangely commutable axis of tremor which allows paradoxical movement to reduce itself and reappear in the relationships between the characters and their self-undoing modes of expression. Clov reflects on himself and says 'sometimes I wonder if I'm in my right senses. Then it passes off and I'm as intelligent as ever' (*CDW*: 128). Does this mean that to remain intelligent one should not question that intelligence; or does it mean that 'as intelligent as ever' was only ever a measure of the 'meremost minimum' (*NO*: 103)? The statement suggests either and, indeed, both. Of course, this is not a new mode for Beckett. In the early short story 'Ding-Dong' (written in 1933), the 'sinfully indolent' Belacqua defends his method of proceeding through 'moving pauses' (Beckett 1970: 41). He goes out, not with the aim of getting anywhere, but merely to experience the 'charm of this pure blank movement' (41) denuded of its itinerary. The narrator comments on Belacqua's description of these 'moving pauses' by stating simply: 'He had a strong weakness for oxymoron. In the same way he overindulged in gin and tonic water'

(41). Like Murphy defending 'his courses of inaction' (Beckett 1993: 26), the idea of the 'moving pause' is a comic oxymoron. But the fact that Belacqua's predilection for it manifests itself as a 'strong weakness' tells us something about the structure of the oxymoron itself which is a tremor of unresolved antitheses – 'an expression, in its superficial or literal meaning self-contradictory or absurd, but involving a point' (*OED*). If, as we have seen, comedy occurs in the border space where the limits of the laws of congruity and expectation are both transgressed and restated, the oxymoron and the figure of 'strong weakness' become a highly suggestive trope for describing this tense, irresolvable relationship between the conceptual mastery in humour and the conceptual play that allows incongruities to appear at all. For limits are not finally or permanently transgressed in such comedy; instead, they are made to vibrate or shake.

So the oxymoron of the endgame, which elicits the appearance of a stuttered 'perhaps', is preserved in the text according to shapes and pulsions, the contours and vicissitudes, of the comic. But if this is true, it is important to note that it is not just the relationship between these two contradictory logics of ending and gaming that is comic; rather, these logics express themselves as seemingly contradictory but crucially conjoined comic techniques that use the paradoxes of the endgame form to create analogously hesitant occasions of affect. What follows will be a detailed analysis of the motility of the comedy of *Endgame* which describes and forces both characters and audience to experience the potentiality of comedy to ossify and objectify otherness according to the temporality of 'the end', while it simultaneously loosens that taut fixity to embrace comedy as a dialogical instant where self and other must face each other without submission to the logic of a final resolution or solution – the temporality of 'the game'. In the oxymoron of the endgame, the comedy of ending, or the comedy of tragedy in which there is a desire to put an end to the other and the self, and the tragedy of gaming in which the end will never come, are forced to inhabit the same theatrical space.

Unhappiness: Nothing Funnier

So for Hamm and Clov, making an end consists of abrogating the ludic relationship of one to the other: 'If I could kill him I'd die happy' (*CDW*: 105), states Clov, gloomily. But, despite their seemingly mirrored desires, both insist on carrying on the 'slow work' between them (97). Clov hits Hamm with the dog:

HAMM: He hit me!
CLOV: You drive me mad, I'm mad!
HAMM: If you must hit me, hit me with the axe. Or hit me with the gaff, hit me with the gaff. Not with the dog. With the gaff. Or with the axe.

(130)

Clov's frustration with being a pawn in Hamm's game, no more than his dog, expresses itself through violence – a violence that suggests he wants to finish for good. But the blow is insufficient, not eliciting an end but simply another kind of playing. Hamm, too, is looking for a blow that might kill him, but as he ponders on the relative merits of the dog, the gaff or the axe as weapons, he starts up another kind of game. So although Clov implores him to 'stop playing', Hamm can neither give up the game nor relinquish the desire to abandon it: he cannot 'play and lose and have done with losing' (132). Hamm's response to Clov's plea that they should stop the game is simply 'Never!' (130), although only a few seconds later, he is crying, again, plaintively: 'Then let it end! With a bang' (130).

Now it is clear that the characters' persistent yet unattainable desire for an end produces a comedy of failure rather than a failure of comedy. At the rehearsals in Berlin for *Endspiel*, Beckett indeed stated that Nell's dictum '[n]othing is funnier than unhappiness' (*CDW*: 101) was this work's most important sentence (Gontarski 1992: 54), affirming both the centrality of humour to the play and the historically tenacious sense of laughter as an alibi for violence and aggression. It remains true that the confrontations between the characters in which an end is attempted are humorous insofar as they function as assertions of a 'sudden glory' or conceptual victory in which the butt of the joke is constructed as an object, refused the position of subject within the exchange. Attempting to assert his own power, Hamm asks Nagg: 'Scoundrel! Why did you engender me?' (116). Nagg's response is blackly comic, but it also serves to mark his momentary superiority over his tyrannical son:

NAGG: I didn't know.
HAMM: What? What didn't you know?
NAGG: That it'd be you.

(116)

When Clov asks Hamm whether he believes 'in the life to come', Hamm fashions a last word to which Clov is unable to respond. Hamm states: 'Mine was always that', and, as Clov exits, he adds a triumphant passing shot – an acknowledgement that the steel trap of a joking mechanism has been sprung: 'Got him that time!' (116).

This comic dialogue that seeks to create ossified occasions of domination finds itself mirrored in a structural emphasis on static posture and mime that reifies the characters' lack of freedom. Beckett as director was particularly keen to emphasise the representation of what he termed 'frozen postures' (Gontarski 1992: xx), just as he displayed an overwhelming tendency to fix and control the material theatrical space. Bolstered by the authority of the author's aesthetic statements on the 'extreme simplicity of dramatic situation' (Harmon 1998: 24) in *Endgame*, many critics have followed Alain Robbe-Grillet's lead in asserting that Beckett's characters are simply 'alone on the stage, standing up, futile, with no future or past, irremediably present' (1975: 115). And there are ways in which the comedy of superiority might be aligned with the sensations of presence that *Endgame* seems to precipitate, as particular forms of joking seem precisely to confer a traumatic fixity upon the object of the comic exchange. Homi Bhabha explains, for example, how colonisers attempt to dominate and objectify their others through specific discursive practices, with the repetitive appearance of the comic stereotype pinning the colonised person to the terms of a predetermined representation. Citing Edward Said, he states: 'The tense they employ is the timeless eternal; they convey an impression of repetition and strength . . . For all these functions it is frequently enough to use the simple copula *is*' (Bhabha 1994: 71). Of course, one of the most tenacious discursive uses of the stereotype occurs precisely in the ethnic superiority joke: the English Irish joke, the American Polish joke, the French Belgian joke, among many others.[1] The stupidity of others is asserted, re*present*ed, objectified and supposedly corrected through laughter, as the laughing subject fixes what is most often a threateningly proximate social group as their risible comic object.

The desire to objectify and annul an other in *Endgame* seems then to echo this particular kind of joking in its repetition of an ever-renewed present that enforces an entrapping corporeality onto these characters, compelling them, momentarily and painfully, into being. In the joke about the 'life to come' Hamm and Clov are both compelled to inhabit a traumatically renewed, clenched, present tense that resists the past which is long ago, half-forgotten, while simultaneously refusing the inconceivable future. Significantly, however, and as Bhabha has revealed in relation to the comic colonial stereotype, the assertion of laughing superiority does not simply occur once and for all; the characters do not succeed in annihilating each other, thus ending the game. As Freud suggests, comic superiority may be an alibi for the murderous aggression prohibited by the reality principle, but, as such, it indicates a fundamentally attenuated form of sadistic power – one in which the subject does not completely destroy its other. Comic superiority is indeed a profoundly weakened form of aggression that thus demands repetition; it is a contraction always to be preceded and followed by a dilation in which the other persists – insists. The fact that, as Beckett stated, the play 'ist voller Echos, alle antworten einander [is full of echoes, they all answer each other]' (Gontarski 1992: xxi), indicates that within this comic drama, the fixity of an end is never produced; instead, the end has played.

This immanent incompleteness or failure of the comedy of mastery for the characters does not destroy the comic structure of *Endgame*, however. For there are moments when the characters, who are both laughing subjects and risible objects for each other, suddenly seem to gain a meta-theatrical awareness of being the object of a wider comic gaze:

> CLOV: [*He gets down, picks up the telescope, turns it on auditorium.*] I see ... a multitude ... in transports ... of joy. [*Pause.*] That's what I call a magnifier. [*He lowers the telescope, turns towards* HAMM.] Well? Don't we laugh?
> HAMM: [*After reflection.*] I don't.
> CLOV: [*After reflection.*] Nor I. [*He gets up on ladder, turns the telescope on the without.*]
>
> (*CDW*: 106)[2]

At this moment, Hamm and Clov suddenly seem to sense that, even as they thought they were subjects in the drama, they are being as much laughed at as laughed with. Clov's laugh that follows Hamm's speculation as to whether the two of them are 'beginning to ... to ... mean something' is a laugh of recognition, then, indicating a meta-theatrical awareness of their dramatic plight. But it cannot and does not last: 'Mean something! You and I mean something! [*Brief laugh.*] Ah that's a good one!' (108). Character laughter dies, then, at precisely the place where audience laughter emerges.

Laughter may offer a sense of solitary power and mastery; as Helmuth Plessner puts it, the sound of laughter offers a sense of virility to the subject, '[it] is the power of self-affirmation: one hears oneself' (quoted in Iser 1993: 172). But that mastery is seemingly confirmed and strengthened as it becomes part of a resounding chorus. In Bergson's model of the comic:

> Laughter appears to stand in need of an echo. Listen to it carefully: it is not an articulate, clear, well-defined sound; it is something that would fain be prolonged by reverberating from one to another ... It can travel within as wide a circle as you please: the circle remains, none the less, a closed one ...

laughter always implies a secret freemasonry, or even complicity, with other laughers, real or imaginary. (1911b: 5–6)

This rendering of laughter confirms its social basis, its demand for that community of 'co-despisers' that Freud also illuminates. But it also indicates laughter's risky, reverberative contagion. For, of course, contagions, infections and reverberations are not perfect repetitions of an original. An echo is not an absolute replication of the sound that it follows; rather, it is that sound subject to an interference as it is reproduced. And as characters and audience in *Endgame* attempt to laugh together, the reverberative crescendo seems to disaggregate, shuddering into voices that are not necessarily laughing in tune with one another, or to the same rhythm.

Endgame seems precisely to play out the risky potential of reversal that haunts communal laughter as it is transmitted and shared. If the laughter of mastery indicates a temporary '*absence of feeling*' (Bergson 1911b: 4) or a 'momentary anesthesia of the heart' (Bergson 1911b: 5), there are, as we have seen, ways in which that anaesthesia infects the laughing subject with mechanical inhumanity. Because the characters laugh with maniacal insistence but do not learn from the unremitting failure of their repeated attempts at comic mastery, they begin to resemble that which was previously coded as risible. And it is within such moments of repetition that Bergson implicitly brings together his thesis on laughter and his famous philosophy of temporality or duration. Bergson asserts that repetition is laughable because a truly living life 'is the continuous evolution of a being growing ever older; it never goes backwards and never repeats anything' (1911b: 88). In *Creative Evolution* (1907), he describes duration as not simply one instant replacing another; instead, the present is always engorged with the past, and this is what makes absolute repetition impossible for a human consciousness:

[C]onsciousness cannot go through the same state twice. The circumstances may still be the same, but they will act no longer on the same person, since they find him at a new moment of his history. Our personality, which is being built up each instant with its accumulated experience, changes without ceasing. By changing, it prevents any state, although superficially identical with another, from ever repeating in its very depth. (Bergson 1911a: 5–6)

The person who seems to be repeating, in the face of the impossibility of absolute repetition, represents a disfiguring of duration and of the human, then, that should, for Bergson, be policed and corrected by laughter. This is a negative model in which something repeats by virtue of what it is not, or what it does not have. In Deleuze's terms, '*one* repeats because one does not know, because one does not remember' (1994: 295). The comic is thus a judgement upon a form of repetition that 'presents it[self] to a spectator who contemplates it from without. It suppresses the thickness in which repetition occurs and unfolds' (Deleuze 1994: 271).

So it is after their 'deadly' (*CDW*: 106) and clownishly repetitive games with the ladder and the telescope that Hamm and Clov display an awareness of being placed under a painfully objectifying comic gaze. As the audience laughs (and empirical evidence suggests they usually do) at Clov's ironic characterisation of them as a 'multitude in transports of joy', the characters suddenly realise their own status as laughable objects subject to repetitions that the audience finds comic, but also, perhaps, painful and 'deadly'.[3] The characters lose their laughter because they find themselves being played by the logic of a game that now has more players, more putative masters in the form of spectators rather than the seemingly longed for less. And yet, even this does not make an end. After Clov admits that he cannot have a 'good guffaw' again today, Hamm pauses, only to submit to the necessity of continuation: 'Nor I', he concurs, '[*Pause.*] I continue then' (122).

Playing for Time

So in the face of these inexorably renewed moments of objectification represented by Hamm's anguished, obsessive question, '[w]hat's happening, what's happening?' (*CDW*: 98), comes Clov's cryptic response: 'Something is taking its course'. Time *is* passing: 'Grain upon grain, one by one, and one day, suddenly, there's a heap' (93). Time's passage can also be measured by the entropic decline of Clov's progressive stiffness, Nell's death and Nagg's retreat – markers that differentiate 'that bloody awful day' from 'this bloody awful day' (113). For despite Clov's statement that there is 'no more nature', Hamm asserts that 'we breathe, we change! We lose our hair, our teeth! Our bloom! Our ideals!' (97). Entropy is increasing and time moves inexorably forwards due to the perpetuation of those games between characters which end only to be reborn in the next moment.

In a world where the conventional markers of time have broken down (alarm clocks seem inherently unreliable and Clov's seeds will never sprout), the passage of time appears most clearly in the delay or the lag that exists as self and other discourse with one another. Although it is important to remember that Beckett insistently pared down the dialogue between the characters,[4] Hamm continues to call to Clov, submitting himself to the unknowable future where Clov might come or he might not. Clov asks questions of Hamm, and although they are the old, interminable questions whose answers are mostly known, there is always the possibility of change that identifies an exposure to contingency. For surely it is the possibility of new answers, of answers that could lead to an end, that drives forward the anxious repetition of the questions. Any finish is nevertheless refused by the terrified insistence on the continuing relationship between the characters: 'Keep going, can't you, keep going!' (*CDW*: 122), implores Clov. As Hamm says to Clov: 'Gone from me you'd be dead', and Clov replies, 'and *vice versa*' (126), and it is indeed precisely the dialogical nature of gaming that disavows the possibility of finality:

> CLOV: I'll leave you.
> HAMM: No!
> CLOV: What is there to keep me here?
> HAMM: The dialogue.
>
> (120–1)

As Beckett wrote to Schneider:

> 'Keep going etc.' means 'Keep asking me about my story, don't let the dialogue die.' Repeated ironically by Clov a little later with the same meaning. Cf. 'return the ball' in *Godot*. I think this whole passage . . . should be played as *farcical parody of polite drawing-room* conversation. (Harmon 1998: 23)

Discursive contestation, linked here explicitly with game playing ('return the ball'), becomes a submission to contingency that resists the end of a known future.

As we have seen, for Levinas time becomes intimately bound to the notion of alterity or otherness. In *Time and the Other* (1948), begun when he was a prisoner of war in Germany and originally delivered as a series lectures at the Collège Philosophique in an immediately postwar Paris, Levinas forges an account of time figured as what might be termed the ethical future. Critiquing Heidegger's notion in *Being and Time* that the future of Dasein, its death, is the 'possibility-of-Being in which the very Being of one's own Dasein is an issue' (Heidegger 1962: 284), Levinas states that death is not an 'event of freedom' (1987: 70) or 'that *possibility that is one's ownmost, which is non-relational, and which is not to be outstripped*' (Heidegger 1962: 294); rather, death makes the 'assumption of possibility impossible . . . we ourselves are seized' (Levinas 1987: 71). Levinas determines that in its relationship with the other the self is opened onto a future beyond itself, that cannot be grasped, that can never be reduced to its own projects. In Levinas's terms, then, the 'other is the future. The very relationship with the other is the relationship with the future. It seems impossible to speak of time in a subject alone, or to speak of personal duration' (Levinas 1987: 77). And just as Hamm and Clov have nothing with which to measure time except each other, Levinas explicitly affirms that 'time is not the achievement of an isolated and lone subject . . . it is the very relationship of the subject with the Other' (Levinas 1987: 39). As Beckett is to restate it in the radio play *Embers* (1957), Henry only has Ada and their dialogue to mark time's fleeting passage: 'Keep on, keep on! Keep it going, Ada, every syllable is a second gained' (*CDW*: 262). For it is the contretemps – etymologically derived from a fencing move made at an inopportune moment, a move that is literally out of time – that occurs between the characters that elicits a moment that cannot be reduced one's own, singular time.

The existence of the self-identical subject creates what Levinas terms 'hypostatized time' – a time that becomes an assertion of the present and of the 'existent's mastery over existing' (Levinas 1987: 55). The self, like the one that would objectify the other through the representation of its own 'now', asserts 'I am master, master of the possible, master of the grasping of the possible' (Levinas 1987: 72). Such a hypostatised, clenched and contracted laughing subject who asserts his own self-identity by fixing and refusing dialogue with the other, is manifested at times in Hamm:

> HAMM: . . . Did anyone ever have any pity on me?
> CLOV: What? Is it me you're referring to?
> HAMM: An aside, ape!
>
> (*CDW*: 130)

Hamm attempts to assert his mastery over existing, achieving the solitude of a unity which contracts and disavows any relationship with the future and the other; he consistently desires to know, to tell his own story, and to represent his own freedom and virility as a subject. For '[a]s present and "I", hypostasis is freedom. The existent is master of existing. It exerts on its existence the virile power of the subject. It has something in its power' (1987: 54), Levinas suggests. Hamm's refusal, at times, to acknowledge the sentience of others becomes just such an attempt to assert his sovereignty: 'Can there be misery – loftier than mine? No doubt. Formerly. But now? My father? My mother? My dog? Oh I am willing to believe they suffer as such creatures can suffer. But does that mean their sufferings equal mine?' (93). It is his suffering, his narrative that attains primacy – a move that requires Clov, Nagg,

Nell to be objectified as insentient slaves, ossified in a perpetually rep-*resent*ed now. But if such solitude, such hypostatised time, becomes a 'pure event', a perpetual present rather than a relationship with the other as the future, it can no longer be perceived as a relationship of time as such. Such '[s]olitude' is thus 'an absence of time' (1987: 57), states Levinas.

Of course, *Endgame* persistently demonstrates that Hamm is never simply a subject and, as we have seen, he hesitates before his end, before the terminal moment of solitude and time without duration. If the whole dynamic of the play is the tension created by the games of Hamm and Clov – Clov desperate to return to his kitchen or to leave despite his incapacity to do so, Hamm desperate to maintain control over Clov even as he desires an end to the game – then their relationship is cemented by a fear of solitude and the terror that all play will cease. Although Hamm commands Clov to 'be off' (*CDW*: 98), he acknowledges that Clov's resistant incapacity means that their relationship, alongside time's forward movement structured by it, persists. Hamm's vaguely comical '[w]e're getting on' (99) captures precisely this sense of time determined through and as a relationship between self and other.

So even as Hamm imagines Clov leaving, he acknowledges that he would then have to split himself, divide himself from solitary self-containment in a way that would produce more time:

> All kinds of fantasies! That I'm being watched! A rat! . . . The babble, the babble, words, like the solitary child who turns himself into children, two, three, so as to be together, and whisper together, in the dark. Moment upon moment, pattering down, like the millet grains of . . . that old Greek. (*CDW*: 126)

Hamm must submit himself to being object, an other, who never achieves the full presence or mastery of an existent, in Levinas's terms. He must cast aside his virility and allow himself to be played. At times, then, Hamm positions himself as Clov's object and allows the slave a momentary victory:

> CLOV: You shouldn't speak to me like that.
> HAMM: Forgive me. I said, forgive me.
> CLOV: I heard you.
>
> (98)

Clov also perpetrates several deceptions in order to place Hamm in the position of risible object and in the exchange that follows the relationship between subject and object submits to an inversion:

CLOV: Why do you keep me?
HAMM: There's no one else.
CLOV: There's nowhere else.
HAMM: You're leaving me all the same.
CLOV: I'm trying.
HAMM: You don't love me?
CLOV: No.

(95)

Yet it is their final words that recognise the irreducibility of the relationship between self and other:

HAMM: I'm obliged to you, Clov. For your services.
CLOV: Ah pardon: it's I am obliged to you.
HAMM: It's we are obliged to each other.

(132)

They need each other, for neither Hamm nor Clov can laugh alone: each requires the other to remain in the game.

Clov asks Hamm why he always obeys his blind master; neither understands why he does not leave or rebel. Hamm's answer, although ironically pompous and denuded of the 'pathos' that Beckett stated would be 'the death of the play' (Gontarski 1992: 65), is suggestive of what seems like an ethical obligation: 'Perhaps it's compassion [*Pause.*] A kind of great compassion' (*CDW*: 129), he says to Clov, acknowledging the continuing dialogue that both binds and deforms their relationship. It is this gaming, the *ur*-condition for dialogue, and for comic dialogue in particular, that holds open a time lag in which the other remains at least partially unknown. And this, amid all the laughing violence, enables the comic to bear within itself at least the trace of the ethical relationship to futurity that Levinas is at pains to identify. Indeed, in the later *Totality and Infinity*, the ethical relation of obligation to the other is precisely figured as a discursive one: 'The relation between the same and the other, metaphysics, is primordially enacted as a conversation (*discours*), where the same, gathered up in its ipseity as an "I", as a particular existent unique and autochthonous, leaves itself' (Levinas 1969: 39). Even though language can function, in its content, as an attempt at mastery, as long as 'the dialogue' continues, there is, in Hamm's terms, always '[t]ime enough' (103).

The cultural historian Johan Huizinga, who influentially described the play element of culture in *Homo Ludens* (1938), is insistent that play and games are precisely determined by their need to be demarcated in space and time – their need for an end: 'Play begins and then at a certain moment it is "over". It plays itself to an end' (9). The goal becomes a vital structuring factor of the game, then, something towards which it tends, but the end is simultaneously the moment the game finds itself extinguished. Samuel Weber's analysis of Nietzsche's conception of gaming and struggle suggestively teases apart this paradoxical quality of games. He identifies two seemingly contradictory logics in Nietzsche's essay 'Homer's Contest', describing how, 'on the one hand, struggle is seen as a means, is subordinated to a finality determined outside the game (whose goal is thus identified with victory); on the other hand, the game (or struggle) is regarded as an end-in-itself' (Weber 1985: 106). The first model is the *Vernichtungskampf*, an extermination struggle; 'the second . . . is designated as *agon* properly speaking, as *Wettkampf* (joust)' (Weber 1985: 106). But Weber presses on a revealing ambivalence that Nietzsche finds in games. For, as Nietzsche puts it, the notion of the joust 'abominates the rule of one and fears its dangers; it desires, as a *protection* against the genius, another genius' (1968: 37). 'Those who, by their superiority, would threaten the status of the joust as a game are banished' (1985: 106), Weber states. As such, 'the game is necessarily ambivalent from the start' (Weber 1985: 106), for its ludic quality – its back and forth through time – in which otherness is preserved in the name of play, is precisely, and curiously, also dependent on a violence, on the ostracism of those who would, by their strength, make all too quick an end.

If Hamm's power over Clov is absolute, if he is assured of winning, then playing becomes, in Nietzsche's terms, the *Vernichtungskampf* or the extermination struggle – a game which, at best, can only be played once and whose very status as a game is at risk if there is no real contest and the winner is already known. Beckett explicitly reminds Schneider that this play is emphatically not an extermination struggle, however: 'death is merely incidental to the end of "this . . . this . . . thing." . . . I do not say "deathgame"' (Harmon 1998: 22). Hamm's hesitation before such an end means that the game continues as a *Wettkampf*, a joust, rather than a struggle of terminal domination. But, as we have seen, agonistics is always an ambivalent process: '[it] always contains an element of domination, a desire to lay hold of the other, to curtail the otherness upon which the agonistics nevertheless depends', Weber determines (1985: 107). Weber goes on to suggest that 'Nietzsche's conceptions lead us to ask whether it is not rather ambivalence, a certain *tension* between unity and disunity – that characterizes all games as such' (113). For, paradoxically, to play a game is to be orientated towards an end, and to enter into those relationships of power, justice and law which are both violent (but not so violent that the end is achieved and the game effaced) and ethical (but not so ethical that there would be nothing to drive forward the play and the relationship between self and other would be transmuted into Levinasian traumatic passivity).

Now this seems to get to the heart of Derrida's critique of the Levinasian ethics of *Totality and Infinity*. As Derrida suggests in 'Violence and Metaphysics' (1964), pure non-violence is the impossibility of a violent relationship and a refusal of the moment of victory. But because any meeting will necessarily be marked by a violence insofar as neither self nor other remains unchanged, absolutely the same, following it, the pure non-violence of a non-relation is paradoxically also the impossibility of ethics, the impossibility of the rupturing of self-identity ethics demands:

> *We do not say pure nonviolence.* Like pure violence, pure nonviolence is a contradictory concept ... Pure violence, a relationship between beings without face, is not yet violence, is pure nonviolence. And inversely: pure nonviolence, the nonrelation of the same to the other (in the sense understood by Levinas) is pure violence. Only a face can arrest violence, but can do so, in the first place, only because a face can provoke it. (1978: 146–7)

Endgame, though, resists interminable agonistics, pure game playing, just as it resists the pure end. The problem is restated in *Play* as the man asks of himself, his fellow interred figures and the audience, 'when will all this have been ... just play?' (*CDW*: 313), and it seems the only imaginable response is 'never'. There is no fantasy of a 'just' game played purely for its own sake, in a space of freedom where there could be no others; instead, each character remains violently held, bound to one another, in their tortured scene. In *Endgame*, then, Being and presence enact the subject's freedom to end but also lay bare its solitude; they offer the pleasure of laughing self-assertion but the pain of the loss of the other, virility and despair. The game, on the other hand, is a moment of becoming, of staving off mastery in a rhapsodically ethical relationship to the future and the other that cannot be grasped. But pure, just play might also be a moment where the relationship with the other is lost. The paradoxical and conflictual pairing of the endgame thus seems to recognise both the structural violence and the ethical possibilities that must inhere within relationships, within being played by the rules of the game. As such, it materialises a form that resists conceptual synthesis to remain a strained and sustained antithesis.

The Play of the Audience

Like his unfinished three-legged dog, then, Hamm is a figure that Beckett leaves on the tilt. Caught between a desire to inhabit the absolute centre of the room he is in and the injunction that this achievement should be '[m]ore or less! More or less!' (*CDW*: 105), Hamm can never march fully in time with himself; but it is precisely in his balanced unbalance, in his tremor of 'strong weakness' that materialises the action of delaying, that more time is forced into passing. Beckett writes:

> What H is doing here is putting off, with the help of such "business" as the gaff, toque, glasses, verse and story, the moment when he must whistle for Clov ("call") and call out to his father, i.e. the moment of his definite dereliction ... [H]e cannot be *absolutely* certain until he has whistled and called in vain ... It is this absolute and final certainty that H shirks from with his 'business'. (Harmon 1998: 30)

It is through his 'strong weakness', his insistence on dialogue with Clov and Nagg, that temporality gets implicated into the scene. Beckett revised the English edition of the text at this point, having Hamm shift from saying 'a few more gags like that and I'll call' to 'a few more squirms' (133) (Harmon 1998: 30). 'Squirms' perhaps emphasises the wriggles and the temporal wrinkles of delay that might be forgotten in the normative comic sense of 'gag', but both words highlight the degree to which interruption and the insertion of time remain vital to the play's foundational comedy. To 'call' and to be left alone would finally be to 'call time' on this scene, but when Hamm calls he suspects he is still not alone but is, instead, making another move in the game. Things are complicated further by an ineluctable meta-theatrical sense – Hamm's sense of being a player with another audience outside of this place whose presence leaks into the scene. For in his final 'gag' Hamm throws his whistle towards the auditorium, offering it up to these others '[w]ith my compliments' (133). It is precisely the audience, then, alongside Clov, who are invoked in the final line '[y]ou . . . remain' (134). It is indeed the audience, as much as the other characters, who are engaged and affected by these 'squirms' and thus give form to the openness and uncertainty of the play – the dilation of the time of the other and the otherness of time, that drives all forwards into the experience of duration.

In terms of the production of comedy, affect must always be materialised in the minds and bodies of an audience, and here they indeed act as the alternately entertained and tortured witnesses of the scene. So although *Endgame* may mark the passage of time through entropic decline, the eliciting of affect in the play suggests that *Endgame* cannot simply be represented as a closed system in which new energy, new organisation, does not enter. Michael North has suggested that readings of comic permutation in Beckett tend to emphasise repetition within a torturously closed system in which the nothing new appears as the only alternative (2009: 159–60). He points out, however, that Beckett's permutations always contain intimations and representations that gesture towards the excess of infinite permutation within a necessarily finite series; consequently, '[t]here is something comic in the infinity opened up within the series because openness means variety, newness, surprise' (North 2009: 162). What North does not make explicit, though, is that the energy to churn through an infinite series, that which is therefore capable of producing the new, must necessarily come into such a system from outside if the second law of thermodynamics is to be obeyed.

The second law of thermodynamics is explained by James Clerk Maxwell's famous passage in the 1872 *Theory of Heat* as follows:

> It is impossible in a system enclosed in an envelope which permits neither change of volume nor passage of heat, and in which both the temperature and the pressure are everywhere the same, to produce any inequality of temperature or pressure without the expenditure of work. (1872: 308)

In other words, in a closed system entropy increases as fast, hot molecules, and cold, slow ones, gradually settle into a homogeneous mixture denuded of local configurations of order. The inevitability of this entropic process and its irreversibility (unless work is put into the system from the outside, which would mean that the system is no longer closed) has, as Beckett knew, been described as marking the arrow or direction of time.[5] Of course, it is clear that Clov's desired order should be understood more as final, entropic uniformity than organisation: 'I love order. It's my dream. A world where all would be silent and still and each thing in its last place, under the last dust' (*CDW*: 120). Nevertheless, he senses that he would be fooling himself if he were to take comfort in that final disordered order – the mixed grey or 'light black' of heat death. Beckett confirms this in his Riverside notebook, for Clov is not in a closed system; something has been added: 'C perplexed. All seemingly in order, yet a change. Fatal grain added to form an impossible heap . . . Last straw' (Gontarski 1992: 197). It is also clear that Clov's new flea, as Hamm suspects, opens the closed system in which there is the hope that all is moving towards an end, to the unpredictability of innovation, of creation: 'But humanity might start from there all over again! Catch him, for the love of God!' (108), he cries. Hamm also envisions, albeit ironically, a world of nature, of open living systems capable of drawing energy into themselves from their environment, that might still exist outside of this seemingly sealed place. 'Flora! Pomona! Ceres! (111), he imagines, ecstatically.

Clov suggests, even more alarmingly, the possibility of a 'small boy' (*CDW*: 130), a 'potential procreator' (131), who prises open glimmers of potential within the play – a new beginning or an 'underplot' (130). And an 'underplot' suggestively implicates an interpreting audience able to recognise the small boy's innovation into the scene – an audience who can precipitate the 'new' through their acts of engagement. The most explicit examples of the 'openness' of *Endgame* as a system indeed appear at moments when characters sense an occasion of interaction with the audience or with others who reside outside of this place. In this world where there are no more bicycles, painkillers or sugar plums, and old people live in dustbins, Hamm asks Clov, as if he were a social secretary, 'No phone calls?' (97). 'Who would be ringing?' one is tempted to ask of this *'polite drawing-room* conversation' (Harmon 1998: 23). Hamm's question is followed by a '[*pause*]', and as in the moment that follows Clov's turning his telescope on the 'multitude in transports of joy' (106), the same stage direction is given. On both occasions (97, 106), the pause is followed by a question. 'Don't we laugh?', says Hamm, to which Clov replies, simply: 'I don't feel like it' (97). It seems likely that what happens in this pause to cause both Hamm and Clov to question their ability to respond with laughter is that the audience recognises the comedy of the situation and laughs, communicating something to the characters. So Hamm and Clov's questions as to whether they too laugh become responses to the delivery of laughter from an audience of observers who are outside of this seemingly closed system but able to add new energy, perhaps even new ordering or interpretative possibilities, into it. Although Adorno insists in the appendix to *Aesthetic Theory* that in *Godot* and *Endgame* '[t]he spectator's laughter fades away in the face of the laughter on stage' (1997: 466),[6] in the play text there is a strong implication that it is precisely audience laughter that produces something new for the characters – an awareness that they are comic objects. Of course, this cannot easily be recuperated into that more socially acceptable 'laughing with', as the characters refuse to admit or mark the fact that they are acting with any comic intent. Against that confirming sense of synthesis and presence offered by shared communal laughter, the play offers an occasion of characters and audience falling out of time with one another's intentions and expectations. And precisely in this moment of syncopation, something new is added to the repetitiousness of the nothing new of the scene.

In one way, perhaps *Endgame* is simply using comedy to draw attention to something that must always be true of literary and theatrical texts. Because texts mark a passage, a channel of communication between author and reader or audience, texts necessarily contain conditions of engagement, unpredictability and newness; they can never be thermodynamically closed systems whose fate of heat death is sealed.

Of course, as we have seen, the comedy of Beckett's early texts worked to close down sites of affective uncertainty, even as those works were developing an interest in uncertainty's more epistemological manifestations. In 'Dante . . . Bruno . Vico .. Joyce' we saw Beckett sneering towards the baffled readers of Joyce's 'Work in Progress', 'if you don't understand it, Ladies and Gentlemen, it is because you are too decadent to receive it' (*D*: 26), while simultaneously deriding their attempts to comprehend the work's occluded content above its disintegrative form. Superiority barged to the centre of the content of those early essays, contracting permissible affect in the reader while nevertheless ironically reproducing a certain affective unpredictability through their lack of formal comic measure.

In *Endgame*, however, Beckett seems determined to open out a more strongly indeterminate space of comic feeling, to solicit what Sianne Ngai calls, after Susan Feagin, 'meta-feelings' (2005: 10), in which emotional or affective audience response shudders into a complex 'feeling *about* the feeling' (2005: 10). But such 'meta-feelings necessarily emerge from and take time. As time is dilated, in the temporal lag in which one could feel something about feeling, uncertainty, ambivalence and the doublings of irony leak in to displace the grander, more sudden and intentionally directed states normally marked out as 'emotions'. So, for example, the audience of *Endgame* cannot simply enjoy laughter as cognitive mastery, as it becomes clear, given time, that the very conditions of difference between laughing subject and mechanical object necessary for comedy always risk being written out of jokes that are nothing but rigid comic violence. Just when the subject seems to be secure in its laughter, then, laughter threatens to force that subject out of coincidence with itself, into a spasm that mirrors the affective state of the players. A distending temporality, a falling away from itself, is folded into the instantaneity, the brevity, that usually characterises secure laughter, then, producing a layering of different states and a 'meta-feeling'. This shuddering into a vertiginous affective confusion that Ngai calls 'suspended agency' (2005: 2) thus replaces a determined feeling of confirmed amusement in *Endgame* that is clearly present and then is equally clearly gone. It is in and through the passage of time raised to the level of consciousness in the play that it becomes clear that even the laughter of superiority fades out if comic mastery synthesises its elements so completely that all tremors of difference and incongruity disappear from the scene. But as paradox and incongruity are retained in the structure of affect, perhaps the conditions for the production of new forms of comedy to shudder into life are ironically preserved.

Now it is precisely the uncertainty of comic affect for the audience that Wolfgang Iser's meticulous study defines as structurally central to *Endgame*. But alongside Iser's clear sense that audience laughter flares up and is then toppled as the spectator realises that it is his or her own interpretations, or attempts at laughing mastery, that are subject to rigorous collapse by the 'counter-sense' of the play (1993: 152–93), there is also a vital possibility of openness and uncertainty implicated into the play by the fact that the audience may not 'return the ball' in precisely the way it was thrown. Because the audience is compelled to respond in ways that are drawn out over time – materialised by the structure of the play as temporal dilation and distension – the possibility that they might find themselves being moved unpredictably ensures that the putative violence of a fully stable representation or a last word is never achieved. Instead, the passing pleasures and transitory dysphoric affects of the comic materialised in *Endgame*'s audiences demonstrate a certain care towards the structure of comedy itself, which seems able to preserve glimmers of incongruity, of possibility, continuation and change, even amid its presentation of laughing violence.

Because of this, *Endgame* is not what Adorno would call a lamenting tragedy that 'raises a claim to the positive meaning of negativity, the meaning that philosophy calls positive negation' (1992b: 253). But neither is Beckett's simply a 'lighthearted' art that refuses to take part in the violence of the world. As Adorno points out, Beckett's art no longer admits the alternatives of the lighthearted or the serious; instead, he cryptically suggests that it 'moves ahead into the unknown, the only art now possible' (1992b: 253). But within the interstices of the lighthearted and the serious, Adorno does admit that humour persists. He writes, finally, that '[h]umor is salvaged in Beckett's plays because they *infect* the spectator with laughter about the absurdity of laughter and laughter about despair' (Adorno 1992b: 253, my italics). In being infected, in being affected, with the uncertain comedy of Beckett's work, the spectator finds him or herself being moved, anxiously, and with a particular forceful care, in a manner that materialises the violence of the social world that persists both within and outside of the text. But it also forces that violence to wear itself out and submit to loss in ways that allow further humour to appear, alongside, perhaps, other new possibilities that it cannot yet name. Instead of laughter as catharsis then – a moment of shared yet subjectively bolstering release which appears and then is over, resolved – *Endgame*'s laughter shudders into an odd, passive and played, momentarily equivocal form of affective experience even amid its most violent assertions. Where Aristotle's account of catharsis emphasises its suddenness (Ngai 2005: 6–7, 13), which might usefully be linked to a Hobbesian contracted laughter of 'sudden glory', *Endgame* remains resolutely anti-cathartic in its dedication to the materialisation of shuddering affects drawn out over and through a dilatory, distended experience of time.

Just Play

So *Endgame* seems concerned with the comic as a sometimes painfully manic, sometimes dully dysphoric, site of affect that evokes the 'suspended agency' in both characters and audience identified by Ngai (implicitly following Adorno) as particularly relevant to the social experience of mid-twentieth-century modernity (2005: 1). Despite this, however, it is clear that the modern, mid-century, biographical Beckett was not neutral or equivocal about play; indeed, he found pleasure in it and threw himself into games with relish. A fine cricketer and piano player, Beckett particularly loved chess, and James Knowlson offers details of the Irish writer's chess battles with Marcel Duchamp in 1940 as both men were holed up in Arcachon on the Atlantic coast while the Germans were marching down the Champs-Elysées (Knowlson 1996: 298–301).

This idea of two artists playing chess has seemed suggestive for Beckett studies.[7] Certainly, Beckett insisted that *Endgame* could be thought of through the lexicon of chess, noting in his Berlin diary that

> Hamm is the king in this chess game lost from the start. He knows from the start that he is making senseless moves. For instance, that he will not get anywhere at all with his gaff. Now at last he's making a few more senseless moves, as only a poor player would; a good one would have given up long ago. He's only trying to postpone the inevitable end. Each of his motions is one of the last useless moves that delay the end. He is a poor player. (Quoted in Gontarski 1992: 49)

Hamm has indeed been likened to a Red king ('*Very red face*' (*CDW*: 92)), who corresponds to Black in those more modern and standardised Staunton sets with less of the Lewis Carroll about them.[8] But a link can also be forged between Beckett's play and the chess battles with Duchamp because of the latter's tantalising fascination with the dynamics of a particular form of endgame. In 1932 Duchamp wrote a book with Vitaly Halberstadt entitled *Opposition et Cases Conjugées sont Reconciliée* (*Opposition and Sister Squares are Reconciled*) on the subject of a rare situation that can occasionally occur in the final phase of a chess game. The authors describe the Lasker-Reichelm position, detailing how in this particular endgame, Black, like Beckett's Hamm, cannot win. He can only delay, but with competent play can always force a draw. With White's four pawns blocked by Black's three, the Black and White kings are still free to make their limited moves. Even hampered and disabled as he is, Black can still play a defence, however, by beginning to mirror White's moves, occupying the sister square (a place of symmetrical opposition) to that of White, and thus keeping the correct distance from those squares White could attack. Only the main-tenance of exact opposition – a literal 'suspended agency' – can force a draw from this position.

These situations are, of course, extremely unusual in chess because competent players rarely get themselves into such a limited kind of stalemate. It is likely that only a 'poor player' like Hamm would end up in such an endgame. But it is equally true that weak players should not get into this position either, for one would expect the poor player to have haplessly lost position sufficiently to have been beaten long previ-ously. Just like Hamm, then, Duchamp's Black must be strong enough to hold out for the draw – not to give up on his ability to block the other's victory. And although there is no evidence that Beckett read this obscure text of Duchamp's, a link can perhaps be forged between it and Beckett's insistence that '*Endgame* will be just play. Nothing less. Don't worry about enigmas and solutions. For these, we have well-equipped universities, churches, cafés du commerce and so on' (Beckett, quoted by and trans. Rabaté 2010: 102). For Duchamp also remarked to Pierre Cabanne on the odd singularity of the endgames that interested him:

> The endgames on which this fact turns are of no interest to any chess player: and that's the funniest thing about it. Only three or four people in the world are interested in it, and they're the ones who've tried the same lines of research as Halberstadt and myself . . . [C]hess champions never read this book, because the problem it poses never really turns up more than once in a lifetime. These are possible endgame problems, but they're so rare that they're almost utopian. (Cabanne 1971: 77–8)

What might link this 'utopian' *no-space*, subtracted from everyday concerns, with Beckett's text, however, is the fact that this endgame problem stages a consideration of a form of 'just play' that denudes chess of any overriding emphasis on the teleology of winning or of problem-solving. Duchamp's endgame is chess reduced to that particu-lar, somewhat violent, abstracted purity of gaming without end – chess as a game of failures, of *échecs*.

Looked at in this way, Duchamp's endgame problems seem more properly aesthetic than ludic, as the antagonism and vectors of resolu-tion on which games of chess are necessarily based are flattened out in favour of symmetry and the maintenance of equilibrium that produce a game that hovers between closure and openness, consummation and continuation. Hubert Damisch certainly connects Duchamp's fascination with these endgames with the fact that the Dada artist relinquished art for chess. Drawing on a dominant late nineteenth- and twentieth-century idea of art's purposeless, its autotelic refusal to be subordinated to the logic of the social world or to the exchange of commodities and profit from which it nevertheless emerges (at least in Adorno's account of things), Damisch suggests that Duchamp gave up art for chess because it represented the possibilities of art in a purer form (1979: 9). Damisch indeed quotes Duchamp's affirmation that the 'competitive side of [chess] has no importance' (9), alongside his insistence that chess players might be thought of as artists because of their refusal to subordinate all to the perception of certain kinds of advantage: '[t]hese people are completely cloudy, completely blind, wearing blinkers. Madmen of a certain quality the way the artist is supposed to be' (quoted in Damisch 1979: 9).

Of course, the blind Hamm might be just this sort of madman: someone capable of forcing art from the idea of play driven forward by the logic of the rules of the game who nevertheless refuses the possibility and *telos* of the end that seems to determine his actions. The madman and chess player totally uninterested in victory appear even more clearly, however, in the figure of Mr Endon in the earlier *Murphy*. He is dressed in a 'scarlet gown' (Beckett 1993: 134) (so, like Hamm, assuming the position of Black), and his poor, random play consists of attempts to move his pieces forwards and then backwards to their initial, symmetrical state without ever engaging his opponent. The narrator describes both Murphy and Mr Endon as having 'very Fabian methods' (106) – Quintus Fabius Maximus (whose moniker was 'Cunctator', 'the delayer') being a Roman general who waged wars of attrition but avoided frontal assaults or final decisive battles. Murphy admires Mr Endon because his mind is 'a closed system, subject to no principle of change but its own' (105). In him Murphy hopes to find a reflection that would offer freedom from his own 'unredeemed split self' (106) by reflecting his own nature back to him as similarly and symmetrically closed. But Murphy's very first engagement with Mr Endon, his moving forward of a pawn that cannot then be reversed, produces a game – a relationship that is not one of simple mirroring. The movement of a pawn rather than a knight, which could be retracted, is indeed 'the primary cause of all White's subsequent difficulties' (137); it represents an irrevocable incursion into Mr Endon's space that precipitates involvement and a necessarily temporal relationship between self and other. Although Murphy finds Mr

Endon's mind 'so limpid and imperturbable that Murphy felt drawn to it as Narcissus to his fountain' (105), here there is a reversal of the myth of Echo and Narcissus in which symmetry is mistaken for a relationship by both figures (Echo with Narcissus, Narcissus with himself). For as much as Murphy may attempt to mirror Mr Endon's symmetries (as indeed he does in the beginning to mid sections of the game), the illusion of two perfectly self-contained systems facing one another in space is untenable.

This is because Mr Endon, in mirroring White's first move with a pawn, acknowledges, at least minimally, that he is also involved in a game which can never be that perfect self-sufficient back and forth that he desires. Play through time cannot be reversed to become a manipulation or playing with time, however much the players would like it to be. For moving any pawn, which allows pieces other than knights into play, initiates the beginning of a game rather than a simple play of spatial mirroring. Mr Endon, of course, refuses the game after his opening move; he does no more than produce the 'pure blank movement' of a 'moving pause', as 'Ding-Dong' has it (Beckett 1970: 41). Mr Endon, as Black, ignores Murphy's increasingly desperate sacrificial offerings, seems to place Murphy in check by mistake, and frustrates Murphy's engagements sufficiently that White – another 'poor player' – finally throws in the towel, breaking the hermetically demarcated space between the two when he is one move away from checkmate. For Murphy has stumbled upon the paradox inherent within desiring a relationship with another self-contained system to confirm his self-sufficiency. The need for the other precisely demonstrates that he is not himself closed and 'imperturbable'. Caught as they now are in a game, then, Murphy's only choice is to surrender if the fantasy of confirming symmetry is to be at least partially preserved. In *Endgame*, however, it is precisely the desire to beat the other over and over, not to let the 'dialogue die' and to keep the other in the game sufficiently that a victory can be imagined – and indeed its trajectories of violence can be materialised – that means there is neither final triumph nor total surrender. There are no resolutions in *Endgame*: no 'solutions', in Beckett's terms.

When Beckett and Duchamp played chess together, however, there was surely a winner, and it seems likely that it wasn't Beckett.[9] But the fact that both artists were already interested in endgames, in defences and 'Fabian methods' denuded of an orientation towards victory resonates suggestively with the historical conditions under which their games took place – conditions materially orchestrated by the grinding machine of war. For Beckett did not stay playing chess in Arcachon; both he and his partner Suzanne returned to Paris and Beckett became part of the Resistance network 'Gloria SMH', processing and translating information into English until the cell was betrayed (Knowlson 1996: 307–14). At that point, Beckett and Suzanne fled the approaching Gestapo and finally arrived in Roussillon, bunkering down into a life of waiting and worrying about the scant availability of vital provisions. Andrew Gibson, among others, has noted that *Waiting for Godot* is at least partially concerned with this experience of war, but Gibson also registers a specific reference to the French attitude of *attentisme* – a position opposed to the Vichy regime that nevertheless felt it necessary to defer, to delay, any final decision as to whether France should rejoin the war until 'the situation "clarified itself"' (2010: 103). Gibson reads *Godot*'s evocation of this ambivalent *attentisme* as a response to the crude triumphalism and the heroic rhetoric that characterised the mood of Gaullist postwar France and – a rhetoric from which the complications of the actual political positions during in the war had been purged (2001: 108). If this is so, though, perhaps part of the postwar *Endgame*'s obsession with anxious and extended play in which both attack and defeat must be refused, alongside its evocation of the affect of 'suspended agency' through comedy, might also be read as imbricated with a historically specific refusal of the rhetorical spoils of victory.

This position of suspended agency that sometimes slips into a particular neutrality is something which, when aligned specifically with the effects of the comic, emerges first in Beckett's work from a revealingly material and historical set of circumstances. In 1945 Beckett enrolled in the Irish Red Cross and went to the devastated and hollowed town of Saint-Lô, which the French called 'the capital of the ruins', to help in a hospital. In a piece of the same name written for broadcast by Radio Éireann in June 1946, Beckett offered up the idea that a smile was the only response to 'humanity in ruins' and that it somehow showed 'an inkling of the terms in which our condition is to be thought again' (*CSP*: 278). After detailing the decimated condition of the town, alongside the vestiges of modern medicine still preserved in the Irish hospital, Beckett makes a surprising move. He determines that 'the therapeutic relation faded to the merest of pretexts' (277):

> What was important was not our having penicillin when they had none, nor the unregarding munificence of the French Ministry of Reconstruction ... but the occasional glimpse obtained by us in them and, who knows, by them in us (for they are imaginative people), of that smile at the human conditions as little to be extinguished by bombs as to be broadened by the elixirs of Burroughes and Welcome [*sic*], – the smile deriding, among other things, the having and the not having, the giving and the taking, sickness and health. (277)

Although Critchley specifically claims this smile for the ethics of the *risus purus* with its shrugging acceptance of human finitude (2002: 111), others have noted something obscene in this neutrality.[10] What kind of ethical stance, particularly an ethics with any relation to politics, is to be found in the affirmation that material conditions of pain and want in which there is no more penicillin, just as in *Endgame* there will be no more painkillers, are something to be derided and transcended with a sardonic smile at a universally shared fate?

In returning 'The Capital of the Ruins' to its time, however, something emerges that is more revealing of Beckett's particular and historically informed sense of ethics to which this smile might bear some witness. Gibson takes the piece back to its material history by suggestively placing it within the context of the Liberation of France, a new chauvinism, the purge of French men and women deemed to have collaborated with the Vichy regime and trials in which 'Gaullists, Communists and socialists all used the courts for political ends' (2010: 112–13). In this context, Beckett's calls for mutual understanding and an internationalism of spirit, for a way of going on forged by 'the establishment of a relation' (*CSP*: 277) between Irish and French, becomes, for Gibson, explicable as something resistant to 'Gaullist Franco-centrism' (2010: 118) and a politics of revenge against the defeated that merely perpetuated the wages of war. Returned to that context, the smile is, by implication, not simply the rather factitious and aloof response to the 'having and the not having' of penicillin that it might at first appear to be. It is, rather, in not holding Irish gifts over French ideas nor, by implication, one group over another – winners over losers in the broader French context – that at this very particular historical moment, 'in this universe become provisional' (278), the question of how to live and how to go on with others amid the rubble of buildings and ideas of European history without an intellectual and material alignment with victory was staged.

In 1946, it was the sense of non-violent mutuality to be found in a smile rather than an assertion of masterful superiority that seemed to offer Beckett 'an inkling of the terms in which our condition is to be thought again' (*CSP*: 278). The difficulty with such a position, which speaks of a smile but certainly does not engage with the highly unpredictable affect of the comic, is that in its absolute passivity, it might, in the end, still be inattentive to pain, inequality and need. It seems, somehow, to gesture towards the unacknowledged violence of a position where the rhetoric of victory is refused but all is flattened out into the balanced blindness of 'just play'. The later *Endgame*, however, in remaining comic and affectively and structurally on the move, in refusing the stillness of absolute equivocality, restates the need to materialise violence and want, while acknowledging the implication of thought, and certain kinds of aesthetic form, in a material history in which an extermination struggle had become a seeming inevitability.

The philosopher Michel Serres, who like Levinas characterises himself as an irenic thinker (a thinker of peace rather than of war), articulates something particular about the experience of the generation formed, in intellectual and somatic terms, by the traumatic passivity of being children of conflict:

> This tragic atmosphere began in 1936 . . . with the war in Spain, with unspeakable horrors, and culminated with the bloody settling of accounts after the Liberation in 1945; the colonial wars and some episodes of torture brought this era to a close in the early 1960s . . . For us power still only means cadavers and torture. (1995: 4)

Here, for Serres, the game-playing of childhood has been contaminated by the exercising of adult power that can lead only to pain and death. Although older and able to participate in events rather than passively witness them, the Beckett of Saint-Lô (like the ex-prisoner of war Levinas) also seems allergic to the rhetoric of victory and the violent tit-for-tat of revenge. But by the time *Endgame* is being staged, Beckett seems to have given up his equivocality. Instead, he represents and forces the audience imaginatively to experience structures of combat in the sordid triumphs of a particular type of humour, while, paradoxically, using this materialisation of violence to give just enough strength to the scenario to drive the play on towards a future in which things might change.

It is suggestive that for Serres, as for Levinas, it is a temporality that cannot be reduced to the production of winners and losers – which for him is the precipitate of a Hegelian dialectic – that preserves something of the otherness of the world from progress and knowledge represented here as a form of violence. Serres insists that 'time alone can make co-possible two contradictory things' (1995: 49): 'Hegel's error was in reversing this logical evidence and in claiming that contradiction produces time, whereas only the opposite is true: time makes contradiction possible' (50). Hegelian time, Serres suggests, is not time at all, it is simply a line:

> It's not even a line, but a trajectory of the race for first place . . . This isn't time, but a simple competition – once again, war. Why replace temporality, duration with a quarrel? *The first to arrive, the winner of the battle, obtains as his prize the right to reinvent history to his own advantage.* (49)

For Serres, then, it is the irreducible time that lies unpredictably curled between people, and between a subject and the object world, that preserves something of that world from the putative violence of thought that, for at least one strand of postwar French intellectual culture, is inexorably imbricated with the wages of war. 'No one that ever lived ever thought so crooked as we' (*CDW*: 97), Clov avers, seeming implicitly to recognise the furled time of thought and life formed in the bonded relationship between him and Hamm. And for Beckett, it is precisely a compulsive refusal of victory, or of time as a 'line', in favour of the temporality and paradoxical 'utopianism' of a particular sense of gaming and play, that performs a resistance to the idea and experience of war, revenge, *telos* and to the thought that seems to subtend it. Of course, as we have seen, in *Endgame* Beckett has also constructed a kind of play that cannot be absolutely 'just', for it must both evoke and bear witness to oppression and pain in its refusal of absolute and aloof equivocality. As such, though, it resists both the injustice of victory as extermination and the shrug of pure play; it creates an endgame rather than an end point of victory or disinterest.

Dialectics at a Standstill

There is a striking turn to the concept of play as something central to human sociality and culture in the period just preceding and following the Second World War, for it accords with twentieth-century modernity's at least partial sense of itself as deformed by conflict, increasing industrialisation and the capitalist reduction of time to work and leisure (both of which drive forward its systems). Huizinga's famous 1938 account of the human as *homo ludens* and of the 'play element' as a determining force in human culture indeed emphasises that play 'is free, is in fact freedom' (1955: 8); it is an 'intermezzo, an *interlude* in our daily lives' (9), which has a structuring influence on the formation of cultural life that both precedes and goes beyond the demands of survival or economic well-being. For Huizinga, it is upon the freedom of play that all human culture – and art in particular – depends.

Now *Endgame* is clearly not pure play in Huizinga's terms; in many ways it seems like the antithesis of that freedom. As we have seen, the stage seems explicitly delimited by external impositions experienced as compulsive obligations, while the implication of the audience into the scene ensures that the play space is uncertainly open rather than safely closed. And yet, the notion of play loosened from an emphasis on victory is important, as Duchamp seemingly intuited, in terms of an art that might, at least partially and in formal terms, resist subordination to the logic of instrumentality – that would resist resolving paradox in any dialectical fashion. Although Beckett's much quoted pronouncements on the determined requirement to 'refuse to be involved in exegesis of any kind' are often taken to be a personal predilection, it is possible to see how this idea of an assertively autotelic art might also be understood as emerging from particular material and intellectual historical conditions. Beckett famously affirms of *Endgame* that

> my work is a matter of fundamental sounds (no joke intended), made as fully as possible, and I accept responsibility for nothing else. If people want to have headaches among the overtones, let them. And provide their own aspirin. Hamm as stated, and Clov as stated, together as stated, *nec tecum nec sine te* [neither with you nor without you], in such a place, and in such a world, that's all I can manage, more than I could. (Harmon 1998: 24)

But this work that hopes in the resistant shape of the relationship between Hamm and Clov to refuse to turn a profit is born from a particular 'world', just as it bears a particular world within it. And 'such a place . . . such a world' is one still ravaged by the sense that exegetical rationality and the dialectical syntheses of linear history had led European culture to a solution that seemed inevitably to have been final – one from which all play disappeared in the voiding collapse of victory as extermination.

In his essay on *Endgame* from 1961, Adorno cannot see out of this point of history, this telescoped contraction; consequently, the idea of play as freedom becomes obscene. He finds humour to be an 'obsolete' and 'repulsive' aesthetic medium, 'without a canon for what should be laughed about, without a place of reconciliation from which one could laugh, and without anything harmless on the earth that would allow itself to be laughed at' (1991b: 257). Adorno is right that from this play that refuses all stable positions, that declines conceptual synthesis and that instantiates what he, after Walter Benjamin, calls 'dialectics at a standstill' (274), there is a significant resistance to a rash reconciliation that would offer either a position of laughing mastery or a safe play space. Nevertheless, there remains a sense in which laughter should and must persist in a world so determined and marked by incongruity, and this perhaps leads to Adorno's later hesitation about the disappearance of laughter in 'Is Art Lighthearted?' (1967) alongside his determination that laughter is 'salvaged' in Beckett's plays. In a world that imagines its chief feature as a persistent lack of reconciliation held against the awareness that things should be otherwise, humour might offer itself up as a witness to this fragmented condition.

But even in 1961, Adorno is actually rather ambivalent about laughter: he will sometimes allow that *Endgame* has approximations of jokes,

jokes that are nearly there. These jokes are 'damaged', however, resistant to any easy payoffs: 'They no longer reach anyone; the pun, the degenerate form of which is there a bit in every joke, covers them like a rash' (Adorno 1991: 258). In one sense, puns are more obviously akin to jokes that have made it too well, that make their way with a facile ease, rather than the hobbled forms that become part of Beckett's aesthetic signature. The pun is all too neatly synthetic; it is a false short cut between two terms – a reconciliation without much work or conceptual labour. As Bergson puts it, '[i]n the pun, the same sentence appears to offer two independent meanings, but it is only an appearance; in reality they are two different sentences ... claiming to be one and the same because both have the same sound' (1911b: 120), and, with its rash syntheses, its false reconciliations, it isn't hard to see why Adorno is suspicious of it too. Nevertheless, one can see why Adorno detects the logic of the pun in *Endgame*; it does inhere within the play's laughing violence, in the laughter of ending that risks causing an end to laughing. This joking that risks its finale either by being too violently insistent or by being too weak to achieve the mastery of comic synthesis, was characteristic of the *Trilogy*, but it persists in *Endgame* too, in Hamm's incessant 'warming up for [his] last soliloquy' (*CDW*: 130) that, of course, never arrives. *Endgame* does, however, remain fundamentally a comic form, for within the persistent presentation of incongruity, something like comedy's conditions of possibility emerges.

So if, as Adorno suggests, 'parody means the use of forms in the era of their impossibility' (1991b: 259), then *Endgame* shows the existing forms of the comic to be worn out and self-defeating, but it does so in such a way that comedy still has some use value. What remains in the tremors and convulsions of *Endgame* is comedy reduced to its bare life, and as the basal conditions of comic incongruity persist, they open up a space in which a glimpse of the world as violent, unequal, unreconciled can, at least momentarily, be tolerated enough to be thought. It is not cast off with a shrug or a smile, nor is it reconciled in a pun. Adorno admits that in all of Beckett's work there is little actual movement towards a changed world; nevertheless, it does 'touch on fundamental layers of experience *hic et nunc* [here and now], which are brought together into a paradoxical dynamic at a standstill' (2002: 30): 'the *need* for progress is inextricable from its impossibility. The gesture of walking in place at the end of *Godot*, which is the fundamental motif of the whole of his work, reacts precisely to this situation' (Adorno 2002: 30, my italics), he writes. In this endless repetition of the paradoxical moment of 'perhaps', in this comic modality of tremor, a space and time is hollowed out for the conceptual and affective labour that would go on in both recognising and refusing the incongruities and paradoxes of the world as it is.

The insistence of the comic within *Endgame* ensures that despite its certain abstraction, the dialectics at a standstill presented remain powerfully informed – sites of force, of domination and of resistance in structural and affective terms that guarantee there is enough energy in the closed system to set off one more act of playing so that there is no simple violence of victory, no consummation in a mercifully quick death. To allow a finish, a denouement more attuned to a realist aesthetic, the text intuits, would be to submit to the way things are, perhaps taking a little pleasure and false comfort from it. For, as Adorno sees it, in truth:

> An unreconciled reality tolerates no reconciliation with the object in art. Realism . . . only mimics reconciliation. Today the dignity of art is measured not according to whether or not it evades this antinomy, but in terms of how it bears it. In this, *Endgame* is exemplary. (1991: 250)

So *Endgame* repeats a historically specific experience where violence and domination seem to stalk the world entire, but it illuminates the minimal temporal difference within such a repetition that enables it to be seen and felt as such. This awareness that things are not reconciled thus uses comedy to view and affectively materialise both the violent assertions of power in 'such a world' and the total incongruity of those attempts at domination and final victory.

There is no synthesis, then, no final coming to one's senses in *Endgame*; instead, 'the end is in the beginning and yet you go on' (*CDW*: 126), as the play stutters towards a closure to which, in its desperation, it always seems to be drawing near, but its obsessive repetitions seem indefinitely to defer. *Endgame* indeed materialises what we might think of as a syncopated dramatic moment in which strong beats become weak and its weak become strong. As such, perhaps it makes sense that it should be the comic – a form that always betrays a tendency towards mastery that is necessarily deferred or interrupted – that seems fundamentally to structure this dramatic game of mastery and loss, freedom and restriction. Any comic pleasures offered up will necessarily remain uncertain, always subject to an unexpected stifling that might cause them to gutter and extinguish themselves. Nevertheless, because Hamm and Clov continue to play with one another and this is witnessed by an affected audience, tiny moments of change and unpredictability are allowed into the dramatic scene: little breaths of oxygen seep into the text that might yet allow humour and pleasure to reignite, offering the merest glimmer that things might one day be different. 'This is not much fun', says the seated Hamm, gloomily, as he cannot make either a comic or a tragic end, nor can he leave for he cannot stand: 'But it's always that way at the end of the day, isn't it Clov?' (98). Clov, who cannot sit, cannot make an end here and stay, simply concurs, as Hamm's equally powerful, equally weak other. 'Always' (98), he states.

Notes

1. Christie Davies (1996) reads these jokes as an attempt to assert and maintain a clear distinction between social groups that are 'near neighbours' and are thus troublingly alike.
2. Beckett cut this scene and all allusions to the audience in the 1967 Schiller production (Gontarski 1992: xviii).
3. The risk that audience laughter in Beckett's plays might also troublingly duplicate laughable mechanisation and begin to stagger is considered later in the chapter and in detail in Chapter 5.
4. Beckett stated: 'We have to retrench everything even further, it's got to become simple. Just a few small precise motions' (quoted in Gontarski 1992: xvi).
5. In 1936, Beckett took notes in French from Poincaré's 1902 *La Valeur de la science* in his 'Whoroscope Notebook' that briefly detail the principle of the dissipation of energy and its relationship to the arrow of time (1930s: 42).
6. Merle Tönnies (1997) emphatically demonstrates, however, in her exhaustive taxonomy of comic effects, that audiences do laugh in a reasonably sustained fashion in performances of *Endgame*.
7. See Hugill (1992), Restivo (1997: 118–23).
8. James Acheson notes that Hamm's red face marks him out as a Red king, but is quite wrong to suggest that 'red and white are the same side in chess' (1980: 33). As Lewis Carroll's *Through the Looking Glass and What Alice Found There* makes clear, Red and White chess pieces are on opposite sides of the chess board.
9. Duchamp had won the 1933 Paris Tournament and served for many years on the team representing France at the Olympiad (Damisch 1979: 6, 8).
10. Cronin finds Beckett's position troublingly detached (1996: 352), while Connor asserts that 'only the humanity of Beckett's later explorations of the inhuman condition could rescue the insufferable, sarky highmindedness of stuff like this' (1998b: 125).

Chapter 4

Comic Tremors: The Late Prose

In terms of comic instants, the late prose is closer to being Beckett's least funny work than to being his most. Refusing the jokes and poker-faced, faded vaudeville of the earlier work, these texts demand we make do with little, with only tiny linguistic maladjustments of fit, muster-ings of affect and palpitations of placement and timing that seem to offer the sensation of the comic despite never quite drawing themselves into a joke that one would be able to grasp or 'get'. A work such as *Ill Seen Ill Said* indeed asks explicitly, and equally within the texts and the affective arena, '[a] smile? Is it possible?' (*NO*: 89), while the eye that observes the old woman within the text, mirroring the eye of the reader, is desiccated, denuded of both its fluid and its sense of comic life: 'No trace of humour. None any more' (81). Somehow, comedy does remain, though, and if laughter is infectious, if it is threateningly transmissible, then, like malaria, the humour that so insistently marks Beckett's earlier work never entirely goes away, although the infection returns in weakened and scarcely recognisable forms. This flickering of comic embers, this funny kind of funniness, is perhaps like the humour Nell describes in *Endgame*: 'we laugh, we laugh, with a will, in the beginning. But it's always the same thing. Yes, it's like the funny story we have heard too often, we still find it funny but we don't laugh any more' (*CDW*: 101). For *Ill Seen Ill Said* is funny after its own enfeebled fashion, but any jokes that remain appear as if their timing is all wrong, anachronistic and wound down, fading in and out through a form of stuttering interruption. Certainly, the comedy that remains is not so driven and demanding as that of the earlier work; it is far less central to the structure and affect of the writing. Nevertheless, I will argue that a 'tenacious trace' (*NO*: 96) of the comic does obtain within these etio-lated scenes, detectable in their textual musterings and slowings above a baseline of stillness. It remains, not as a primary drive, but as a trace that nevertheless adumbrates something essential. As a stilling, quivering, structural and affective reverberation that gives form to something that no longer seeks to appear clearly, for reasons that the text both reveals and occludes, the peculiar, tremulous comedy of the late prose indeed matters and signifies, permitting a glimpse of the obsessive aesthetic and ethical demands that constellate there.

Weller identifies the trajectory towards moments of radical indecision in Beckett's late work as a 'voiding that is neither liberally nor illiberally humorous, but anethically posthumorous, in which one is left to ask not only "does one ever know oneself why one laughs?" [*CSP*: 54] but also whether there is any laughter left at all' (2006: 133). Significantly, for the argument here, the possibility that laughter has evacuated the scene is brought together with the suggestion that such 'posthumorous' indecision also determines a space of the 'anethical'. For Weller, because it stages the failure to know whether any laughter, following judgement and the establishing of secure positions, can occur, the posthumorous qualities of Beckett's late work form part of a radical and thoroughgoing uncertainty. But this moment of indecision is not ethical in itself, Weller insists; rather, it enacts a

> failure either to establish the difference between the ethical and the unethical ... [I]t involves the opening of the anethical as the experience of that particular nothing the filling of which can be justified only through an appeal to values that will always negate the very things they are there to save. (2006: 194–5)

There is, of course, a profound dimming of comic effects and affect within Beckett's late fiction. This chapter will indeed precisely explore the ways in which a late fictional text like *Ill Seen Ill Said* asks whether there is any laughter left at all, while, seemingly coextensively, manifesting an uncertainty as to whether a secure difference between the ethical and the unethical can be found. For Weller, the post-Holocaust ethics in whose name Beckett's work is most commonly brought to bear witness is part of an attempt to 'think a saving alterity' (2006: 2) that is irreducible to the violence of the Same in Levinas's thought, or identity-thinking in Adorno's. But, he argues, Beckett's work is, in fact, moving towards the 'anethical', a space of indecision, of 'shuttling or shuffling to and fro', within which 'the disintegration of both art and ethics might be rendered visible – or audible' (Weller 2006: 194). But I will suggest that it is too strong a critical move to reach for Weller's neologisms of the posthumorous and the anethical and the particular neutrality of nothing towards which these terms tend. If a text persists in asking whether any laughter or anything comic obtains, the answer need not necessarily be 'no', and, in fact, probably isn't absolutely 'no', if the question remains as one that is posed at all. Similarly, ethical philosophy is always, at least partially, a meta-ethics that seeks to define and debate the nature and substance of ethical properties or evaluations, as much as to prescribe modes of the good. If it is always part of the purview of ethics to ask what might be ethical, then Beckett's later work remains in the space of ethics in that it persists in asking these questions, even if it partakes of a historically specific scepticism as to the possibility of gaining any satisfactorily recoverable or representable answers. Although traced through by a marked diminution of comic affect and angry critique, I will argue that in the space of tremulous indecision that remains in the late fiction, the comic and the possibilities of ethical thought and action still shadow one another, although both are shading and shifting in and out from under spectre of their occulting impossibility. The relentless necessity of posing the question of the ethical that appears alongside and through an indefatigable interrogation of the comic indeed insists in the late prose, as both emerge as the products and the producers of uncertainty.

Embers and Ashes

Beckett's late fictions frequently plot narrative and imagine spaces that are determined by little save repeated oscillation. The 'cylinder pieces' – *All Strange Away* (1963–4), *Imagination Dead Imagine* (1965), *Ping* (1966), *Lessness* (1969), *The Lost Ones* (1966, 1970) – indeed come to embody vibration, to materialise a compulsively hesitant aesthetic that posits a fictional space and its inhabitants, while dramatising the resistance to and painful impossibility of any stable representation. In *Imagination Dead Imagine*, oscillation is figured through the temperature and the 'convulsive light' that rises and falls in variant rhythms in the white rotunda, the bodies within, by turns, 'sweating and icy' (*CSP*: 184, 185), while in *All Strange Away*, although light is similarly fluctuant, this time the dimensions of the indefinite cube/rotunda in which Emmo/Emma and the figures on the wall are confined alter, agitating and squeezing those within. This space of enclosure in *All Strange Away* expands and contracts, it lightens and darkens, as the body within explores its limits. But as soon as a position is reached where the body is imagined – it blinks, it murmurs, perhaps it crushes a ball, and a still point of presence is implied by a relieved, almost triumphant 'aha' – the narrative itself turns back on itself; it continues to imagine and represent, to confirm presence by saying more, and in so doing confounds the stability of the previous utterance:

all contained in one hemicycle leaving other vacant, aha. All that if not yet quite complete quite clear and little change likely unless perhaps to complete unless perhaps somehow light sudden gleam perhaps better fixed and all this flowing and ebbing from full to empty more harm than good and better unchanging black or glare one or another or between the soft white unchanging but leave from the outset and never doubted slow on and off thirty seconds to glare and black any length through slow lightening and darkening greys from nothing for no reason yet imagined. (*CSP*: 179)

In *The Lost Ones*, too, although the dimensions of the space are relatively stable, oscillations are endemic here, as light and temperature are 'shaken by a vertiginous tremolo between contiguous extremes' (Becket 1995: 205). Even in its attempt to imagine a 'last state' in the cylinder, all cannot yet be quite still: 'the persistence of the twofold vibration suggests that in this abode all is not quite yet for the best' (223). There is neither absolute absence nor full presence here, then, only the oscillations enacted to effect their asymptotic approach.

Despite leaving the environment of the cylinder, the late works of *Company*, *Ill Seen Ill Said* and *Worstward Ho* refuse to relinquish this modality of tremor. Such as they are, the narrative events in *Ill Seen Ill Said* describe a '[s]low systole diastole . . . Rhythm of a labouring heart' (*NO*: 75). Between 'coming and going' (62), the old woman with trembling face and hands traces a path between extremes, '[a]s smooth and even fro as to' (78), just as the objects that appear momentarily only to fade from view in the ill-saying of this ill-seeing – the buttonhook, the house key, the curtain – faintly quiver and tremble, vibrating in sympathy with her, that other object of sight. For these objects have no more consolidating permanence than she does and thus they appear only to 'dimmen'. Here, ill-seeing and ill-saying are thematically and formally bound to one another, with the distinct yet dissolving paragraph structure describing and mirroring the clearing and fading of the scene. As all begins to shake, this tremolo of assertion and retreat reverberates inwards, infecting each sentence or group of sentences with a microscopic syntactical quavering. So, as in *Endgame*, the dramatic tension in the structure of the work seems to replicate itself in the minima of the text, producing those same self-consuming textual utterances that Critchley describes as comic collocations of 'weak intensities, antithetical inabilities' (1997: 169). For Beckett's deviations from the logic of non-contradiction such as the statement that '[s]he who looks up no more looks up and sees them' (69), do have a humour, of sorts, as all is subject to (un)expected reversals, confusions, dead-pan arrhythmic denials and reassertions. All indeed 'trembles faintly without cease. As if here without cease the earth faintly quaked' (65). Comically ill said – determinedly ill seen; '[a]s though outlined by a trembling hand' (59), the scene is drawn by a discourse that disavows representational certainty.

As we have seen, Carla Locatelli reads Beckett's comedy as part of a rhetoric of ill-saying that renders 'semantic closure' (1990: 85) impossible, but she neither fixes on nor explains why such tremulous resistance to certainty is funny and, consequently, why a text like *Ill Seen Ill Said* should be comically paradoxical and paradoxically comic, rather than more simply problematic. Perhaps this is because what makes a comic instant funny rather than illogical, paradoxical or even troubling is something that seems to pull away from Locatelli's account. Funniness lies precisely within the fact that comic transgressions are understood, and discrepancies and incongruities brought together within a certain, temporary resolution. As Alenka Zupančič's Lacanian reading of joking makes clear, the point of the joke, its structuring finality determined by the punchline, 'operates through the mechanism of what Lacan calls *le point de capiton*, the "quilting point" – that is to say the point at which an intervention of a Master-Signifier . . . retroactively fixes the sense of the previous signifying elements' (2008: 133). In Lacan's terms, *le point de capiton* is where the slippage of signified under signifier that is part of language's potential indeterminacy is momentarily held in place and time; it is where, despite their structurally arbitrary relationship to one another, 'signifier and signified are knotted together' (Lacan 1993: 268). The punchline of a joke, or the moment of comic payoff, uses its force, then, to pucker the linguistic fabric and stuffing behind it, working like a *point de capiton* – an upholstery button – to create a node of sense that stops the material behind drifting away into unrecuperable nonsense.

Of course, it is Freud who explains the mechanism behind why this puckering, this folding back in of incongruity, might be affectively funny. He suggests that jokes and the unexpected mental activity they produce defuse the necessary expenditure of energy on repression, functioning as psychical reliefs as the bound 'cathectic energy used for the inhibition has now suddenly been lifted, and is therefore now ready to be discharged by laughter' (1905: 148). The understanding which precipitates laughter, the awareness that Freud's energy-saving short circuit has been effected, is thus a moment in which the extension of the joke is folded back in, gathered in comprehension, representation. To be sure, most poststructuralist readings of Beckett have concentrated on its movement towards unrecuperability – on diachronic folding outwards rather than synchronic folding inwards or folding over – but as Arsene reminds us in *Watt*, such directions are always subject to a confounding in Beckett's work: 'the coming is in the shadow of the going and the going is in the shadow of the coming, that is the annoying part about it' (Beckett 1976: 56). The comedy of *Ill Seen Ill Said* indeed seems to quiver between two seemingly (although not ultimately) antithetical possibilities: the synchronous gathering that causes incongruity to be funny, and the diachrony along the syntagmatic chain enabling any comic incongruity to appear as such. The comic trembling that appears in this text is not simply a shaking apart, then; rather, as seen in the convulsive body, it describes a disintegration that is nevertheless integrated – a dissolution that is simultaneously bound and held in place.

So if comedy and joking are always and obsessively about timing, the comedy of *Ill Seen Ill Said* seems to oscillate between two seemingly incommensurable temporalities. For joking seems to require the gathering, puckering or folding in of time into something that resembles a point – 'brevity', in Freud's terms. Such condensation, the economy of expenditure of psychical energy, produces the laughing instant, and indicates, by implication, the collapse of temporal diachrony (syntagmatic incongruity) into synchrony (its marking in the light of comprehension). Of course, *Ill Seen Ill Said* contains very few jokes, excepting perhaps the groaning homophone of a window with 'nothing but black drapes for its pains' (*NO*: 61), although it can occasionally muster itself for a minimised sight-gag as the curtains are flung open in this scene of incessant drawing out with the comic incongruity of an abracadabra – a 'flash. The suddenness of all!' (66). Mostly, though, the incongruous contortions mime something like those comic discrepancies that might lead to a joke, but the gathering terms are denuded of their itinerary: 'And man? Shut of at last? Alas no' (59). Elsewhere, these joking traces begin with a binding together but move towards their own ruination and dampening of affect, dissolving back into the incongruity of the comic field, as the folding in of joking sensation is matched and marred by a contiguous folding out: 'Such – such fiasco that folly takes a hand. Such bits and scraps. Seen no matter how and said as seen. Dread of black. Of white. Of void' (75).

As the joking instant is played by the relentless onward pulsion of the text there is in this diachrony, as Locatelli rightly points out, a defection from 'clôture' (1990: 87). But for Locatelli, this refusal of determination, this lack of linguistic exclusions, is precisely the humour of the text, that which allows incongruity to appear, even though, like Nell, one might not feel quite able to laugh. The comedy of *Ill Seen Ill Said* thus seems caught in a dialectic without synthesis of mastery and loss, synchrony and diachrony, in which, contradictorily, each side of the binary appears as both the event of humour and its ruination. Overlaying instantaneity and the dilation of duration, there is an accretion of half-presences in the text, then, but no coming into presence through the progression of linear time. For this ghostly half-life of comedy fluctuates between appearance and disappearance, reignition and forms of dampening down: 'On the one hand embers. On the other hand ashes' (*NO*: 82). Comedy and laughter thus fade in and out of the text like every other effect in this quivering scene.

So the assertion that a 'moor would have better met the case. Were there a case better to meet' (*NO*: 60) has a humour, of sorts, that marks out a limping movement of assertion and retreat, statement and then confounding qualification. Part of the comedy here is due to the incongruous relationship between the colloquial blandness of a 'moor would have better met the case' and the pseudo-philosophical gravitas of '[w]ere there a case better to meet' – the possibility that what is being represented here is the limit instance of disaster. Although such a phrase holds the sensation of black humour, a marked and markable incongruity, there is, however, an overdetermination of elements, a more radical kind of ill-saying than that which can be worked through a Freudian laughter due to psychical economy. 'Were there a case better to meet' – is it suggesting that there could be no case worse than that which we are meeting, or that there could be no case better, that this is the apotheosis of cases? Of course, it is suggesting either, or rather both, working through that same oscillating economy that the best might be the worst, and the worst best, that becomes familiar in *Worstward Ho*. There is even the suggestion that this infamous case may not even qualify as a case at all. The whole phrase is rather reminiscent of the scene in *Murphy* where the protagonist's points come unstitched and the stuffing behind bulges outwards:

> Sometimes Murphy would begin to make a point, sometimes he may have even finished making one, it was hard to say. For example, early one morning he said: 'The hireleth fleeth because he is a hireling.' Was that a point? And again: 'What shall a man give in exchange for Celia?': Was that a point? (Beckett 1993: 16)

Of course, the example from *Murphy* reveals that such contradiction, such excess, can be stitched back into the comic by being marked as such. But the phrase from *Ill Seen Ill Said* bears only the faintest echo of the humour in *Murphy*; it seems to be engorged with elements that might be effectively condensed in the brevity of the joking instant, just as in other cases phrases are voided of terms that might be brought together in a punchline. There is no straightforward binding under a higher principle of congruity; instead, the text offers a deep asymmetry in which mastery and loss fade and phase in and out, offering stabilities that both produce and confound laughter, alongside movements of elapse that enable and overdetermine the comedy. Clearly evaluative distinctions that are usually made between presence and absence, the best and the worst, are replaced in Beckett's late prose by what one might think of, following Sianne Ngai, as 'modal differences' – those 'not-yet-qualified or – conceptualized difference[s]' – that insist between the 'worst' and the 'worser worst' (2005: 252–3). As such, the evanescent trace of uncertain comedy materialises portions of affective experience that do not submit themselves easily to what might be termed value judgements.

So such an oscillation does not describe an on/off movement between antithetical extremes of the comic and the serious, 'stasis' and 'on', synchrony and diachrony, then; instead, as the text itself continually demonstrates, there are no stable limits, no ultimate certainties here: even the woman's body, '[w]hen it seems of stone. Is it not ashiver from head to foot?' (*NO*: 74). And, curiously, this mechanism of enfolded and enfolding oscillation is given a material form by the most literal trembling with which the text is concerned – the physical movements of the old woman. Some critics have suggested that the ghosted figure in *Ill Seen Ill Said* could be an occluded representation of Beckett's mother (Graver 1992: 148; Knowlson 1996: 669), although others have insisted that there is no specific evidence to link this figure with May Beckett other than her implied widowhood (Bryden 1993: 154–8). There is, however, a link to be made between the trembling of the old woman that comes to infect the text as a whole as her body defines and delimits the oscillating environment and object world that surrounds her, and the illness which was listed as May Beckett's cause of death in 1950 – 'paralysis agitans' or Parkinson's disease.

Hugh Culik has noted that symptoms of Parkinson's disease recur with uncommon regularity in Beckett's work: 'in *Watt*, the notoriously diseased Lynch family includes a "Sam" whose mother is afflicted with "Parkinson's palsy"; the May of *Footfalls*, the V of *Rockaby* and the woman of *Ill Seen Ill Said* all embody symptoms of his mother's disease' (1989: 45).[1] James Parkinson's description of 'the shaking palsy' in 1817 lists the key symptoms of the disease as 'tremulous agitations' (tremor), 'the almost invincible propensity to run when only wishing to walk' (a festinating gait), the tendency towards the alternations of relentless pacing (acithesia) and profound rigidity (akinesia), and a loss of expressive capability in the facial muscles (leaden facies) (1817: 25).[2] The woman in *Ill Seen Ill Said* could clearly, then, be subject to a Parkinson's diagnosis, for she displays an 'imperceptible tremor unworthy of true plaster' (*NO*: 95); she continually crosses the threshold of the cabin, walking '[h]ither and thither' (79); she walks with a 'fluttering step as if wanting mass' (70); her movements oscillate between tremor and rigidity, as when in 'her faint comings and goings she suddenly stops dead' (62); and her face is characterised by a 'livid pallor. Not a wrinkle. How serene it seems this ancient mask. Worthy of those worn by the newly dead' (70–1). Culik uses his diagnosis of the recurrence of Parkinsonian symptoms as a sign of a tenacious return to the figure of the maternal in Beckett's work that 'hide[s] a quest for an integrated maternal imago' (48); here, though, I want to suggest that the complex and contradictory collocation of pulsions and restrictions that define and deform the Parkinson's body function as an embodied materialisation of the distorted relationships of strength and weakness, mastery and loss, that define and deform the text. The Parkinson's body, which Beckett would have witnessed, incarnates, gives flesh and a resistantly revealing though nevertheless occluded shape to a writing strategy and effect with which Beckett's corpus has remained consistently concerned. The Parkinson's body indeed offers opacity and thus a visibility to what Beckett cryptically described fifty years previously as those 'unseen vicissitudes of matter' (1930s: 84) – the unseen forces that produce form.

Oliver Sacks's description of post-encephalitic Parkinsonism in *Awakenings* describes how the tremor characteristic of the disease appears in conjunction with sudden speedings and slowings that quiver between limit instances – extremes of acathisia (restlessness) and akinesia (profound rigidity and paralysis of will). For the embattled patients caught between these antithetical pulsions, Sacks writes, citing Jean-Martin Charcot, '[t]here is no truce'; rather, the tremor, rigidity and akinesia of such patients can be seen as 'the final, futile outcome of such states of inner struggle' (1991: 7). In *From an Abandoned Work*, Beckett's narrator describes a congruent embattled tension between extreme slowness of movement and a sudden tendency for sprints: 'No, with me all was slow, and then these flashes, or gushes, vent the pent, that was one of those things I used to say, over and over, as I went along, vent the pent, vent the pent' (*CSP*: 158). Sacks's patient, Leonard L., with an almost Beckettian flourish, describes how it feels to be caught between the compulsion to 'pent' and to 'vent': '"There's an awful presence," he once tapped out, "and an awful absence. The presence is a mixture of nagging and pushing and pressure, with being held back and constrained and stopped – I often call it 'the goad and halter'"' (1991: 205).

Although trembling is usually identified with and as enfeeblement – as the opposite to the physical expression of will through purposive action and ability – Leonard L.'s description of the 'goad and halter' reminds us that trembling can never be a sign of absolute weakness. It demands a relationship with strength, even if that strength is necessarily attenuated and deformed by its intercourse with inability. As Connor puts it, trembling occurs as a 'strength meets a weakness [that] is not quite weak enough simply to absorb it, to collapse and vanish under the blow' (2000: 4), and there is a way of thinking of Parkinsonism as materialising, with the ruthlessness of disease, a congruent mode of 'strong weakness'. Sacks suggests:

> patients suffer simultaneously (though in varying proportions) from a pathological absence and a pathological presence. The former cuts them off from the fluent and appropriate flow of normal movement (and – in severe cases – the flow of normal perception and thought), and is experienced as a 'weakness,' a tiredness, a deprivation, a destitution; the latter constitutes a preoccupation, an abnormal activity, a pathological organization which, so to speak, distends or inflates their behaviours in a senseless, distressing, and disabling fashion. Patients can be thought of as *engorged* with Parkinsonism. (1991: 10)

So the seemingly antithetical states of rigidity and agitated movement are not, in fact, contradictory; instead, pathological 'weakness' and 'pathological organization' are bound together. Festination (the forced hurrying of walking, talking, speech or thought), represented by Beckett in the woman's 'fluttering step' (*NO*: 70), is consequently not the opposite of stasis, the 'rigid Memnon pose' (78); rather, rigidity is exorbitant festination: 'steps tend to become smaller and smaller, until finally the patient is 'frozen' – stepping internally, but with no space left to step in' (Sacks 1991: 391). One might be reminded of Murphy 'work[ing] up' his rocking chair: 'the rock got faster and faster, shorter and shorter . . . Most things under the moon got slower and slower and then stopped, a rock got faster and faster and then stopped' (Beckett 1993: 9). The motionless figure in *Fizzles 7: Still* (1972–3), who is 'not still at all but trembling all over. But casually in this failing light impression dead still' (*CSP*: 240), mimes the same possibility. And although it seems as if matter is more likely to crack under forces than to sway, Sacks notes that states of profound Parkinsonian akinesia (rigid stasis) can also suddenly shudder into a manic *hyperkinesia* 'most apt to occur . . . where there seems to be an intense constrained or curled up pressure' (Sacks 1991: 363).

Rigidity is not rest, then, any more than the activity of festination is freedom; instead, each is the exorbitant extreme of a tension between a weakness that is too strong and demanding to be denied and a strength that is too weak to enable unreserved affirmation or purposiveness. Rigidity and festination thus become curiously interconvertible:

> *Parkinsonism* itself can be visualised as a . . . curved surface, bipolar, like a figure-of-eight . . . The patient with Parkinsonism is enthralled on this surface, which is a dynamical surface, an orbiting surface in time. Every so often this orbiting will take him, tantalisingly briefly, through a few seconds of 'normality,' or into the mirror state of hyperkinesia, only to return him to the immense 'gravitational' attraction of that powerful attractor which (in dynamical terms) is the 'cause' of Parkinsonism. (Sacks 1991: 364)

Less like a two-dimensional figure of eight and more like the three-dimensional Möbius strip which is a topological figure that must be described by temporal movement, Parkinsonian space is 'infinite yet closed'. Caught in the endless movement between seemingly irreconcilable yet enfolded limits, it would seem that the temporal structure of the woman's embodied oscillation between 'stasis' and 'on' materialises and gives a revealing shape to *Ill Seen Ill Said*'s tremulous attempts to 'say' while 'ill-saying' – that process of simultaneous determination and disablement that traces and is traced out by the wrinkles of comedy that define and scar the narrative surface. This is not, then, the articulation of a contradiction that can be worked through time, with one oscillation following another; rather, it is the paradoxical interruption of one temporal logic with another – a syncopation of strong and weak beats that manifests itself more globally as a structural tremor.

Of course, Parkinson's disease is not obviously humorous and one might wonder why writing that assumes and represents a dynamic of pathological embodiment might have any commerce with the comic. Zupančič has, however, used the spatial and temporal oddities of the topological figure that make sense of the bipolarity of Parkinsonism to explore something structurally central to comedy. The Möbius strip has two sides but only one surface. By tracing that surface through time one side becomes the other immanently, so to speak, without any need for transcendence. At every point, though, there is paradoxically an other side, a seeming opposite – something that lies outside or beyond any particular point on the surface. And Zupančič implies that this figure models something particular to the experience of the human – a mode of being that understands itself to be nailed to a surface, to finitude, and yet remains capable of understanding itself as a being that can see itself from and as constituted by an outside, an other side, into which it can neither be lifted up completely nor from which, in a movement of absolute reduction, it is totally separated. For Zupančič, what makes the comic so important a form for understanding the shape of human experience is that '[c]omic incarnation is a surprising sort circuit between the two sides' (2008: 55); it is 'the sudden intrusion of the other side, followed by an "impossible articulation" of the two sides in one and the same frame' (2008: 56). It is 'the impossible sustained encounter between two excluding realities' (2008: 57), and, one might add, between two seemingly opposing drives – the human's tendency towards infinitising (to be more than matter) and its ineluctable finite materiality that will always trip up any 'tireless desire'.[3] Comedy renders visible the 'joint articulation' of modes of human experience that nevertheless remain mutually exclusive – the doubleness or 'strong weakness' that is never quite 'visible in the given reality, yet is constitutive of it' (Zupančič 2008: 59). It is this rather profound dialectic that refuses synthesis but assumes the form of a syncopated interruption, that finds itself hesitatingly whispered in Beckett's late comic stutters and solicitously formed as matter in the trembling body of *Ill Seen Ill Said*.

Imagination at Wit's End

To return to the form of the text, if the comedy of *Ill Seen Ill Said* is both produced and disturbed by interruptions of synchrony and diachrony, this syncopation appears perhaps most significantly in the peculiar rhythms and cadences that mark its modulations of tempo. Here, gatherings of affect or possibilities of representation assert themselves only to be subject to a seeming winding back or down: 'Quick beforehand again two mysteries. Not even. Mild shocks. Not even' (*NO*: 94). Both a mustering and a slowing can be perceived: 'Praying if she prays. Pah she has only to grovel deeper. Or grovel elsewhere' (81). 'Praying' – assertion; 'if she prays' – a slowing, a confounding qualification; 'Pah she has only to grovel deeper' – profound quickening, a gathering and working through of the impossibility of hopeful prayer into comic bathos of weakened grovelling; 'Or grovel elsewhere' – a retarding and dissolving of even that certainty. In terms of narrative register, such modulations are marked by the oscillation between the even-paced simplicity of colloquial speech and a slow and ponderous drawing out: 'Still fresh the coffer fiasco what now of all things but a trapdoor. So cunningly contrived that even to the lidded eye it scarcely shows. Careful. Raise it at once and risk another rebuff. No question' (82). The comic timing of *Ill Seen Ill Said* thus performs a series of temporal arrhythmias, caught between a slow hyperactivity and a hyperactive slowness. Just as the woman oscillates between a slowing and a quickened exorbitant movement, both of which can lead tremor into petrifaction, time, too, interrupts itself or trembles here – it 'slows all this while. Suits its speed to hers' (70).

Any reading of the modulations of tempo and timbre in *Ill Seen Ill*

Said as forms of intensification and weakening, quickening and delay, or, indeed, of the interruption of one with another, suggests there is a general rhythm or speed of elapse against which such aberrations can be measured. After all, rhythm is not a discrete form, reducible to being observed as a spatialised instant; rather, as Nicholas Rand and Maria Torok remind us, rhythm is instead a 'series of acts: the perception of an initial temporal emergence, the expectation of its repetition, and the integration into the repetition of any supervening accidents or surprises' (Abraham 1995: xi). In other words, for a rhythm of a text, even a syncopated one, to be perceived, it must be experienced by a temporised consciousness and held in reference to the future of the completed rhythmic project. As Nicolas Abraham's phenomenology of a rhythmising consciousness suggests, then, rhythm only appears to the degree that there is a consciousness present to transmute basic sequence or recurrence into a recognisable form with a project – a consciousness that is 'rhythmizing from the start. From the first emergence, it is the expectation of a return ... *the first emergence already entails the project of its reproduction*' (Abraham 1995: 79). A rhythmising consciousness does not appear in response to an essential rhythm; rather, consciousness materialises rhythm.

Now this expectation and demand for reproduction drives rhythm forwards; as such it is 'characterized by increasing tension and oriented toward completion' (Abraham 1995: 80). For Abraham, any apprehension of rhythm is indeed dependent upon perceiving the relationship between the pole and place of the tension's resolution and the set of emergences leading up to this resolution. Rhythms may be end-oriented, then, but they do not demand an absolutely uniform progression of elapse. Abraham distinguishes between odd and even rhythms: '[even rhythms], with their multiply-even teleutēs [places of resolution], offering perfectly harmonic rhythmic phrases, realize temporal structures of equilibrium, tranquillity, serenity ... [odd rhythms], leaving us continually unsatisfied, represent modalities of impassioned life' (90). But, significantly, odd and even rhythms are not necessarily discrete. As Abraham notes, a single emergence of rhythm can belong simultaneously to both even and odd modes, thus creating a form of disagreement that 'endows such rhythms with a shimmering, shifting ambivalence' (1995: 90). And if one were to define the comic rhythms in *Ill Seen Ill Said*, they could be said to assume something of this 'shimmering' quality, as unpredictable comic asynchronicity is forced into an interruptive commerce with those highly structured forms of synchronous binding demanded by forms that are perhaps rather closer to jokes. Such interruptive rhythm is not simply 'on the side' of incommensurability and the ruination of form;

instead, rhythmic interruption forces incommensurability and measure into a deforming compact with one another.

Like jokes, then, rhythm is necessarily oriented towards completion. But if this is so, the rhythms of *Ill Seen Ill Said* must play themselves out according to an underlying project of elapse. The text is indeed clear that the woman disappears, but her fading seems precipitate, and thus she persistently reappears: 'Time to go again. Where still more to change. Whence back too soon. Changed but not enough. . . . To all the ill seen ill said. Then back again. Disarmed for to finish it all at last. With her and her rags of sky and earth. And if too soon go again. Then back again' (*NO*: 90–1). The very fact that her disappearance is consistently represented as 'too soon' must imply a lawful speed limit against which her 'progress' towards dissolution can be measured.

This book has been arguing that Beckett never really seems to write about resolutions, achievements or underlying principles, whether ethical or otherwise, that find themselves faithfully demonstrated; rather, the work fudges its way around tendencies, hesitant yet compulsive drives, that both demand and seem always to resist a playing out to their conclusion. It is possible, however, to pick out the trace of an end in *Ill Seeen Ill Said*, which, although never achieved, orientates the oscillating movements within many of these late texts. And that end is unbeing – death, perhaps. 'Neither' (1976), for example, that consists of little save recursion and wound-down oscillation, describes what it means to be caught between extremes of self and unself. In the text, a stillness is approached – an 'unspeakable home' that might be death or, in a coincidence of contraries, the inanimate calm that precedes life:

> till at last halt for good, absent for good from self and other
> then no sound
> then light gently unfading on that unheeded neither
> unspeakable home
>
> (*CSP*: 258)

But there is no entering this 'unspeakable home'. As Beckett puts it in a poem from 1948 known as 'je suis ce cours de sable qui glisses', one might hope for a peace where one could 'cease treading these long shifting thresholds' and live in the time and 'space of a door / that opens and shuts' (Beckett 2002: 67) with determined finality. But the oscillations of the late prose, while maintaining the magnetic poles of 'that unheeded neither / unspeakable home', determinedly refuse the idea that such refuges might be penetrated.

So in *Ill Seen Ill Said*, too, if there is the sensation of progression (or regression) towards a conclusion that determines textual rhythm, that conclusion is never achieved, although it obtains as a trace towards which the text limps. *Ill Seen Ill Said* implies the possibility of a final state, though, by describing a marked movement towards ultimate petrifaction, even though it never appears in the text: 'So on. Till fit to finish with all at last. All the trash. In unbroken night. Universal stone' (91). Time is, indeed, passing: 'everywhere stone is gaining. Whiteness. More and more every year. As well as every instant. Everywhere every instant whiteness is gaining' (*NO*: 72). Phil Baker has suggested that much of Beckett's work stages a movement towards unbeing, and that unbeing is manifested in the antitheses of dissolution and petrifaction, rubbish and stone (1997: 137). Here, however, rubbish *is* stone, in that *Ill Seen Ill Said* is littered with more or less organised heaps of minerals: 'White stones more plentiful every year. As well as every year' (71). And it is this tendency towards '[u]niversal stone' (whether organised into a deathly stasis or a disorganised and mutable form) that might be linked to the proper pole and lawful speed of elapse that structures the text's progression – what Beckett himself called '[man's] congenital yearning for the mineral kingdom' (Büttner 1984: 67, n. 20).[4]

As Gottfried Büttner makes clear, for Beckett this essential yearning for the mineral kingdom recalls Freud's articulation of the death drive in *Beyond the Pleasure Principle* (1920) – a work for which Beckett apparently had a fondness. Freud's essay does not speak of the mineral kingdom exactly, or '[u]niversal stone', but it articulates the *'urge inherent in organic life to restore an earlier state of things'* (1920: 35) – the desire to return to 'the quiescence of the inorganic world' (61).[5] We know from his psychology notebooks that in the 1930s Beckett encountered a version of the Freudian death drive in his reading of Otto Rank's *The Trauma of Birth* (1924).[6] There, Rank effects a compelling elision of the pleasurable experience of an intra-uterine calm and what must be a fantasy of the experience of death, as, after all, it can never be grasped as an experience:

> What biologically seems to us the impulse to death, strives again to establish nothing else than the already experienced condition before birth, and the 'compulsion to repetition' arises from the unquenchable character of its longing, which exhausts itself in every possibility of form. This process is what biologically speaking we call 'life'. (1929: 196)

Weller rightly notes that Beckett's interest in the 'wombtomb' appears in *Dream*, thus preceding his reading of Rank (2006: 187); nevertheless, the running together of the signs of the maternal that appear in *Ill Seen Ill Said* with the tendency towards (rather than achievement of) '[u]niversal stone' does seem to force an echo of a specifically Rankian version of the Freudian death drive. Whether the pole of '[u]niversal stone' represents an orientation towards the final extinguishment of death or an intra-uterine calm, there is a way in which *Ill Seen Ill Said*'s uncertain economies of pleasure and Freud's *Beyond the Pleasure Principle* can be seen to begin to read one another.

The Freud of *Jokes and Their Relation to the Unconscious* asserts, unsurprisingly, that jokes and humour can be identified with the pleasure principle (1905: 117), and Beckett notes just this Freudian point in his transcriptions from Jones's *Papers on Psychoanalysis*: 'Wit (economy of expenditure on inhibition) . . . [distinguished from] humour (transformation of pain-producing into pleasure-producing energy, economy of expenditure in feeling)' (Beckett 1934–5: 8/3). Freud is also clear in 1927 that humour 'signifies not only the triumph of the ego but also of the pleasure principle' (1927: 161) as it rebelliously denies reality, at least momentarily. For in Freud's model, as we have seen, joking and humour represent the momentary victory of the pleasure principle in the face of the reality principle that requires the social adult to emerge as a repressed being.

It might be expected, then, that the drive that asserts that '*the aim of all life is death*' (Freud 1920: 37), would undo the primacy of the pleasure principle to which the comic is bound in service. One thing *Ill Seen Ill Said* demonstrates, however, is that even if it is at least partially governed by Thanatos, the pleasure principle is not completely overridden, as its arrhythmic comic traces maintain a complex, non-dialectical, relationship to the movement of elapse that the text describes. This rather paradoxical state of affairs might, in turn, be explored by noting that *Beyond the Pleasure Principle* and *Ill Seen Ill Said* are characterised by remarkably similar hesitant or stuttering writing effects that complicate any stable oppositional relationship between the comic (or the pleasure principle) and its other (which might, provisionally and imperfectly, be identified with the death drive). For *Ill Seen Ill Said* offers up the progression towards a last moment, it is 'on the way to inexistence. As zero to the infinite' (*NO*: 93). But something comic still inheres in the text, retarding and deferring the achievement of death, even squeezing a kind of sensuous pleasure from the performance of retention:

> Then in that perfect dark fore-knell darling sound pip for end begun. First last moment. Grant only enough remain to devour all. Moment by glutton moment. Sky earth whole kit and boodle. Not another crumb of carrion left. Lick chops and basta. No. One moment more. One last. Grace to breathe that void. Know happiness. (97)

As Moran implies in *Molloy*, there may in fact be a pleasure principle attached to death – a 'fatal pleasure principle' (*T*: 99). I will go on to argue that it is precisely in the weakened, though structurally preserved, comedy of the text that the complex non-dialectical relationship between life and death, the pleasure principle and the death drive, with which the text is more fundamentally concerned, gropes its way towards being represented patiently, hesitantly, gently – without its simply being reduced to a theme or lifted up into the category of knowledge.

As Jacques Derrida has elaborately shown in his reading of *Beyond the Pleasure Principle*, 'To Speculate – on "Freud"', Freud's text determinedly works to complicate the 'step beyond' implied in its rather disingenuously straightforward title. For in *Beyond the Pleasure Principle*, the death drive does not simply override or pass beyond the pleasure principle, indicating 'tendencies more primitive of it and independent of it' (Freud 1920: 16); instead, each is consistently and chiastically twisted and folded into the other as the text compulsively trembles, hesitating before the space of the 'beyond'. In Derrida's reading, Freud's complex adumbration of the detours through and by which the pleasure principle dominates, alongside his uncertain consideration of whether anything escapes it, ensures that the text remains 'athetic': it is a *'pas de thèse* which advances without advancing, without advancing itself, without ever advancing anything that it does not immediately take back ... without ever positing anything that remains in position' (Derrida 1987: 293). In the final section of his text, Freud's own suggestion that his work has become a form of 'limping', a forward movement which is always retarded, always approaching the possibility of backtracking, offers Derrida a way of moving to centre stage the strangely compelling *fort-da* game which is so oddly sidelined in Freud's text. For Freud's method of proceeding through his argument itself takes the form of a back and forth, a 'démarche' – a proceeding that does not ultimately proceed. And Derrida notes that if there is a 'theme' rather than a thesis to Freud's essay, 'it is perhaps *rythmos*, and the rhythm of the theme no less than the theme of a rhythm' (406).

For Derrida, *Beyond the Pleasure Principle* is thus both patterned and structured by a trembling progression in which there can be '[n]o *Weg* without *Umweg*' (Derrida 1987: 284). First, Freud suggests that there seem to be principles that oppose the pleasure principle, such as forms of neurotic unpleasure and the so-called 'reality principle' that serves the ego's instincts of self-preservation but impinges on sexual enjoyment. But he soon states that these principles do not offer a glimpse of the 'beyond'. Neurotic unpleasure is caused simply by 'the process by which repression turns a possibility of pleasure into a source of unpleasure'; in other words, it is 'pleasure that cannot be felt as such' (Freud 1920: 10). Neither, of course, does the *fort-da* game played by Freud's grandson that performs and repeats the unpleasurable experience of the disappearance of his mother indicate an opposition to the pleasure principle; rather, the compulsion to repeat stages a kind of mastery of the traumatic event because the child is active in the game rather than merely 'experiencing it [the unpleasure] passively' (34). Indeed, as Freud himself admits, 'repetition, the re-experiencing of something identical, is clearly in itself a source of pleasure' (35). The reality principle, too, although it appears to inhibit pleasure, does not finally abandon that aim; it simply postpones satisfaction by mortgaging some of the possibilities of gaining pleasure 'as a step on the long indirect road to pleasure' (9). One might note, here, that the proto-reality principle that appears in the Joke book also functions to impinge hostile and sexual impulses and thus seems, on one level, to reduce pleasure. 'Since our individual childhood, and, similarly, since the childhood of human civilization, hostile impulses against our fellow men have been subject to the same restrictions, the same progressive repression, as our sexual urges' (1905: 101), Freud argues. But this impingement on primary pleasure both allows and enables the psychical reliefs experienced in jokes, as they *evade restrictions and open sources of pleasure that have become inaccessible*' (Freud 1905: 102). Although the reality principle inhibits the pleasure taken in the expression of primary impulses, it offers other and new sources of pleasure due to the fact that it can find itself and its repressions momentarily relieved. As Derrida puts it, the reality principle offers 'no definitive inhibition, no renunciation of pleasure, only a detour to defer enjoyment' (1987: 282).

Freud then attempts another step forward by suggesting that there is a more primary, more unmasterable compulsion to repeat which appears in the psyche. Living substance has an essentially 'conservative nature' (Freud 1920: 35); it has no wish to change, and, if conditions remained constant, it would happily persist as it is. But as this blissful, inert state is disturbed by the complex, tension-inducing forces and detours of life – what emerges from the very trauma of birth itself, in Rank's terms – the inanimate state becomes something to be desired. For Rank, pleasure's aim is to return the organism to the state of quiescence that precedes the trauma of birth, to allow the 're-establishment of intrauterine primal pleasure' (1929: 17). But Freud goes on to unbind any simple opposition between Thanatos and Eros through a reconfigured reading of the 'reality principle' in which the instincts of 'self-preservation, of self-assertion and mastery', are not working in opposition to death. Instead, they are

> component instincts whose function it is to assure that the organism shall follow its own path to death, and to ward off any possible ways of returning

to inorganic existence other than those that are immanent in the organism itself ... What we are left with is the fact that the organism wishes to die only after its own fashion. Thus these guardians of life, too, were originally the myrmidons of death ... [T]he living organism struggles most energetically against events (dangers, in fact) which might help it to attain life's aim rapidly – by a kind of short-circuit. (Freud 1920: 38)

The 'reality principle', which was first described as working outside the pleasure principle, now remains in the service of a death drive.

So the detours of life instituted by the death drive produce unpleasurable tensions in the organism whose aim is 'to free the mental apparatus from excitation or to keep the amount of excitation in it constant' (Freud 1920: 61). But just as sexual pleasure is produced by the 'momentary extinction of a highly intensified excitation' (Freud 1920: 61), the fact that tension has been produced at all serves the pleasure principle by ensuring that the corresponding discharge at the moment of death will be all the more satisfying. As Connor puts it:

In avoiding the short-cut to death via accident, it is as though the organism had recognized that oblivion will be *all the more complete* a nothingness, or, to adopt an appropriate Beckettian word, a 'lessness', for the fact that life has intervened. The longer the organism can hold out against negativity, the sweeter it will be in the end. (1992: 63)

By impeding a headlong rush to death, by drawing time into the organism according to the vacillating logic of the pleasure principle, more pleasure is produced. And there is a moment early in Freud's work that seems suggestively to mime this peculiar and somewhat contradictory entwining of principles and drives in which pleasure might be elicited from deferral and the binding of primary impulses. For it is the Joke book that proleptically, as it were, suggests that pleasure might be increased if cathectic energy is tightly bound and then released. Freud replaces his initial notion that jokes are based upon an economy of psychical expenditure on inhibition with the thought that it is the release of dammed-up tension that is significant. He suggests that 'the discharge of an inhibitory cathexis is ... increased by the height of the damming up' (1905: 154).

But, true to his hesitant aesthetic, as *Beyond the Pleasure Principle* progresses Freud withdraws his assertion that the 'reality principle' works to serve the death drive, suggesting instead that the self-preservative instincts have a libidinal character and are part of the life instincts that pull against it. The dilemma effected between these two contradictory principles enforces a suggestive rhythm in the organism – a trembling:

It is as though the life of the organism moved forward with a vacillating rhythm. One group of instincts rushes forward so as to reach the final aim of life as swiftly as possible; but when a particular stage in the advance has been reached, the other group jerks to a certain point to make a fresh start and so prolong the journey. (1920: 39–40)

If the life instincts in the organism, which demand a union with the living substance of a different individual, increase tensions, 'introducing fresh *vital differences* which must then be "lived off"' (54), then life finds itself in opposition to the dominating tendency of mental life to reduce, keep constant or remove internal tension – the pleasure principle. Yet again the death drive does not function as a 'beyond'; instead, the death drive becomes the pleasure principle's most primal expression. Of course, as we have just seen, the increased tension and release initiated by the life instincts that demand the hydraulic 'living off' of 'vital differences' are themselves to be folded into the embrace of the pleasure principle. As it turns its face from or perhaps towards the light, the pleasure principle reveals itself to be, like the duck-rabbit illusion of gestalt psychology, the death drive too.

As Derrida notes, for Freud pleasure is thus caught in a double bind. The organism limits its pleasurable primary processes, the instinctual impulses of the unconscious, in order to reduce tension and thus to increase secondary pleasure in the conscious. But if it limits itself absolutely, it disappears: 'if it liberates something as close as possible to the *PP* (a theoretical fiction), thus if *it does not limit itself*, not *at all* [pas du tout], it limits itself absolutely: absolute discharge, disbanding, nothingness or death' (1987: 401). Pleasure is thus only produced in the binding of the unbound, the unbinding of the bound; it is a *fort* which is always a *da*, a *da* which is always a *fort*. But Derrida reminds us that this oscillation has no *relève*, no *Aufhebung* in Hegel's terms; rather

> the irresolution of the scene of writing that we are reading is that of a *Bindung* which tends, stretches itself and ceaselessly posts (sends, detaches, displaces, replaces) to the extreme without conclusion, without solution, without acting, and without a final orgasm (rather a series of orgasmic tremors, of enjoyments deferred as soon as obtained). (397)

Pleasure is not an achievement; pleasure is a process. Pleasure is the process by which the organism lives by putting off death, by which it contains and takes its own time, instead of evacuating its life into a stillness beyond all experience.

One can also read *Ill Seen Ill Said* as modulated by a rhythm of interruption that seems to have death as its final end point. By not rushing towards a denouement, however, *Ill Seen Ill Said* uses pleasure as a mode that forces time to be taken both structurally and in terms of the reader's affective experience. Its comic embers function as stutters that seize time, interrupting any measured or indeed precipitate progression towards death. For as in Freud's text, there is no simple oscillation between pleasure and death. Even at the last, most petrified and desiccated moment, there remains a trace of pleasure both within the scene and within the space of its reception: 'a smile? Is it possible?' (*NO*: 89). Death is forestalled by the introduction of 'vital differences' – final sputtering incongruities – so that the last wrinkles of pleasure can be traced over in this pleating in the fabric of elapse, before all is flattened into absolute imperturbable stillness: 'No. One moment more. One last. Grace to breathe that void. Know happiness' (97). Death's achievement, as a final and absolute extenuation, will be neither pleasurable nor unpleasurable, as, by its nature, it can be neither grasped nor experienced. To '[k]now happiness', then, just before extinction, is to experience at the limit of experience itself. The comedy that so palpably though unexpectedly obtains in *Ill Seen Ill Said*'s compulsive hesitations and recursions, its stuttering rhythms that carve out the impossible possibilities of life and death in this pared-down scene, thus both echo and materialise the fundamental concerns of this late work. Just as the compelling rhythm of *fort-da* that remains so peculiarly tangential to the main argument of *Beyond the Pleasure Principle* comes to infest both its substance and rhetoric, in *Ill Seen Ill Said*, perhaps the comic diversion also becomes the theme – the funnies become the lead story.

Of course, the trembling endemic to *Ill Seen Ill Said* is no longer compulsive in quite the way it was in *Endgame*. Less angry, less concerned with sudden discharges of tension and moments of comic mastery, less infected by a drive which orients the texts towards persistence and critique, *Ill Seen Ill Said* is also markedly less funny. This text is much more evenly balanced, the musterings of mastery more minimal, more tempered by dissolution, than those that inhere in the earlier work. Nevertheless, a comedy of sorts remains, as we have seen, alongside a set of seemingly ethical obligations described and performed within the text to which this somewhat neutered comedy bears witness. For if the text were merely describing the manifestation of drives or tendencies, why then the repeated injunctions of 'Careful', 'Gently gently', 'No more!' and 'and yet', which distend and retard the woman's progression towards both full presence and absolute absence? Although such hesitation may be driven, it seems to be figured more clearly here as an obligation in which drive is itself husbanded, becoming, indeed, a drive to husband. For the demand to ill-say as ill-seen is represented as a particular form of obligation that demands the resisting of any definite movement towards comprehension and crystallisation. Ill-seeing and ill-saying indeed 'defend[s]' the old woman from the eye through fidelity to ineluctable elapse, fading, senescence and dying rather than death, for what is it that 'forbids divining her. What but life ending?' (*NO*: 64). But there is also a holding back from the purity of absence and absolute dissolution that would be the mere dialectical antithesis of stable representation through the structural and seemingly ethical obligation to produce more textual time: 'Absence supreme good and yet' (96).

So by materialising tremor within the text and by using oscillating economies of pleasure that work to contain the drive towards absolute evacuation – the rush towards death – *Ill Seen Ill Said* does not simply play with time; instead, it draws time as contraction, dilation and distension into itself, allowing its passing to be experienced as such, just as the compact between the pleasure principle and death drive allows the organism to live and die according to its own time, 'after its own fashion'. This movement is not totally alien to those compulsions and obligations of the *Trilogy* that were profoundly evacuatory and driven by a furious, retentive anality that held back in order to attempt all the more complete an expulsion – these compulsions that irrupted into the texts as comically engorged incorporation followed by bulimic bathos.[7] The time of the body taken into the texts was indeed marked by 'motions' that materialised an angry back and forth – a deeply driven expulsion and frantic incorporation that led to a finally purposeless propulsion. Here, though, the drives to split off and expel – the compulsions of emetic and enema – followed by gagging sensations of forced-feeding seem to have been far more thoroughly laid down. Time is not forced into the body but rather is taken in, retained or contained, and then released according to modes seemingly more determined by 'care' and 'gentleness'. The oscillations of pleasure that defer the death in which neither pleasure nor anything else can be felt are no longer compulsively evacuatory and manically incorporative; in *Ill Seen Ill Said* they are, instead, experienced as an obligation that remains driven to shepherd something for the right period of time (even as it is clear things might not be all gentleness and care here), and then to allow a release. In *Ill Seen Ill Said*, then, the pleasure and rhythm given their form by a crepuscular comedy become central to its mode of solicitous containment.

Ill Saying, Ill Said

As we have seen, much of Beckett's work stages dilemmas below the threshold of ethical prescriptions of a normative or foundational sort.

Indeed, to Charles Juliet's suggestion in 1973 that 'the artist's work is inconceivable without a strict ethical sense', Beckett responds by revealing just how far he hopes his artistic practice is from ethics as value judgement or moral prescription:

> What you say is true. But moral values are inaccessible. And they cannot be defined. In order to define them, you would have to pass a value judgment, which is impossible. That's why I could never agree with the notion of a theater of the absurd. It involves a value judgment. You cannot even speak about truth. That's what's so distressful. (Juliet 2009: 23–4)

Although we will return to this, in *Company* (1980), which is the first part of what was collected as Beckett's late Trilogy, it seems that moments of more normative ethical anxiety do appear – anxieties that are primarily concerned with how a self relates to otherness. A narrator describes the scene: 'To one in his back in the dark a voice tells of a past' (*NO*: 5). The voice that appears offers the figure 'company', of sorts, by representing a putative present and what seem to be the figure's memories; as such, more and more company (both other people and scenes) extrudes into the dark. If the ethical, even in its most straightforward configurations, is necessarily concerned with relations between selves and others – relations of company – it is significant that here there is both a demand for and a horror of what it means to forge a connection between voice and prone figure. And this, in turn, materialises obligations seemingly inherent within connections staged through acts of representation. The voice somehow needs the figure to admit his implication within the scene. There is indeed a compulsive desire to fix the cords of connection between representing the voice and the obstinate body of the figure within whom these scenes of memory cannot finally settle: 'If he were to utter at all? However feebly. What an addition to company that would be! . . . In the end you will utter again. Yes I remember. That was I. That was I then' (16–17). Yet in the final scene of the text, there is the sense that although representation admits the relationship between a subject and company – a relationship which is the stage upon which all ethical relations appear – it might be better, it might ironically be more ethical, in the end, to leave well alone: 'And how better in the end labour lost and silence. And you as you always were. / Alone' (52).

Here, to '[i]magine', to represent, is to undertake an act that fills the void with company, with images that flash with the brief, fragmented, cathected intensity of home movies. In one sense, one could say that all representation expresses a perturbation within solitude, a fixing of material beyond the self in a way that is always for an other, even if it is the self as other as in *Krapp's Last Tape* (1958). But an anxiety emerges that whatever drives the compulsion to represent and thus to take a certain responsibility for a relation to an other also enacts a violence. The voice reminds the figure of a hedgehog he once found:

> You take pity on a hedgehog out in the cold and put it in a hatbox with some worms. This box with the hog inside you then place in a disused hutch wedging the door open for the poor creature to come and go at will ... Kneeling at your bedside you included it the hedgehog in your detailed prayer to God to bless all you loved. And tossing in your warm bed waiting for sleep to come you were still faintly glowing at the thought of what a fortunate hedgehog it was to have crossed your path as it did. (*NO*: 23–4)

But there are consequences in imposing a care, especially a care that was not asked for, and which turns out to be more of a care of the self than of the other. The child begins to wonder whether 'rather than do as you did you had perhaps better let good alone and the hedgehog pursue its way' (24). Paralysed by this sense of ethical unease, he returns to the box weeks later to find only 'mush' and 'stench'.

The sense that ethical action might more properly be a form of letting 'good alone and the hedgehog pursue its way' that this late text considers should be understood, I think, as a profoundly post-Holocaust articulation of the ethical that refuses an ethics of knowledge or judgement which might turn otherness into an object of understanding for the self. It should also be thought of as part of a historical moment that reads ethical anxiety and representational crisis as strikingly imbricated. For in 1947, Theodor Adorno and Max Horkheimer famously describe an account of Enlightenment knowledge that reaches its end point in the domination of all otherness, of the object world. In *Dialectic of Enlightenment* Adorno and Horkheimer suggest, first using nature as a synecdoche of otherness, that the necessary disenchantment of the natural environment that enlightened rational and scientific thought demands in order to obtain knowledge leads to a denuding of the sensuous particularity of that world. The world of natural objects becomes, simply, 'nature', and 'nature' becomes nothing but a reflection of reason's abstracting categories, a set of resources there to be used. 'Men pay for the increase of their power with alienation from that over which they exercise their power. Enlightenment behaves towards things as a dictator toward men. He knows things in so far as he can manipulate them' (Adorno and Horkheimer 1997: 9), they write. But to historicise explicitly Adorno and Horkheimer's profoundly historical argument, this domination of the object world by a rational subject represents a particularly postwar, and a specifically post-Holocaust, anxiety about Enlightenment knowledge in which thought has become devastatingly instrumental, seemingly proven to be as fatally abstracting and abstracted as the world of late capitalism that it both produces and reflects. For the later Adorno of *Negative Dialectics*, such putatively rational thought, which could convert all otherness into an instrumental abstracted identity, indeed finds its apogee, but also its point of voiding collapse, its absolute irrationality, in Auschwitz. The appearance of hyperbole in reaching for Auschwitz in one sense enacts a resistance to a seeming rationality that would seek to repress violence into a place fundamentally distinct from itself. But Adorno is insistent; there is a link between rational thought, knowledge and mass murder: 'Genocide is the absolute integration. It is on its way whenever men are levelled off ... until one exterminates them literally ... Auschwitz confirmed the philosopheme of pure identity as death' (1990: 362).

Of course, for Adorno and Horkheimer, ethical thought does not simply oppose this Enlightenment rationality, for an exterminating irrationality has already become the modus operandi of rationality itself. They demand instead that Enlightenment thought should reflect upon itself, return to a rationality that would be able to think a relationship to a world of objects and otherness that would allow alterity to appear in its all material, sensuous specificity. As Adorno puts it in *Negative Dialectics*, there must be an attempt to think and to reconcile the subject-object dichotomy that would allow something of the unexpected, the unthought character of the world to appear for and as itself: '[such reconcilement] would open the road to the multiplicity of different things ... Reconcilement would be the thought of many as no longer inimical' (1990: 6).

For Adorno, and maybe also for the Beckett of *Company*, an ethical relation to the world would see otherness as something that could not simply be lifted into the light of thought, placed within pre-existent containers of reason, something like a hatbox, perhaps, and made to confirm the subject in a complacent 'glowing' care that risks becoming a domination of all that remains outside of it. For Adorno, the non-identity of object and concept is not to be overcome, turned into identity. But there is, nevertheless, the necessity for a recognition and reconciliation of object, concept and subject in their difference, if another world is to appear. And the idea that ethics might consist in offering a regard that could leave something of an other alone, for and as itself, is worried away at in *Company*, but it is also held against the acknowledged impossibility of any absolute enactment of laissez-faire.

Texts like the *Trilogy* and *Endgame*, I have argued, are concerned with forging a resistance to the given world, while nevertheless displaying all its violent administrations; in Adorno's terms, they are marked 'by the same distortion and indigence which [they] seek to escape' in order not to negate the world, dialectically, but to interrupt it by presenting a standpoint removed from the given world 'by a hair's breadth' (1974: 247). If Beckett's late *Trilogy* is less comical than this earlier work, that is because, at least on one level, this mastery of critique is far more completely laid down here. And it is laid down in favour of a more determined and clear exploration of what is represented as a necessarily ethical demand that a relationship be formed with alterity. Ethics, here, is not a question of making 'value judgment[s]', as Beckett himself put it; ethics is instead concerned with the particular shape of the relationship of self to otherness – a relationship that is found and explored not just in dialogue but within the act of representation itself.

In *Company* to be is always to be perceived by an other. The voice in *Company* indeed seems compelled not to leave the figure alone; instead, they are bound to one another, just as text becomes bound to its reader, to the injunction of '[i]magine', and to the relentless compulsion of company. Even the '[a]lone' of the end of the text, which seems to step away from the feared violence of representation and of knowledge, in fact only establishes an illusion of the cessation of representation rather than a final achievement. For as a word reproduced in a text, 'Alone' is never alone: by representing it implicates itself within a scene of others. As we have seen in *The Unnamable*, both within the characterisation of textual voices and as a text which not only implies a reader, but also self-consciously dramatises the existence of others who bear witness to the text as a fictional representation, there can be no voice, especially no represented voice, which is only for itself – fully self-present without the temporal lag of its being formed in a relationship. Even as company seems to threaten violence, there is no voice that can exist without the company and the time that allows it to think and experience itself as such.

On one level, language remains insistently suspect for Beckett. He never quite gets over the Bergsonian position expressed in his early lectures on French literature that 'language can't express confusion' (Le Juez 2008: 35). Language, as Bergson has it, organises and spatialises: 'the word with the well-defined outlines . . . which stores up the stable, common, and consequently impersonal element in the impressions of mankind, overwhelms or at least covers over the delicate and fugitive impressions of our individual consciousness' (1910: 131). Language thus violently deforms that temporal quality of living human experience in which 'we change without ceasing, and that the state itself is nothing but change' (1911a: 2), as Bergson famously puts it in *Creative*

Evolution (1907). And yet, as Beckett's writing career progresses, it becomes clear that language can produce complexity, disturbance, discordance, as all is never quite stilled 'for good' or turned into the stability of space. Beckett's later writing indeed remains singularly compelled to knead air-pockets of time (and perhaps otherness) into itself through linguistic repetitions, recursions, dislocations, oscillations.

It is, I think, because Levinas also stages this specifically post-Holocaust anxiety about a violent subsumption of otherness immanent within representation, while acknowledging the fact that the subject always emerges in relation to company, that a suggestive symmetry can be discerned between his writing and the late Beckett's. Both articulate a demand to recognise an alterity that might persist in its absolute otherness; nevertheless, both remain wedded to the coexistent necessity of articulating an ethics that registers the unbreakable bonds between the human and its other, or others – the demand of company and of representation. And just as Levinas turns to an interruptive, linguistic relation to enact this demanding ethical situation in the densely recursive *Otherwise than Being or Beyond Essence*, so, for Beckett, it is language that materialises the ungainsayable relations between self and other – bearing witness to the violence of representation while allowing that something might appear in its irreducible particularity.

For Critchley, Levinas's vital distinction between Saying and Said in *Otherwise than Being* represents a 'linguistic or deconstructive turn' because rather than enabling writing about ethics, the oscillating distinction allows 'the performative enactment of ethical writing' (1999b: 8). Relocating the nudity of the face, that transcendence beyond all language that is the locus of the ethical in *Totality and Infinity*, into the space and time of representation, Critchley describes the relationship between Saying and Said:

> The content of my words, their identifiable meaning, is the Said, while the Saying consists in the fact that these words are being addressed to an interlocutor. The Saying is the sheer radicality of human speaking, of the event of being in relation with an Other; it is the non-thematizable ethical residue. (1999b: 7)

The Saying is the quasi-transcendental condition that enables ethics, while the Said is its incarnation and 'immobilization' within the tangible world of paraphraseable meaning, knowledge and history.

In temporal terms, the Said

> recuperate[s] the irreversible, coagulate[s] the flow of time into "something", thematize[s], ascribe[s] a meaning . . . takes up a position with regard to this

"something" fixed in a present, re-present[s] it to itself and thus extract[s] it from the labile character of time. (Levinas 1998: 37)

This is the logic of the Said that one finds in 'the time that marks historiography, that is, the recuperable time, the recoverable time, the lost time that can be found again' (Levinas 1998: 36), as the relationship between present and past is synchronised through representation and reminiscence into 'absorption', 'death' and 'inscription' (Levinas 1998: 36). Not in a strict opposition to the Said, but existing instead in a trembling relationship of indiscrete tension, the Saying, however, is the possibility of ethical language, even though that possibility will always be 'betrayed' – transformed into identification and meaning by the concretising language of ontology. Levinas insists that the approach of the other, which is both phenomenal and transcendental coextensively, can be enacted within language, but through language as interruption rather than a representation of essence. The Saying is the fact that before the face, as I am exposed to the other as fleshly and corporeal, I cannot remain silent. As Levinas puts it in *Ethics and Infinity*, I do not simply remain there contemplating it:

> I respond to it . . . It is difficult to be silent in someone's presence; this difficulty has its ultimate foundation in this signification proper to saying, whatever is said. It is necessary to speak of something, of the rain and fine weather, no matter what, but to speak. (1985: 88)

Of course, there are ways in which this sounds like a Beckett text; one is perhaps reminded of the Unnamable's necessarily repeated linguistic acts of definition or the compulsion of dialogue in *Endgame*. But, for Levinas, it is the addressivity of the Saying that is significant, over and above any necessity for self-expression. Saying 'is communication, to be sure, but as a condition for all communication, as exposure' (1998: 48), he writes. It precedes our entry into the world of the social and communicates little but the desire and necessity of communication. It is the openness between self and other that enables language, although it is not the act of speaking, of forming consensus, or even of exchanging information. It is, instead, language's possibility: 'a saying holding open its openness, without excuses, evasions or alibis, delivering itself without saying anything said. Saying saying saying itself, without thematizing it' (Levinas 1998: 143). This Saying is something like the radical *ur-*condition of speech; it signifies nothing but the possibility and necessity of the self opening responsibly and responsively to the other. With an astonishing attention to the corporeal, Levinas describes it as being 'like a cellular irritability; it is the impossibility of being silent, the scandal of sincerity' (1998: 143). The Saying is the uncovering of the self that exposes it to trauma and vulnerability.

So the Saying is, in Critchley's terms, 'my exposure – corporeal, sensible – to the other, my inability to refuse the Other's approach' (1999b: 259–60) that acknowledges an ethical relation that necessarily precedes a determinedly thinking consciousness. As such, Levinas produces what Critchley describes as a *'material phenomenology of subjective life'* (1999a: 63) that unfolds and exposes itself in the Saying:

> Not saying dissimulating itself and protecting itself in the said, just giving out words in the face of the other, but saying uncovering itself, that is, denuding itself of its skin, sensibility on the surface of the skin, at the edge of the nerves, offering itself even in suffering . . . In sincerity, in frankness, in the veracity of this saying, in the uncoveredness of suffering, being is altered. (Levinas 1998: 15)

Levinas's non-foundational ethics is thus not the appeal to universals or maxims; rather, it is lived experience that opens up another possibility – an ethics that would refuse to confirm the position, power and status of the subject.

As the Saying disturbs the plenitude of the self, 'interrupting the for-oneself' (Levinas 1998: 56) and the very time of its being, the I can no longer be a generalised concept, a *res cogitans*, an idealised self-consciousness. For the I is a pre-reflective sensibility before it is a thinking self; it submits itself to the call of the other rather than remaining an autonomous subject that freely possesses its own experience. And this subjection pleats a disturbance of temporality into the subject because that subject is 'required . . . by responsibility, and is always wanting with respect to itself . . . This diachrony of the subject is not a metaphor. The subject . . . is not in time, but is diachrony itself' (Levinas 1998: 57). Such passivity thus interrupts the synchronous time used by philosophy and its alibi, the thinking consciousness, to confirm itself;

> The lapse of time is also something irrecuperable, refractory to the simultaneity of the present, something, unrepresentable, immemorial, pre-historical. Before the passive syntheses of apprehension and recognition, the absolutely passive 'synthesis' of ageing is effected . . . It is the impossibility of the dispersion of time to assemble itself in the present, the insurmountable diachrony of time, a beyond the said. (Levinas 1998: 38)

Crucially, though, this Saying is not the antithesis of the Said. Saying can only be manifested in terms of the Said (every Saying retains a trace of the Said that will allow it into being, if only by being a singular Saying, rather than simply Saying in general), but the Said will always be interrupted because Saying, as the very possibility of language, precedes and outlasts the intelligible consciousness that speaks in the Said. Attempting to express the ethical, but unable to oppose philosophy due to the possibility of recuperating such negativity as a mere mirror image, *Otherwise than Being* is thus marbled and marked by a stuttering writing effect, a trembling non-coincidence, as terms are represented in the Said; but the Said is then forced to oscillate, distort and metamorphose, as the irreducible trace of the Saying interrupts the stable language of philosophy. Andrew Gibson has precisely read the suggestively congruent struggle in *Ill Seen Ill Said* to leave the scene half-said through repetitions and dislocations alongside Levinas's terms of the Saying and the Said.[8] But while Gibson worries that the linearity of Levinas's philosophical text still privileges the Said over the Saying, with the Saying remaining a secondary disruption in the work,[9] he asserts that certain kinds of literary language might not remain so enthralled to the synchronic linearity of the Said but might 'properly hover in an enigmatic, indeterminate or undecidable space between Saying and Said' (Gibson 1999: 140). Gibson indeed excavates an ill-saying in Beckett's text that functions as a form of gentleness, describing and performing a relationship with the other which forgoes the mastery of representation, effecting a 'suspension of the Said' and describing a space where 'the immediate appeal of the Saying displaces and even refuses the ontological fixity of the Said' (140).

There is much that is convincing in this reading but, as we have seen, *Ill Seen Ill Said* is certainly not all gentleness – 'quick seize her where she is best to be seized' (*NO*: 63) – caught as it in the desire to represent the woman (despite the unattainable determination that she should remain 'pure figment' (67)) and to grasp her, even as it evades violence by misrepresentation, only ever offering the penultimate moment. Such seizure figures the necessity of holding back from the 'void', from the dissolution of all ontology, despite the fact that it is given the chance to appear, quiveringly: 'Grace to breathe that void' (97). Equally, though, neither is the appearance of the ethical in *Otherwise than Being* a manifestation of pure Saying. In an oscillating economy that is never gathered in representation, the ethical is not the Saying; instead, it appears in the interruption of the synchronic Said by the diachronic Saying (and vice versa). The terms are never brought together in equivalence, never submitted to sublation; rather, the unthematisable trace of Saying within Said, Said within Saying, is maintained. Thus, if there is an Levinasian ethics of ill-saying to be found in *Ill Seen Ill Said*, it will appear in the trembling, stuttering interruptions of synchrony and diachrony, seizure and dissolve, which appear and evaporate, never achieving resolution.

So the Said does appear in *Ill Seen Ill Said*; it is present enough to be interrupted. The text is positively brimming with resinously identifiable props – windows, curtains, coats, buttonhooks, keys, lambs, books, soup, spoons, and one might recognise the old woman in a police line-up – despite all being subject to a fading out and fading in. There is indeed the desire to define and represent, but after the description of the woman's hands the text begins to ask anxious questions: 'Who is to blame? Or what? They? The eye? The missing finger? The keeper? The cry?' (*NO*: 76). But even as the 'eye rivets the bare window' (66), there is a holding back through the seemingly ethical injunction to resist full representation. 'Careful' (67), it enjoins, which then shudders strangely into a residually comic resistance to the finality of definition: 'Winter evening. Not to be precise' (68). In the description of the 'zones' of this landscape, dimensions are offered which might attain the status of Said. Even though a Saying does interrupt to (un)clarify the scene through further inadequate and inappropriate descriptions, the revelation of the absurdity (yet compulsive necessity) of all measure comes from the marking of this incongruity that effects a reappearance of the Said's certainties: 'The two zones form a roughly circular whole. As though outlined by a trembling hand. Diameter. Careful. Say one furlong. On an average. Beyond the unknown. Mercifully' (59). And yet, such comic incongruities could not be experienced without the interruptive Saying that drives forward the disparities in scale and affect – this Saying that puts into question any smug satisfaction that the 'absurd' has been coded as such, ordered and understood. For it is this very sundering of the synchronous time and space of the Said (what is 'said of' a subject) that enables the diachronic time and asymmetrical space of the Saying to effect its comic work. These comic moments are, nevertheless, like everything else in the text, subject to a fizzling out; they appear only to shimmer and dissolve. As such, the spectral half-life of the comic that remains when so much riotous, libidinal affect has been attenuated, along with the uncertain quavering pleasure it produces, works to drive forward and to retard what must be understood as a historically specific compulsion to represent, alongside a philosophically and aesthetically driven obligation to resist the violent assimilation of the scene through knowledge.

Ill Seeing

If Saying is always a 'saying to' rather than a 'said of', one might ask who or what is the unknown addressee of *Ill Seen Ill Said*? There are a number of silent others in the text: the 'imaginary stranger' maintains an uncertain existence, enabling the woman to be posited as not present ('[m]otionless against the door he listens long. No sound ... Returns at last to his own and avows, no one' (*NO*: 61)), while the mysterious figures of the 'twelve' observe her even though she does not give herself up to representation. But of these others possessing an 'eye of flesh' which 'digests its pittance' (69) and perpetually returns to the scene of 'its betrayals' (72), it is the text as subject that seems most securely sighted and which, through the putative violence of representation,[10] brings the scene into being.

Ill Seen Ill Said's anxiety about the violence within a seeing and saying linked to a particular kind of knowing accords with a more general suspicion of modes of vision and representation that appear in Beckett's later work. In *Play* (1962–3), for example, stage lighting violently forces expression from those tormented, infernally repeating, adulterers, imprisoned in their urns. The stage directions of *Play* are unequivocal: 'speech is provoked by a spotlight' (*CDW*: 30), with the first female figure registering an assault by an interrogatory theatrical gaze as she enjoins both dramatic text and audience to '[w]eary of playing with me. Get off me. Yes' (317). In *Not I* (1972), Mouth is similarly riveted to and by the spot that enforces her traumatic repetitions, while in *Film* (1963) the eye, dissociated here from linguistic expression, explicitly becomes a hunter of objects: 'the protagonist is sundered into object (O) and the eye (E), the former in flight, the latter in pursuit', Beckett writes (1990: 323).

Why precisely Beckett should so determinedly figure visibility and representation as tainted with violence comes rather more into focus if it is understood as part of an intellectual tradition that associates vision, especially the light of knowledge drawn from Enlightenment versions of rationality, with processes of violent control and domination. In *Downcast Eyes*, Martin Jay finds a pervasive anxiety and thoroughgoing critique of 'ocularcentrism' in twentieth-century French thought, represented, most frequently, as a suspicion of a philosophical tradition that finds the ultimate ground for rationality in sight, in a seeing originary and foundational consciousness, whether this is a Kantian subject or the Cartesian self-reflecting *cogito*. Jay traces this suspicion through Alexandre Kojève's reading of Hegel in the 1930s and its monumental legacy within French intellectual culture. There, the account of the master–slave dialectic from Hegel's *Phenomenology of Spirit* which delineates the demand by a self-consciousness to have its reality recognised by an other is reframed by Kojève to emphasise the reciprocal violence within such a meeting rather than mutual recognition. For Jay, a philosopher such as Sartre responds directly to this version of the dialectic, recasting the self's demand to have its own conscious reality recognised by an other specifically into a violently imagined 'register of sight' (1994: 287). Within the Sartrian battle for self-definition, selves and others are indeed figured as duelling for their existence according to an oscillating, sadomasochistic economy of looking.

Angela Moorjani has offered compelling evidence for reading Beckett's early plays as precisely engaging with French intelligentsia's postwar enthrallment to the Kojèvian master–slave dialectic. She notes that in *Eleutheria* and *Godot*, but in texts like *Endgame* too, one could argue, the subject's Hegelian demand to have its self-consciousness recognised by the gaze and consciousness of an other is mocked. Turned into art, the dialectic is 'no more or less than the dependence of actors in any play on the eyes and ears of the audience to exist' (2003: 74). Moorjani is right that the master–slave dialectic emerges as something of a comic scenario, and indeed that any achievement of 'freedom', which is the final precipitate of Kojève's system, is profoundly ironised in Beckett's work. Her 'no more or less' seems rather too equivocal, though, to do justice to the materialisation of the violence involved in acts of looking, recognition and knowledge in Beckett's work. In a textual environment increasingly suspicious of vision, it similary becomes hard to know whether a position could be seen and represented with sufficient solidity from which any straightforward mockery could take place.

For Jay, the determinedly postwar thought of Levinas also represents a turning from what had become a seemingly obvious collocation of knowledge, self-knowledge, and vision, towards a relationship with the other that would resist the violent 'avidity of the gaze' (Levinas 1969: 130). Levinas's properly Hebraic suspicion of the graven image is reformulated at this historical moment into part of an ethical relationship between self and other; as Jay puts it, '[a]lthough Levinas often talked about "face-to-face" encounters, it was the summons to hear the Other's call rather than seeing his or her visage that mattered' (1994: 556). Saying is not primarily a seeing. Ill-seeing, as it appears in *Ill Seen Ill Said*, then, acquires a more thoroughgoing and intellectually precise imbrication with ethics if seen as coming towards the end of a century in which vision and Enlightenment accounts of knowledge and representation had not only been subjected to critique, they had been philosophically implicated within the most systematic forms of violence humans had yet perpetrated on one another. Without ever having read Levinas, Beckett's concern with encounters between self and other emerge from a shared intellectual context which worries away at what it means, after

Auschwitz (in Adorno's provocative terms), for a subject to see and speak so clearly that it turns an other into an instrument for its own purposes.

So *Ill Seen Ill Said* as textual subject wishes to be rid of its eye: 'Close it for good this filthy eye of flesh' (*NO*: 74); for to get rid of the eye would be to void the scene of representation and its potential for violence: 'Ope eye and at them to begin. But first the partition. It rid they too would be. It less they by as much' (92). But something forbids the possibility of finding either a determined presence or an absence underwritten or written off by the seeing eye of the subject: 'What forbids?', the text tremulously asks: 'Careful' (74), it warns. For at least some of the time it seems as though this text is not simply a self-present seeing or saying subject; rather, it enacts a Saying that is addressing itself, speaking to itself as much as any implied reader, enjoining itself to be 'careful', to move 'gently' – folding itself, away from any sighted certainty, and through its language, into the estimate of itself as other: 'what is the word? What is the wrong word' (65).

Within this fractured text, the stuttered representation that uncertainly unsays as much as it enacts anything Said, is always subject to an other's assessment, held hostage to its judgement (even though it is only provisional), and, oddly, alongside the anxieties about violence, this perturbation inserts a little comic incongruity, perhaps even a little comic superiority into the scene: 'Well! Above all not understand' (*NO*: 83), the text, states, nudgingly, after its desperate efforts to represent and comprehend the old woman. Of course, this text that rends itself, holds itself subject to the estimate and judgement of an other, also mimes that structural requirement that joking and comedy must be shared. As such, the retaining and containing of a particular comic moment, might be thought of as part of a drive that turns the text round upon itself, introducing an interruptive and unpredictable otherness into the scene of representation – an otherness against which that scene is measured and to which it is held responsible. Although it might be argued that there is only a formal analogue between the stuttering caesurae of *Ill Seen Ill Said*, in its comic interruptions, and the disruption within the time of representation that Levinas describes as the horizon upon which the ethical will appear, the comic text, as an aesthetic object, precisely and by necessity, shows how form stages encounters between selves and others, and how form produces effects. Form elicits affects.

So *Ill Seen Ill Said*, with its stuttered moments of avowal and disavowal, materialises and forces into consciousness those unpredictable economies of transmission in which structure shudders into effect, form replicates itself as affect. This, in turn, offers a way of soliciting movements which pull away from subjective solitude or the abandon-ment of the world, into a world of 'company' – the place of sociality, sen-suous involvement, of being moved, and the stage on which the ethical demand of a relationship with otherness appears. But these movements and affects also dramatise a holding back from what, at this particular historical moment which senses itself as always after Auschwitz, gets experienced as the dread weight of knowledge, judgement and represen-tation that had so conspicuously failed to preserve even the minimum conditions of an ethics that would allow otherness to persist for itself. Consequently, instead of reproducing the ethics of 'value judgment[s]' of which Beckett remained so suspicious, the text solicits from itself affec-tive conditions under which the anxious necessity of a relationship with alterity, indeed a demand for it, might be felt rather than known.

So it is not a question of *Ill Seen Ill Said* simply describing movements that may be open to ethical interpretations; rather, by creating a stut-tering, interruptive form that manifests itself through and as comedy, in this compulsive 'syntax of weakness', the text takes into itself move-ments and sensations that are solicitous of otherness, or, in Levinas's terms, ethical. In gathering up the passage of time in a way that recalls the temporality of life as one drawn out by the passing economies of pleasure, the text materialises as an affect a sensation of what it might mean to live and die through time, after one's own fashion, while adding the awareness that 'one's own fashion' is compelled to include the sen-sible experience of living with others. What the symptom of tremor indeed offers the Beckett of *Ill Seen Ill Said* is a form of writing that creates a variegated sensation of modulating intensities – of strength and weakness, of representational mastery and its loss, of uncertain comic pleasure and pain and of ethical obligations as they might be felt and experienced over time, rather than as they are known in the fullness of time. For Levinas ethics is not determined by moral prescriptions that call upon a thinking subject to choose them; ethics instead is determined by an openness to the other that renders the subject out of phase with itself and is materialised in a body. This bodily experience, which is 'that by which the self is susceptibility itself' (Levinas 1998: 195, n. 12) and precedes any knowing self, precipitates an ethics determined by feeling, then, or an aesthetic ethics, if one prises the aesthetic away from art and towards an earlier sense of 'things perceptible by the senses (as opposed to things thinkable or immaterial)' (*OED*). Modulating and interrupt-ing itself through and as time, within *Ill Seen Ill Said* the comic and the ethical are brought together as an affective formalism.

This is not to say that these sensations will necessarily be securely felt. It is true that in its unpredictable gathering and dissipating tremors *Ill*

Seen Ill Said, alongside *Company*, has a paucity of clear comic affect, although this seems to allow in more obvious sentiment than most of Beckett's work. Limned with memory and sensations of senescence, the comedy of this late work never quite musters itself into producing the sensation of a good, securely captured joke. Indeed, this atrophied comedy, with its arrhythmic bleeding of extremes, ensures that the conceptual hardening that might allow the texts to be read as, say, 'absurd' is radically undercut by the explicit drawing out of time, or the accelerated running together of extreme conditions, which produces laughter momentarily, but holds humour back from its trajectory and still end point. So the sensation of comic remains here, but it is like Ada's ghosted and tremulous ha ha ha in *Embers* – wound down from having gone on too long, or aborted before it can become an assertion of happiness, freedom or mastery – the expression of subjective will. As Nell says in *Endgame*, one can no longer laugh with the 'will' one once had: 'Yes, it's like the funny story we have heard too often, we still find it funny but we don't laugh any more' (*CDW*: 101). Little more than a weakened convulsion, a spasm of the breath that has never properly been born (recalling us to the passivity of matter and senescence that Levinas describes as the experience of diachrony), it traces out, as in mourning, the possibility and affect of the comic, the convulsive gatherings and dissipations of which body and consciousness are capable. As if it were a slowed down or wildly accelerated ringing of past laughter in the ears (like the buzzing tinnitus of the sea in *Embers*), the stalled, accelerated and distended temporality through which such comedy appears and disappears in the late prose seems to describe and embody the blurred and twisted threshold between cognition and reflex, linguistic representation and corporeality, the intelligible and the sensible, that Beckett's work obsessively traces and erases and that Levinas holds open as the interruptive time in which the ethical relation appears. In the final sentences of *Ill Seen Ill Said*, Beckett writes: 'No. One moment more. One last. Grace to breathe that void. Know happiness' (*NO*: 97). Perhaps it is not possible to know happiness here, to grasp it, but in the penultimate moment where the void is offered the grace to breathe (or is that grace itself voided?), one might at least begin to feel its hesitant approach.

Notes

1. Culik suggests that Cooper in *Murphy* seems to be suffering from Parkinsonism: his inability to sit is humorously described as an 'acathisia [which] was deep-seated and of long standing' (Beckett 1993: 69). Beckett transcribes in his psychology notes at about the same time: '[a]cathisia i.e.,

inability to sit down', from Wilhelm Stekel's *Psychoanalysis and Suggestion Therapy* (1934–5: 24). Maude also notes that Jean Martin, the first actor to play Lucky, studied Parkinson's disease to help him to find the right physical shape for *Godot*'s Lucky. Martin suggested that Beckett approved of the representation, telling him 'to change nothing' (Maude 2009: 107).

2. See also Magalini et al. (1990: 670–1).
3. See Chapter 2.
4. This remark was made by Beckett to Büttner in a conversation on death, petrifying and the 'sclerotic traits' in *Krapp's Last Tape* (Büttner 1984: 67, n. 20).
5. A number of critics have described correspondences between Freud's account of the death drive and the movement towards death and dying in Beckett's work. See, for example: Baker (1997: 128–40), Ricks (1995: 107, 109), Trezise (1990: 86–94) and Watson (1991: 69–80). Katz makes explicit the connection between measure and pleasure in Beckett's work through a reading of *Beyond the Pleasure Principle* (2003: 246–60). See also Maude (2009: 96–7), who connects Beckett's convulsive bodies to Freud's rhythmic account of drive.
6. A short discussion of the death drive also appears in Woodworth's *Contemporary Schools of Psychology*, upon which Beckett took notes: 'The longing for rest or Nirvana was an expression of the death instinct' (1931: 162).
7. See Salisbury (2011).
8. Locatelli similarly connects the Saying and the Said with the later *Trilogy* in a discussion of *Worstward Ho* (1990: 230–1).
9. Gibson asks, importantly, whether interruption is ever anything more than a *'cutting across* ontology', thus remaining secondary to it. 'Doesn't Saying always "come after"?' he worries (1999: 140). This problem can be worked through by remembering that the Saying remains the radical *ur*-condition of all communication for Levinas, and that ethics remains 'first philosophy' because the call of the other precedes the attainment of consciousness; it is not achieved by consciousness. In this sense, the Saying which retains the call of the other also precedes rather than follows ontology.
10. Levinas explicitly sees representation, within which he includes visual art and literature, to be violent forms, in service of the Said (1998: 40).

Chapter 5

Slapstick Echoes: The Late Plays

There is a way of moving forwards that will always entail a retracing of what has gone before. As Beckett's late fiction has demonstrated, there can be no starting over, reinvigorated and refreshed. A place is presented, but imagination is dead: 'A place, that again. Never another question' (*CSP*: 169). As if each newly stuttered text displays an awareness of its position within a body of work, the novelty of the textual performance is tempered by the knowingness of a return to the fold where, like an echo never quite done with resounding, 'the old questions' (*CDW*: 110) can be asked one more time. The correspondences between settings within Beckett's oeuvre are far from exact; nevertheless, the bleakened scenes of *Come and Go* (1965) or *Rockaby* (1980) do retain traces of, say, *Waiting for Godot* (1952) or *Krapp's Last Tape* (1958) in their formal repetitions and sudden stark echoes of a former life, even though their considerations of waiting, memory or the relationship between self and other are Chinese whispered beyond any certain recognition. But despite the fact that aesthetic and affective concerns do reverberate across the *oeuvre*, albeit as diminuendos rather than the gatherings of a crescendo, there are none of the idiomatic old jokes that pepper *Murphy* and *Watt*, nor the failing banter and mistimed slapstick that offer a little local colour in *Godot* and *Endgame*. By returning to the comic moments that punctuate the periphery of the earlier work, however – the circular songs, the repetitive physical exchanges, the desublimating gags through which purposiveness or progress are reduced to fiasco – it becomes possible to notice correspondences between these tired clowning routines where narrative appears to be treading water and the diminishing verbal returns of *Come and Go* or the paced out and exhaustive oscillations of *Quad* (1981). And this chapter will argue that the profound structural stuttering or trembling of these flattened out dramaticules traces out, both in formal and in affective terms, something reminiscent of Beckett's earlier comedy, even though no jokes or slapstick remain. It will be suggested that Beckett's late, attenuated comedy is thus not a marginal effect or simply a way of passing the time; rather, because the failing joke or flailing slapstick produces habits by inaugurating a particular way of passing the time in which a formalism is forced into unexpected commerce with twinges of affect, the barely there trace of the comic offers a way of teasing out the recurrent aesthetic and ethical obligations that punctuate the late plays. If these works represent Beckett's most occult and yet, paradoxically, his most explicit rendering of the way life goes on when all going on is purposeless, then, as the very early 'Whoroscope Notebook' insists, perhaps 'life is a Joe Miller', and the old joke that is on the turn has much to tell us (1930s: 20).[1]

Limping Gags

So it is useful to explore some of these comic moments in the earlier work before moving on to those later plays that seem so suggestively to echo them. In *Waiting for Godot*, Vladimir remarks that 'time flies when one has fun' (*CDW*: 71); nevertheless, it is clear that even this most amusing of Beckett's plays, the one that most approximates the leisurely enjoyments of a pastime, offers itself up as fun only sporadically. The guttering comedy that appears in the songs about dogs, the games with hats and the exchanges of insults certainly passes the time, but time never really seems to fly. Grounded before it could soar through the interminable turbulences of duration, the humour in *Godot* is, instead, kept taxiing on the runway, subject to an endless gathering in which time trundles on according to its own recalcitrant rhythm of elapse. Time passes, but '[i]t would have passed in any case' (46). Yet if humour supposedly performs operations upon time, if it congeals time into a solid shape that can be skated over speedily, then the humour within this play most commonly describes another sense of time that is drawn out and ductile – time as the passivity of waiting and of incapable endurance. And although the gag may offer momentary relief, 'a little canter' (60), it is equally as likely to be 'awful', 'worse than the pantomime' (34). These gags – the hat games, dances, kicks and falls – do, at times, function as hiccups in the time of waiting, small gatherings that allow a minor relief from time's distended elapse. But because the gags seem to be subject to a decline in that they either go on too long or never really get going at all, there is also a sense in which they too, like everything else in the play, describe the slow and arduous passage of time rather than its flight. Tainted over and by time, the incongruities and running gags may be funny, but this comedy already seems a little past its sell by date, or on the turn, as it were. And comedy that is going off, slapstick that doesn't really work, comes, like a slow hand clap, to beat out elapse rather than contract it; it becomes a form of walking on the spot in which waiting is first sloughed off, then measured and finally increased.

Now the comedy of the early plays seems, at first glance, a rather simpler affair than the fading forms of the late prose; as has often been noted, it places itself within a popular and recognisable comic tradition of vaudeville performance and circus clowning.[2] But these are wearied and wearying performances in which the scenarios and props of the circus and the music hall remain but much of the conventional trajectory of the vaudeville act or the circus bill is subject to interference. Robert Knopff has suggested that the shape of the vaudeville bill and the acts within it is that of a 'rising curve' in which the scale and pace of the gags are accelerated (1999: 50); but if this is so, then the very sections of Beckett's plays that, for an audience, most approximate vaudeville, end up least approximating the prized achievement of 'variety', as gags seem to be set up, but are then subject to deflation and collapse before the masterful 'topper' can be reached. In *Rough for Theatre II*, from the late 1950s, the two bureaucrats who are settling the account of a poten-tial suicide's life are subjected to the capriciousness of an unreasonably potent material world as desk lights flash on and off according to their own frustratingly comic logic. But this is a running gag that refuses to go the distance; indeed, by the time the centre of the play has been reached, B blankly asserts: 'This gag has gone on long enough for me' (*CDW*: 244). Similarly, in *Act Without Words II* (1958), the props of a music hall comedy routine appear, but here the vaudeville crook has been transformed into a goad. Rather than humorously disciplining the failing comic, it prods and forces a sack and the man contained within it, demanding and momentarily producing a vigorous, well-performed, comic mime of routine daily mundanities. The goad renders explicit the latent disciplinary violence within the vaudeville crook by becoming sinister, threatening, possibly even torturous. It ruins the comic spectacle with its inhuman, mechanical insistence, and the figure in the sack finally remains still as he is poked, refusing to repeat his humorous mime. The anticipated 'finish' to this vaudeville act becomes the dissolution of its humour and the man's refusal to keep playing his part in the comic spectacle.

In *Endgame*, too, the props of the circus or vaudeville remain, although they become monstrously unwieldy as tools for manipulation within a standard comic routine. The performing dog is of the three-leg-ged stuffed variety, the very antithesis of a dog capable of tricks (*CDW*: 111); the only miraculous circus trick the invisible flea found by Clov is

capable of performing is the blackly comic possibility of a second genesis
(108); and perhaps most strikingly, although the story the audience is
called on to imagine of the crashing tandem bicycle has the formal elements of a pratfall (and Nagg and Nell do indeed laugh), instead of displaying comic resilience to injury, as a circus clown might, the amorous
couple lose their 'shanks' (100). Of *Happy Days* (1960), Beckett wrote
that '[w]hat should characterise whole scene, sky and earth, is a pathetic
unsuccessful realism, the kind of tawdriness you get in 3rd rate musical
or pantomime, *that* quality of *pompier*, laughably earnest bad imitation'
(Harmon 1998: 94). But Willie, who is first dressed up like a seaside
postcard and then a beau or even a villain from the music hall, eschews
any of these recognisable comic roles as he crawls from his hole '[*dressed
to kill*]' (166) and attempts to scale the mound.

Perhaps, though, there is one scene in *Waiting for Godot* that, above
all others, most approximates the vaudeville gag. Vladimir sees Lucky's
hat – the hat that has previously elicited its owner's pseudo-scholasticism
– but where the hat is a catalyst for speaking for Lucky, for Vladimir
it becomes a prop that facilitates the appearance of physical comedy.
Vladimir's hat 'irk[s]' him, so he puts on Lucky's while asking Estragon
to hold his. Estragon then puts on Vladimir's hat in place of his own
hat that he hands to Vladimir. Vladimir puts on Estragon's hat in the
place of Lucky's which he hands to Estragon. And so on. The sequence
ends when, finally, Vladimir keeps Lucky's hat and Estragon keeps his
own, so that the only hat involved in the exchange between the two is
Vladimir's (*CDW*: 67). This scene is comic: that much would appear
to be certain. There is an obvious correspondence with the vaudeville
routines which comedians of silent and early sound cinema drew so
much of their material. When the music-hall veteran Max Wall played
Vladimir at the Royal Exchange Theatre in 1980, he recognised the
familiar gag and enjoyed bringing to the routine other honed techniques
such as rolling the hats down his arm (Worth 1999: 68). Knowlson also
notes that 'this hat-swapping sequence is the standard "three hats for
two heads" music-hall or circus routine as used, for example, by the
Marx Brothers in their film *Duck Soup* [(1933)]' (1993: 15). He tells
us that '[i]t is known that Beckett saw this film' (15). The similarities
between the two scenes are indeed compelling, but the differences are
just as instructive.

In both scenes, much of the humour resides in the unexpected and
incongruous nature of the action. There is an absurd visual violation
of the norms of behaviour, as the relatively simple action of placing the
correct hat on the correct head becomes farcically complicated. Freud
offers an explanation of why such 'extravagant and inexpedient' clown-

ing movements might elicit humour. An observer laughs because, in comparison with the amount of energy the observer imagines he or she would have expended in the clown's place, the 'clown's' expenditure 'is too large' (Freud 1976b: 249). For Bergson, though, physical gags that present quickened, exaggerated movements are comic because flailing corporeality begins to resemble a puppet or an automaton. The mechanically repeating body appears to be cut off from the flux and flow of life, where life is 'evolution in time and complexity in space' (1911b: 88) and, as we have seen, this defection from lived time must be marked and policed through laughter. In a hat gag the swapping of hats will probably not be amusing the first time, nor perhaps even the second, as both events could be figured as a rational move within the narrative. It is only as the movements become part of a speedily repetitive series that the routine relinquishes its narrative purpose, however tenuous, and becomes an exaggerated form, or a 'pure' gag.[3] Indeed, if the comedy of this kind of slapstick exchange lies within formal spatial incongruities, what Beckett referred to as the 'grotesque' 'disparity of size' between the hats (Knowlson 1993: 65) and the obtuse recalcitrance of the physical world, it also lies, more significantly, in the timing of the routine and the acceleration of its tempo.

As Bergson notes, a slapstick routine will invariably be played out in 'a uniformly accelerated rhythm, visibly intent upon affecting a *crescendo*' (1911b: 58), for a decelerated, ponderous movement of hats will likely appear intended, carefully composed and therefore unfunny in this particular context. The visual comic effect is produced because the players involved in this speeding exchange of percussion and concussion no longer appear as 'men of flesh and blood like ourselves', in Bergson's terms; instead, they begin to take on the appearance of 'large rubber balls hurled against one another in every direction' (1911b: 59). For the creation of a gag, then, a certain intrinsic speed is necessary; and indeed, in the revised text for the Schiller-Theater production of *Godot* in Berlin Beckett suggests that the whole hat exchange must be 'rapid and uninterrupted' (Knowlson 1996: 65). Revealingly, within silent film the required acceleration of a gag was often produced in the medium itself. Charlie Chaplin, for instance, would give instructions that at particular comic moments in his films the camera should be 'undercranked'. As the film speed was reduced from twenty-four frames per second to eighteen or sixteen, screen movement was sped up and a comic effect would ensue (McCabe 1978: 170). Extravagance and the simulation of mechanisation – the catalysts for the comic for Bergson – are only emphasised and increased by the quickened tempo of the gag's unrolling.

Now although *Godot* and *Duck Soup* both present rapid and accelerating hat routines, there are some significant differences between these two gags. In *Duck Soup*, there are three characters involved in the exchange of hats rather than two: Harpo, Chico and a stooge or a straight man. Harpo initiates the hat exchange by mixing up his hat with the barrow owner's. Harpo then kicks the stooge's hat to Chico, thus bringing his brother's trademark hat into the routine. All three hats are now rotating, but it is clear that Chico and Harpo are in control of the gag and in powerful sympathy with the suddenly illogically potent material world. Harpo is even able to bounce a hat on a string as if it were a yoyo. The comic incongruity of the scene is intensified, however, by the contrast with the straight man's frustration and impotence in the face of Harpo's mute sheepishness and both brothers' ability to control and create extravagant incompetence. The tempo of the scene is, unsurprisingly, visibly intent upon a crescendo, but, unlike Beckett's gag, the routine is not 'uninterrupted'; instead, the general trajectory of delivery is one of acceleration, but the players offer the audience a little respite from this incremental rhythm – moments of stillness to mark the contrast between the straight man's sensible frustration and Harpo's oscillation between mute naivety and the face-pulling of a knowing trickster. By interrupting the unrolling of the running gag, the Marx brothers offer time and space for comic incongruity to be marked as such and for audience laughter to resound. This is a good and effective gag, then, because its comic tremors are profoundly annunciatory, like the coiled crescendo of wriggling in a cat's hind-quarters as it gathers itself to pounce upon its prey. Their hat routine is an old gag, but nevertheless a good one, because it races towards its physical punchlines – offering a short cut to the pleasure that pleats or folds the experience of duration.

In Beckett's hat gag, however, there is no stooge to mark comic incongruity or to interrupt the rapid unrolling of the gag form; there is no contrast to the poker-faced duo that might mark their lack of frustration as comically inappropriate. Similarly, just as there is no straight man to represent the norms of behaviour that the gag is overturning, neither Vladimir nor Estragon display frustration at the stubbornly resistant object world or at being subordinated to the functioning of the gagging mechanism. They seem to be puppets controlled by gag rather than agents within the comic scene, but neither seems to find or mark the situation out as aberrant or surprising. In his production notes, Beckett makes no mention of expressions, of displays of frustration or of knowing glances to be shot between the players or at the audience, which might mark the skill of the comic performance. Instead, once the gag gets going, the whole exchange is, almost without fail, played as

Beckett stated it must be: 'rapid and uninterrupted'. Where the Marx Brothers build in moments of stillness into the crescendo of the running gag, moments where the grimaces of the stooge or their own knowing expressions mark out the previous action as aberrant to the audience, there is no time for a physical punchline here. As a speedily repetitive series, delivered deadpan, this limping gag seems to be moving but not advancing, marching on the spot rather than running.[4] Repeated without a display of frustration, the gag begins to go off somewhat – becoming a quivering without the climactic event or certain release of comic pleasure that such trembling portends.

As Beckett's hat gag begins to stutter, it becomes stuck in a groove of compulsive repetition in which abstract form is intensified and affect subject to an unpredictable flaring. In 'The Exhausted', Deleuze defines such moments in Beckett's work as ritornellos, although he makes no mention of their comic possibilities. Eliding the distinction between the verbal and the visual, for Deleuze the repeating series of the frog chorus in *Watt*, a patch of starry sky that comes and goes in *First Love*, the trembling rocking chair in *Murphy*, Watt's walk or the exhaustive pacings of *Quad* are all ritornellos because of the 'internal tension' within their formal movements or relationships – their mobilisation of forces into an exhaustive and exhausting form (Deleuze 1998: 159, 161, 162). Within the hat gag, as the rising excitement that could be created by increasing pace is slowly refused by the internal tension of the formal ritornello, as the routine's immanent speed is interrupted by the distended time of its unrolling, comic affect indeed flares up but it is subject to exhaustion – an unpredictable dampening down and fading out. As such, however, these repetitious and weakened gags begin to ask some vital questions of the relationship between form and affect: where are the points of inflection within such ritornellos or repeated series;[5] when and where in what appears to become a purely formal system might affect, sensation and intensity fade in and out for a perceiving audience?

As we have already seen in Chapter 2, if a gag hurries towards a finish, gathering and folding over time so that it seems to pass with increasing speed, then gags placed within a narrative seem to have the opposite effect, revealing another logic of recursion and delay. As Knopff notes, in silent comic films such as those of Buster Keaton or Laurel and Hardy, a gag very rarely advances a storyline or a narrative 'horizontally'; instead, 'the story seems to be treading water in one place as the gag transpires' (1999: 12), as the routine interrupts conventional narrative temporality with its own percussive and recursive logic. But if a gag represents a derailing of narrative by some (perhaps only seemingly) extempore play, the theatrical gag is also not entirely removed from an eighteenth- and nineteenth-century definition in which a gag is 'a "made-up" story; a piece of deception, an imposture, a lie' (*OED*) – a sense which is, in turn, related to the notion of forcibly inducing an audience to 'swallow' a story. For gagging indeed causes a hiccup within conventional theatrical narration, putting one over on an audience by disrupting their expectations and subjecting them to its own contradictory form and speed.

If a gag is denied its place within a broader comic narrative or 'variety bill' and its vertical accumulation of comic routines, however, if it becomes a singular event, the sense of running but not advancing in a paradoxical moment of agitated, active stillness increases. The inability to advance narrative and the emphasis upon formal circularity rather than the adumbration of content similarly grows as the laughter it elicits, the end point towards which the gag orients itself, becomes uncertain. The singular, deflated gag might still pucker or pleat time, but such a fold is no longer simply a short cut, a bridge that passes over a depression; rather, to be placed within that fold might be to be forced to take a detour. Instead of the seriousness of outright failure, or the paradoxical success of the comic gag marked as an expression of skill and dexterity, the display of minor, unmarked, fatigues eggs the audience on with the dangled reward of a graspable failure or satisfying punchline, while simultaneously goading them into giving up on those rewards that it seems will never arrive.

A comic scene from Beckett's *Film* (1963), starring Buster Keaton, illustrates something similar. O (Keaton, the object of perception) attempts to rid a room (his mother's?) of seeing eyes. First, O takes the dog to the door, puts it out and returns for the cat. As he picks up the cat and puts it outside the door, the dog comes back into the room. O then pick up the dog, puts it out, only for the cat to come back in again. And so on until O manages to achieve their final expulsion (Schneider 1972: 60). The relationship between this scene and a vaudeville gag is clear; as Alan Schneider, the director of *Film*, points out, it was 'Sam's feeling that the film should possess a slightly stylised comic reality akin to that of a silent movie' (1972: 68). Keaton was chosen because Chaplin was unavailable, but Keaton had problems with the film from the start. Although Beckett determined '[c]limate of film comic and unreal. O should invite laughter throughout by his way of moving . . . He *storms* along in *comic foundered precipitancy*' (Harmon 1998: 168), Keaton was worried about *Film*'s comedy. As Schneider recalls, Keaton made no effort to disguise the fact that the film not only baffled him, he found it unfunny. He suggested a special walk or a pencil-sharpening gag (all of which Schneider and Beckett rejected) and asserted that only the 'cat and dog business . . . wasn't too bad' (Schneider 1972: 68). Although Beckett's production notes mark the cat and dog scene out as a 'foolish suggestion' (Schneider 1972: 60), it is clear that it was supposed to be a gag; indeed, Beckett even considered an animated version of the scene, although he finally rejected this on formal grounds (Gontarski 1985: 108). But although Schneider notes that Keaton was 'in his element' when filming the scene – '[t]his was straight slapstick, a running gag, the little man versus the mutely mocking world' (81) – Beckett was unhappy: 'Because I don't feel the animal gag at all funny, I find it too long' (quoted in Gontarski 1985: 145).

Certainly, Beckett is right that the gag feels as though it is taking its time, just as when *Godot's* hat gag begins to stutter – as though stuck in a groove – duration is drawn out rather than contracted. If the performer's reaction is the punchline to a physical gag – be it one of frustration as exemplified by Oliver Hardy or the flatly incongruous 'great stone face' displayed by all Keaton's characters when confronted by malevolent objects or hysterical humans – Beckett's *Film* undermines this comic potential by cutting away from that reaction, by closing down the space and time for the incongruities of the gag to be marked as such. As Knopff, who is writing on Keaton rather than Beckett, puts it: 'Schneider literally cuts the gag out from under Keaton by cutting on the take instead of a moment after it, limiting the shot to a split-second view of O's back' (1999: 145). The gag feels too long because it is actually too short; because there are no shots of the 'great stone face', the gag is missing 'three seconds of vintage Buster takes' (Knopff 1999: 146). Within the hat routine, as the rising excitement that could be created by the vertical accumulation of the running gag is slowly refused by the internal tension of the form, or the persistent pace of its unrolling, comic affect flares up as formal incongruity is intensified, but it is subject to an unpredictable dampening down and fading out as the gag falls short of its physical punchline. Laughter occurs momentarily but cannot be retained: it does not resound – it cannot and does not ring out.

It is strange, though, that Beckett should have been surprised by the fact that the cat and dog gag is not securely funny; it is strange that he, the supposed master-creator of scenes or interminable waiting, should have felt that the whole business was going on too long. For, as we have seen, even within Beckett's earlier work, the straight gag that would make time fly rarely appears. Of course, in most comic scenarios, things are usually 'arsy-versy' (*CDW*: 191) – getting a gag right is a way of getting things rightly wrong. But in the fading out of comic certainty within these shaky gags, defections from good sense and corporeal capability are not simply represented as a form of comic mastery over the materially recalcitrant world by the skill of the performance or the meticulous timing of clowning. Beckett's comic fiascos – the mistimed jokes, the gags that might be too long or too short, the comic scenes that never present their punchlines or present nothing else – are indeed punctured and interrupted by a less recuperable kind of failure and an increasing uncertainty as to whether an attenuated form of comic mastery is taking place or whether all mastery is subject to an evacuation. And as form shudders into the production of 'meta-feelings' or uncertain affect, it becomes ever harder to know whether these scenes are experienced as securely funny, or whether more affectively indeterminate feelings of boredom or anxiety begin to infect the scene, pushing comedy towards a place of quivering uncertainty.

Deadpan Demands

Gags, of course, are not the main locus of the comic in *Godot*; rather, the hat game is a sideshow that passes the time while showing how the time interminably passes. The most easily definable comic instants occur instead within the dialogue – the misplaced intellectual antics, the tenaciously misguided bombast and the acutely aimed and deftly timed strokes of verbal violence – although the effect of such dialogue is not altogether antithetical to those moments of uncertain stillness where narrative appears to be walking on the spot. Within the later plays such as *Footfalls*, *Rockaby*, *What Where*, *Come and Go* and *Quad*, however, comedy becomes uncertain to the degree that it becomes difficult to tell whether it is there at all. Clearly there are no recognisable gags left that fall into a vaudeville or clowning tradition. And yet, a trace of the formal structure of the mistimed, exhausting, gag does seem to remain in the smooth and rhythmic oscillations of *Rockaby* and *Footfalls*, or in the peculiarly clown-like obsession with entrances and exits that persists within *Quad* and *Come and Go*. If these late works are reifications of the attenuation of time and of a life that resists its own end, then the formal oscillations that remain might be usefully thought through the figure of the singular, limping gag – a form that is going somewhere and going nowhere coextensively.

Come and Go, written in 1965 and first performed in German in 1966, is described by action and dialogue that has been dramatically minimised. Little overt humour persists, with textual events reduced to a simple formal oscillation, to coming and going. The scene begins with three women sat on a bench – Flo, Vi and Ru who are as abbreviated as their names but 'as alike as possible' (*CDW*: 356). As one gets up and leaves, the other two discuss her fate in faint, muted tones:

FLO: Ru.
RU: Yes.
FLO: What do you think of Vi?
RU: I see little change. [*Flo moves to the centre seat, whispers in Ru's ear. Appalled.*] Oh! [*They look at each other. Flo puts her finger to her lips.*] Does she not realize?
FLO: God grant not.

(354)

Vi then returns to the scene, assumes her place and Flo exits. As Flo leaves the stage space, her fate is whispered between the remaining two, just as Vi's was, in voices '[a]s low as compatible with audibility' (356). The third cycle is played out as Ru leaves the bench and Vi tells, in hushed tones, the news of the impending catastrophe (is it Ru's death?) to Flo. Just as action and dialogue are dampened down, the scene is similarly voided of expressive sound, light or colour, save for the dull violet, dull red and dull yellow of the coats that almost distinguishes the characters, and the startled 'ohs' ('[t]hree very different sounds' (356)) which punctuate the otherwise drab dialogue. Beckett indeed insists in a letter to Schneider that he sees '*Come & Go* [as] very formal. Strictly identical attitudes & movements. The getting up, going, return, sitting, whispered confidence, shocked reaction (sole colour), finger to lips, etc. the same for all 3' (Harmon 1998: 417). Even the stage space is desiccated and denuded of depth. The women sit '[v]ery erect' (354) within a lit area that is narrow and restricting; 'just long enough to accommodate three figures almost touching', but not deep enough for it to be 'clear what they are sitting on' (Harmon 1998: 356), Beckett determines.

There is, however, some evidence to suggest that Beckett was toying with more obviously comic elements for *Come and Go*. At first, he considered calling the play 'Good Heavens' – a sardonic little pun for a play that ostensibly concerns the terminal illness of its three protagonists (1964: 7/16/4). 'Good Heavens' has episodes of dialogue that are informal, conversational even, and a later version of the play includes a character performing a comically inappropriate reading from what seems to be a bad romantic novel – a novel slipping into farce:

POPPY: – reading 'A last maddening kiss & she [word obscured] herself from his knees and disappeared into the bedroom. Aubrey stretched out to the flames his long hairy legs, took a sip of his brandy, relit his cigar and resumed alone the collection of obscene postcards.'
VIOLA: Are his trousers off already then?

(1964: 7/16/5)

By the time the final version of *Come and Go* appears, however, most elements of farce have disappeared. Heaven is anything but good and redemption is never implied; rather, the figures circle one another in an anti-clockwise direction that reminds Keir Elam of an infernal or at least a purgatorial movement (1994: 149).

'Farce' derives etymologically from the French 'farcir', 'to stuff', with the word used metaphorically to describe 'comic interludes "stuffed" into the texts of religious plays' (*OED*). Suggestively like the 'gag', then, farce implies an interruption of conventional narrative patterning. But if *Come and Go* bears an occulted resemblance to farce, it is not as an interruption; instead, the prerequisite pointless complications of concealment and revelation, the deftly timed mistimings that mean that each character misses the whispering of her own fate, and the convoluted impasse between the desire for revelation and its prohibition that drives the action onwards, are moved sufficiently centre stage that it is hard to register them as interruptions at all. Farce typically involves minimal characterisation and relies instead upon the accretive absurdity of its action; reduced to its most basic elements, however, farce is simply a process of coming and going which creates a series of formal incongruities. Coming and going are not unmotivated actions, though; rather, they are the inevitable results of the oscillation between desire and prohibition, be it sexual or material. And within a conventional farce form, this coming and going usually gathers pace. Entrances and exits are shrewdly timed and the trajectory towards a comic finish is clear to the audience who has caught a glimpse of the totality of the plot in all its preposterous complexity. Farce rushes onwards in a crescendo, tripping over itself yet explicitly showing its plot threads to the audience, purposelessly tying those strands into a knot that will finally be loosened as good sense is restored at the end of the play. Although it is exaggeratedly purposeless, then, farce creates the semblance of clear intention by rushing towards its humorous denouement.

Both speed and revelation are dramatically minimised in *Come and Go*, however. Beckett removes the suggestion of a shared sexual secret that appears in one of the drafts (Poppy whispers to Vi, eliciting the response 'Heavens! The croquet champion!') (1964: 7/16/5), and exits and entrances are described as 'slow, without the sound of feet' (*CDW*: 357) as the characters skirt around the occluded centre of the play. Such soundless slowing interrupts the purposive purposelessness of farce and the transparent depth usually demanded of fourth wall drama. Revelation to both characters and audience is indeed partial and contingent, confined within the tightly intertwined chiasmus of self and other that is the final scene of the play. Although a small stagger of the humour of incongruity remains in the syncopations of tone and register – the horrified 'ohs' that pierce the smooth surface of the dialogue – these effects are clearly on the wane as they are replaced by increasingly formalised images, dialogue and action. It certainly seems as if Beckett's late plays are increasingly flattened and spatialised, as though the element of time, upon which the comic depends, is being squeezed out of the frame. Whether gesturing towards an exclamation or a grudging pun, 'Good Heavens' is decelerating, reducing itself to the degree that it is little more than a residual oscillation that plays with an almost abstract incongruity within a flattened space – a simple coming and going that traces out an aesthetic of the deadpan.

Later versions of earlier works bear witness to a suggestively similar movement. Beckett's production notebook for the Schiller-Theater's 1974 version of *Godot* indeed betrays an increased emphasis upon spatial organisation, an emphasis to to be achieved at the expense of the sensation of the slow change through time that might occur between the acts.[6] In his notebook, Beckett traced through various elements of the experience and dialogue of Vladimir and Estragon such as 'Doubts confusions', 'Help', 'Sky', 'Sleep', 'Divisions', to facilitate the achievement of symmetrical patterning; he also drew complex diagrams to indicate the importance of the spatial organisation of the stage image. The San Quentin production of *Godot* also displayed an increased attentiveness to the seriousness of formal symmetry, with gags largely reduced to what Beckett called a few exhausted 'wriggles' (Knowlson 1993: xxii). Such a reduction is echoed in *Krapp's Last Tape*, for although the play text suggests a 'purple nose' for Krapp (*CDW*: 215) that emphasises the 'colour' of a comic scene, the nose was minimised in the first Royal Court performance in 1958 and Beckett later removed this clownish element from the productions of the play with which he was associated. Knowlson indeed notes that in the 1969 Schiller-Theater production, Beckett was 'extremely wary of overstressing the clownish elements in Krapp's physique, dress and behaviour': 'elements of Krapp's costume that recall the circus clown or music-hall comic were deleted: trousers too short for him, large white boots and capacious pockets in his waistcoat' (1992: xvi). The first clownish routine of slipping on a banana skin remained, but in this revised version, the second time the banana skin appears, Krapp throws it away before it can assume its role in a pratfall (Knowlson 1992: xv).

This reduction of humorous possibilities is also echoed in the texts of the late plays and their production notebooks, as Beckett recurrently demonstrates a concern with spatial relationships and symmetries over obvious comic elements. In *Come and Go* and even *Footfalls*, the action of the play is indeed reducible to a deadpan diagram or a repeating mathematical series, reminiscent of the 'J. M. Mime' sketch conceived for Jack McGowran, written as diagram, mathematical solution and error, and abandoned just before *Come and Go* was started. Consequently, the movement towards an expressionless surface in *Come and Go* should not be considered an aberration; rather, it is a version of the smooth, bleached aesthetic that extenuates all the late work and has its apotheosis in the television play *Ghost Trio* (written in 1975).

In *Ghost Trio* there is the now recognisable attempt to denude the text of easily determinable affect, despite the melodramatic or even sentimental subtext of a man waiting for a woman who does not and will not appear. As with 'Good Heavens', the working title of the play was moderated from 'Tryst' (Maude 2009: 120) to intensify the sense of colourless abstraction. For there will be '[n]o shadow. Colour: none. All grey. Shades of grey' (*CDW*: 408), the unpuckered descriptive voice 'will not be raised or lowered, whatever happens' (408), and the strongest injunction in the play is to '[k]eep that sound down' (408). The stage space (chamber, wall, door, window) and props (pallet, pillow, cassette) are similarly denuded of depth and volume – described simply as 'smooth grey rectangle[s]' (408–9). Once again, ill-seeing becomes a central concern as these are blank surfaces that repel the eye that searches for interest or depth within the scene. Even the window is only an '[o]paque sheet of glass' (408)), just as eyes themselves, when they appear in the late fiction, become engulfing and blank surfaces at the limit of dilation rather than apertures. In a move that is without an equivalent in Beckett's *oeuvre*, the eye is momentarily offered a view of the scene as a mock-up seen from above. The arrangement of rectangles, in variously muted shades of grey within the surrounding rectangle of the room, eschews any perception of depth and, like a minimalist painting, refuses the figurative and its ocular illusions of perspective, volume and tonal recession. The lighting, described as 'faint, omnipresent. No visible source' (408), also declines the potential depth to be achieved through visibility, occluding the possibility of contrasts and of hollowing out concave and convex spaces, emphasising instead the restricted depth of field of the television image. *Ghost Trio* thus describes that exhaustively flattened aesthetic noted by Deleuze: 'the whispering voice has become neutral, blank, without intentions, without resonance, and the space has become an any-space-whatever, without depth and with no underside [there is no space under the pallet], having no objects but its own parts. This is the final step of depotentialization' (Deleuze 1998: 167).

The quality of image offered by television is, of course, consonant with a more generalised compulsion to submit to an aesthetic of flatness in the late work. In *Worstward Ho*, for example, all is similarly smooth and dim. But if the text describes the paradoxical compulsion to achieve absolute negation through expression, there is a linked need to grub up and turn over any hidden presence in order to achieve a final voiding. The suspicion remains that the nothing will be all the more complete if it can be measured against a posited presence: words are thus said, missaid and unsaid rather than simply not said at all, while sly shades of presence – figures, bones, grots and, most strikingly, 'a pipe . . . A Tube. Sealed' (113) – are secreted into the 'void'. The pipe becomes a momentary flaw in this text, but by introducing difference, it offers a way of perceiving and measuring the quality of the scene's compulsive and subsequent extension. Space is folded, perhaps even syncopated, by the temporal interruptions of narrative. Of course, the wrinkle in the void is then extended, pressed out, for 'in that pipe or tube that selfsame dim. Old dim. When ever what else?' (113). Its appearance and subsequent disappearance remains in the service of the more powerful demand that the surface of the void should remain undisturbed.

In *Ghost Trio*, the sense of an inexpressive surface is similarly intensified by the complications introduced into the scene: the crescendo and decrescendo of the Largo from Beethoven's Fifth Piano Trio; the fleeting perception that the figure 'hears her' (*CDW*: 410); his movement as he gets up and looks out of the chamber; V's surprised 'Ah!' after she had insisted that her voice would not be 'raised or lowered' (412); the cut to a view of a long, deep corridor (a pipe in the void?); the faint sounds of rain, of a door opening and of knocking; and the appearance of a boy in the corridor who shakes his head. Although these elements are aborted as part of the text's asymptotic approach towards a comprehensively stilled surface, nothing remains quite as flat or still as it first appears. Even the blank rectangles of the window and door are described with an attention to their imminent potential to disrupt the flattened surface: they are, ironically, '[i]mperceptibly ajar' (408), introducing an infinitesimal depth into the space – a depth that is paradoxically both measurable and 'imperceptible' – and a wrinkle of temporal asynchronicity. The door may not yet be perceptible as ajar; nevertheless, measure – of both the human eye and narrating voice – might one day allow it to be seen as such.

Now the window and door that are '[i]mperceptibly ajar' sound like elements of a hoary joke that was maybe once a good one;[7] more significantly, however, as with the early limping gags, there is something exorbitant and exaggerated, pointless even, about this obsessed return to a measurably flat and inexpressive scene littered with unexpected topographical features. The narrator of *Ghost Trio* is certainly not beyond a little joke along these lines. Where depth has been devoured by the flattening eye of the television camera under the exhausting control of the female voice, V suddenly worries, in a deadpan way, that her controlling commentary is excessive: 'Forgive my stating the obvious' (*CDW*: 408), she states, obviously. One wonders how 'stating the obvious' is any more excessive or comically inappropriate than the camera that meticulously renders all space clear, extended or obvious, in a word? The window and door thus materialise the contradictory aesthetic demand that all should be extended but that such extension should be quantifiable, and the comic offers a wrinkle in the scene, a tiny temporal deflection, which functions as a triangulation point from which to measure the play's flatland.

In *Come and Go* all is similarly approaching extenuation as light, colour and sound are dimmed and movement is reduced to a faint and final shimmering. In the last scene all three figures are seated, interlocking arms and holding hands in a chiasmus that extends itself as a reflective surface, like a dilating pupil, over the unuttered centre of the play. Whether this deadpan farce has overshot its 'wow finish' years ago, or whether any finish is still a lifetime away, this arrhythmia through which contradictory forces of push and pull, come and go, have shaken themselves into a flattened stillness creates a final enfolding rather than any denouement. But this metaphorical origami of theatrical space, reminiscent of the schoolgirl paper-folding and fortune-telling game in which complexity is made from one, carefully creased, piece of paper and girls pick a fold under which to peep, enables the unexpected perceptions of difference that allow the text to measure its extenuation without increasing depth. Despite the fact that all is inscribed upon one shimmering surface, each woman, still bound to her memories of 'the playground at Miss Wade's' (*CDW*: 354) and a kneading of a former time into the spatialised present, only has access to the fold that reveals the fortunes of the other two; absurdly, she has no knowledge of her own fate. The flattened aesthetic surface that remains is thus essentially smooth yet complex, punctuated with barely visible folds effected by the shaking force of coming and going, of extension and contraction.

If comedy is all in the timing rather than the spacing (a gag fallen completely flat is hardly a gag at all), the very fact that a minimal incongruity, a reduced comic depth, bleeds back into the flattened scenes of these late works indicates their inability finally to expel the element of time. For although they remain in thrall to a flattened, deadpan aesthetic, as in *Ill Seen Ill Said*, any such achievements must be compulsively charted and measured rather than simply accepted as present. As Molloy experiences with his sucking stones or Murphy does with his biscuits, it is not simply the case that there is pleasure to be gained from measure; instead, pleasure is precisely a way of enacting and enabling measure. Again, implicitly following the Freud of *Beyond the Pleasure Principle*, the late plays seem to intuit that wrinkles and folds implicated into the work as temporality and comic pleasure might bind and release energy in a way that would enable the sensation of an increasingly complete evacuation. Stillness and flatness might be experienced as all the more convincing after being caught in the ruckles and wrinkles of diversion. Never having quite finished with resounding, these oscillations, vibrations or variable interferences thus enable the momentarily achieved deadpan flatness of the end of a play like *Come and Go* to be charted or experienced as such. But if oscillations and vibrations always remain threateningly transmissible in the vibrantly still 'ringing' perceptible at the end of *Come and Go*, it becomes clear that a truly exhausted end has not been achieved. More comings and goings might yet echo, given time. Of course, it is not the characters who are given time here, as they seem unable to retain a past or predict a future in a way that would enable them to experience their repetitions as incongruities. These repeated oscillations do, however, create incongruities for an audience as they are stretched and repeated. And as these formal oscillations are experienced as and through a duration that can be measured, gathered up and experienced according to the affective forces of passing and evanescent pleasure, they begin to perform operations on lived time that make suggestive and strenuous demands on the observing subject.

Gravity and Levity

Many elements of *Come and Go* and the later *Quad* plays (1980–1) might seem incommensurable, but there is a way of viewing these plays as counterpoints to one another. *Come and Go* is an equally appropriate title for *Quad*, as action in both plays is reduced to the oscillation between entering and exiting as the figures rotate around each other. The square dramatic space of *Quad*, seen from slightly above, becomes as flattened and extenuated as that of the earlier work, for there are no points visible outside of what appears to be a two-dimensional quadrilateral hung in the void. Perhaps even the occluded centre of *Come and Go* (the character's knowledge of her own fate) is replicated in *Quad*, although here it is reified as a convulsive swerve in which the central point of the quincunx is compulsively avoided. There is, however, a strong difference in the way time is allowed to play with space in *Quad*. As with everything else in *Come and Go*, time seems caught in a repetitive loop: the women sit 'just as we used to' (*CDW*: 354), and the present, at least for the characters, seems simply a reverberation of a past event – a ringing both in time and in space. Within *Footfalls*, there is the same sense that May is caught in a loop – a loop transcribed both in a temporised space and spatialised time. 'Will you never have done? Will you never have done . . . revolving it all?' (400), the woman's voice asks M, the tattered figure caught in an almost endless purgatorial moment and movement. As Enoch Brater notes, 'time neither progresses nor stands still; like a "metronome", a word Beckett uses to describe walking in this play, time merely continues its rhythmic pacing' (1987: 54). Although there is no play of Beckett's in which the temporal loop is sealed into a pattern of absolute and eternal recurrence, in most of the late plays, any sense of temporal progression is profoundly abbreviated. Time has lost any strong sense of periodicity, as though, as the narrator of one of the *Texts for Nothing* puts it, 'time has turned into space and there will be no more time, till I get out of here' (*CSP*: 132).

Quad is different, though. Space is still closed but time now appears to be open – subject to progression. *Quad* was written in 1980 but it was directed, altered and extended (by adding a second part) by Beckett for the German TV company Süddeutscher Rundfunk in Stuttgart in 1981. *Quadrat I* seems unusually fast, noisy and colourful; *Quadrat II*, however, returns to a more familiar aesthetic surface. 'Yes, marvellous', Beckett was to note, after seeing the colour print of *Quadrat I* on a black-and-white monitor, 'it's 100,000 years later' (Brater 1987: 109). The actors were called back for another shoot; this time, though, the footage was printed in black and white, and *Quadrat II* thus has 'no colour, all four in identical white gowns, footsteps only sound, slow tempo, series 1 only' (*CDW*: 454). There is an implied entropic decline within the repeating series, then, as if the intrinsic motor energy within these figures is winding down. Perhaps it is, as Beckett imagined in his early handwritten draft of the play before the second diminished sequence had been added, as if '[a]n eye suddenly opens, suddenly shuts (can't bear any more)' (Beckett 1980). As a 'quadrat' is 'each of a number of small areas of habitat, typically of one square metre, selected at random to act as samples for assessing the local distribution of plants or animals' (*OED*), the plays indeed seem to offer mere snapshots from a sequence in which time is not looped but extenuates itself, perhaps out into geological tracts.

Now many critics have noted that *Quad* has some potential for comedy, although it hardly produces a sustained effect of amusement.

Mary Bryden suggests that 'amusement gives way to grim concentration and finally hapless resignation' (1995: 110), while Gontarski asserts that although the 'action at first has comic potential . . . [in its] rush toward an apparent collision', the obsessive repetition of the pattern 'shatters whatever comic possibilities were established early on. The final effect is of determined, enforced motion' (1985: 180). They imply that comedy seems to be exhausted by an unending repetition through time. Curiously, though, gags and physical slapstick are usually comic precisely because they are repetitious, and Beckett indeed notes in *Proust* that 'vaudeville . . . inaugurates the comedy of an exhaustive enumeration' (1999: 92). Gontarski is right to assert that *Quad* is as alarming or as pathetic as it is funny, but the basic formal movements of four hooded figures automatically and unconsciously pursuing a course that describes the limits of a square retain suggestive traces of clowning that severely complicate the putative disappearance of comedy. *Quad* may indeed become a pure 'motor ritornello' (Deleuze 1998: 161) that exhausts the possibilities of a tightly defined space and confined image, but this form still suggestively echoes the stutters that punctuate Beckett's earlier work as gagging slapstick.

Within *Quad*, all the world is the stage, a blank plane within that other flattened two-dimensional space of a television aesthetic, although these four players no longer have parts to play; as in clowning all has become secondary to entrances and exits. But as the hooded figures shuttle on and off stage, describing the perimeter and the diagonals of the square as they purposefully shuffle down two sides and into its centre, each player, with a sharp and unexpected deflection or turn, obsessively avoids the central point and the other figures that speedily and incautiously approach it. And there is a minimal comic instant as the centre, the 'Abgrund' or abyss, as Beckett called it (Hiebel 1995: 339), is avoided with the paced out equivalent of an involuntary tic. The figures appear to be tramping with excruciating purposiveness in one direction; however, at the final moment they swerve seemingly involuntarily and are drawn offstage to the beat of a similar mechanical, maniacal rhythm.

Of course, in vaudeville gags as the audience begins to anticipate an identical frightened reaction at the centre, it can become comic that 'these figures continually *forget* [about the centre], like stupid animals unconscious of their movements' (Hiebel 1995: 339). They neither choose their route nor recognise one another, making way for other subjects; it is the centre rather than the other players they instinctually avoid. 'Should solo player avoid E? Yes if centre dramatized tabou [taboo] – this rather than avoidance of collision', Beckett affirms in a draft of the play (Beckett: 1980). But, as almost all the critics note, that comedy of forgetting soon shears away for the audience. As though they are deprived of almost all of their own intention, the figures become little more than genderless puppets, pulled into the centre and pushed out into the black by a rhythmically inverting oscillation of forces, and despite what Bergson seems to suggest, there is little funniness to be sustained from repetitions that maintain an absolute, fully mechanical constancy.

Although Bergson suggests that the 'attitudes, gestures and movements of the human body are laughable in exact proportion as that body reminds us of a mere machine' or 'a jointed puppet' (1911b: 29, 30), it is clearly Cartesian thought that provides the terms for his analysis. Descartes asserts that the body can be thought of as 'a statue or a machine made of earth' in which functions and movements are logically ordered to 'follow from the mere arrangement of the machine's organs every bit as naturally as the movements of a clock or other automaton from the arrangement of its counter-weights or wheels' (1985c: 99, 108). Cartesian dualism thus determines that 'the soul by which I am what I am – is entirely distinct from the body . . . and would not fail to be whatever it is, even if the body did not exist' (Descartes 1985b: 127). Of course, the body, for Descartes, should not have a disjointed relationship with the mind. It is figured as a knot of nerve fibres attached to the brain wherein the instinctual 'animal spirits' and 'the soul' are located. And as these spirits and the soul stir and are modulated by the brain, they are directed through the nerves and into the muscles, 'just as when you pull the end of a string, you cause a bell hanging at the other end to ring' (1985c: 101). The body is thus modelled as a perfectly worked puppet with strings held on the inside.

Many early critical readings of Beckett's texts noticed what seemed to be their parodic Cartesianism,[8] and perhaps the clearest example of a playing with the discontinuities within Cartesian dualism is the joking kick that Murphy experiences in the 'correlated modes of consciousness and extension, the kick *in intellectu* and the kick *in re*' (Beckett 1993: 64). But if the early work resonates obviously with Cartesian discourses and concerns, even in a late play like *Quad*, the non sequiturs of dualism are never quite stilled. For the quincunx is a parody of an ordered, geometrically explicable Cartesian space, mapped in reference to the thinking subject. As Tom Conley notes, Cartesian geography

> resembles the order and process of the *quincunx*, a two-dimensional system of gridding and squaring that places a center (the ego) at the intersection of the diagonals of a surrounding square. When the self moves into space, it transforms one of the corners of the square or rectangle of its periphery into the site of a new center, around which new extremities are established, and so forth, until space is conquered. (1993: xvii)

In *Quad*'s quincunx, however, there is no thinking self that can inhabit the centre; there is no describing and ordering of this space. The hooded figures shuttling to and fro are similarly almost parodic of the famous thought experiment in the Second Meditation:

> If I look out of the window and see men crossing the square, as I just happen to have done, I normally say that I see the men themselves . . . Yet do I see any more than hats and coats which could conceal automatons? I *judge* that they are men. And so something which I thought I was seeing with my eyes is in fact grasped solely by the faculty of judgement which is my mind. (Descartes 1985a: 21)

Watching *Quad*, though, it is perhaps not so easy to judge, against empirical evidence, that these figures are men (or women) rather than automata.

For Bergson, there is an implicit Cartesianism at work in the human imagination that sees dualism in every human form: a 'soul imparts a portion of its winged lightness to the body it animates' and matter pulls against this elevating force, as it 'draws to itself the ever-alert activity of this higher principle, would fain to convert it to its own inertia and cause it to revert to mere automatism' (1911b: 28). And it is precisely this disjunction between the grace of the soul and the stolid materiality of the body that produces humour. As he develops his thesis on laughter, Bergson indeed begins to modify his initial emphasis on mechanisation and absolute rigidity towards a concern with disjunction and asynchronicity – the unpalatable and discomforting traces of a Cartesian dualism within the human subject:

> it seemed to us that the living body ought to be the perfection of suppleness . . . When we see only gracefulness and suppleness in the living body, it is because we disregard in it the elements of weight, of resistance, and, in a word, matter; forget its materiality and think only of its vitality . . . Let us suppose, however, that our attention is drawn to this material side of the body; that, so far from sharing in the lightness and subtlety of the principle with which it is animated, the body in our eyes is no more than a heavy and cumbersome vesture, a kind of irksome ballast which holds down to earth a soul eager to rise aloft . . . The impression of the comic will be produced as soon as we have a clear apprehension of this putting the one on the other. And we shall experience it most strongly when we are shown the soul *tantalized* by the needs of the body. (Bergson 1911b: 49–50)

To see pure gracefulness represents an overlooking, then, an amnesia in relation to the body's desiring materiality and the dual aspect of the human. Where, at other points in the argument, it is a forgetting of the immateriality of the human that produces a comic object, here it is clear that comedy also becomes perceptible through the irruption of the putatively immaterial into the corporeal.

Now this account of the comic, figured according to the disjunctive, asynchronous relationship between human bodies and inanimate matter, comes suggestively clearly into focus in Heinrich von Kleist's 'Essay on the Marionette Theatre' (1810) that Beckett seemingly admired. Kleist's narrator recounts the story of seeing a young man attempting consciously to take on a pose that he had previously assumed naturally, or perhaps, more properly, habitually. He concludes that 'the movements he made were so comical that I was hard put not to laugh' (1981: 17). Although Kleist agrees with Bergson that a lack of grace, or the maladjustment of fit between self-conscious intention and material movement, can produce humour, he suggests, as Bergson goes on to intuit, that it is affectation and excessive thought in human movement, in which 'the soul, or moving force, appears at some point other than the centre of gravity of the movement' (Kleist 1981: 15), rather than any simple simulation of mechanisation, that is derisively comical. Consequently, the marionette is not comical because it possesses no consciousness to disrupt the grace of its movements; the centre of gravity within a movement simply needs to be shifted by the puppeteer and 'the limbs, which are only pendulums, follow mechanically of their own accord' (13). Due to the coincidence of contraries in which the 'two ends of the circular world meet', grace also returns when knowledge has 'gone through infinity' (18): '[g]race appears most purely in that human form which either has no consciousness or an infinite consciousness. That is, in the puppet or in the god' (18). Possessed of neither infinite consciousness nor absolute unconsciousness, however, humans are necessarily caught in a shifting state, in a rhythm that is constantly falling out of step with itself. Although, to be sure, the narrator implies the possibility of transcendence, the human is located here within the jerky arrhythmias of a riven state and the essential ludicrousness of existence in a post-lapsarian world.[9] Despite the powerful immanence of Kleist's model, the human is not yet to be found in either the puppet, or in the god – an infinite rather than a human puppet master, in perfect control of and in harmony with natural law. For grace is perfect coincidence, an absolute synchrony with natural laws such as gravity. To be human, however, is to be humorous. Risky, syncopated forms, beset by intermittence and interference, affectation and the lack of coincidence between self-conscious intention and matter, are the space and time of the human for Kleist, but they are also the space and time of the comic. And if humour is human, then gravity is a law of perfect seriousness: gravity is grace.

Knowlson and Pilling tell us that Beckett, who showed little enthusiasm for the rest of Kleist's work, referred the actor Ronald Pickup to
'On the Marionette Theatre' during the rehearsals for *Ghost Trio*, when
trying to describe how the minimised movements of the play should
be rendered (1979: 277). The story of the young man whose affectation makes the narrator laugh 'particularly impressed' him, apparently.
There are thus, they say, suggestive correspondences between the two
authors; indeed, they go as far as to state that Kleist's essay expresses
some of 'Beckett's own deepest aesthetic aspirations' (Knowlson and
Pilling 1979: 277). For they argue that Beckett's work implies that
material movement, unfettered by the incomplete, 'fallen' and interruptive infections of knowledge, is potentially transcendent.[10] As Molloy
reminds us, '[t]here is rapture, or there should be, in the motion crutches
give' (*T*: 64). 'Or there should be': this equivocation, this hopeful hesitation, is everything. Graceful human movement might tend towards transcendence or the weightlessness of puppets who are 'not afflicted with
the inertia of matter' (Kleist 1981: 16), but Beckett's figures are kept
determinedly within the syncopated realm of the human.[11] And within
the arrhythmic oscillations or quiverings of the strings that effect a slide
and shift between perfected inanimate matter and absolute intention, the
realm of the human also becomes that of the comic.

Perhaps *Quad* remains residually comic, then, precisely because it
retains this sense of interruption. The central deflection of the play
could be an unretainable moment of intention, a necessarily irruptive
glimmer of consciousness or awareness of the danger zone into which
the figures are being drawn that interferes with the simulation of absolutely mechanised movement. The immanent grace of that movement
is similarly thrown off balance by the recalcitrant presence of matter
in the play. Puppets may only 'need the ground only to glance against
lightly, like elves, and through this momentary check to renew the swing
of their limbs' (Kleist 1981: 16), but humans are continually drawn to
the ground; they 'must have it to rest on' (16). In *Quad*, the players
might move with an accuracy and economy that resists affectation, but
the shuffling of the feet remains as an aural trace of the resistance of the
thin plane of matter upon which they are placed and which the mass of
their pacing bodies anchors in the void. The central jerk also confirms
the resistant presence of the ground by the slight change in the timbre
of the shuffling feet within this momentary deflection. For Kleist's narrator, a dancer whose movement is interrupted by self-consciousness
or affectation, whose soul is displaced and out of step with the natural
ellipses of joints that follow merely the law of gravity, is subjected to
an unexpected and rather comic reappearance of that soul in the most

surprising of locations – perhaps in the small of the back or the elbow. Within the central jerk of *Quad*, then, one might be able to detect a 'soul' on the underside of these shuffling feet. But if this is comic, it also echoes something that Beckett expressed as a demand. In *Footfalls*, although the tattered woman might be approaching immateriality, it is clear that the motion of the quasi-infinite pacing is not enough. May must recognise the 'inertia of matter', in Kleist's terms: 'I must hear the feet,' she intones, 'however faint they fall' (*CDW*: 401). And this sense of 'mustness', this sense of a demand, is vital. For when discussing *Footfalls* with Charles Juliet, Beckett precisely emphasised '"that back-and-forth movement . . . " He acts out with his fingers the pacing of the prisoner in his cell, of an animal in its cage' (Juliet 2009: 38), and went on to determine, '"[y]ou must be here," he says, pointing towards the table, "and also," pointing is index finger upward, "millions of light-years away. All at the same time . . ."' (Juliet 2009: 38). The movement of the feet in *Footfalls* imagined alongside constricted matter (emphasised by the shuffling sound) enables a compact between the seeming prison-house of corporeality and the glint and glimmer of escape and transcendence beyond.

Beckett seems clear that this is a demand – a demand that holds the human back from the putative violence of reconciliation that would denude it of its dual capacity for being both more and less than matter. And perhaps this is why comedy persists in this late work. For comedy is a structure that relies on, preserves and renders visible in form, the immanent doubleness in the human. As Zupančič implies, the comic appears in seeing 'the turning of materiality into pure spirit and of pure spirit into something material as *one and the same movement*' (2008: 47). Comedy thus repeats an excess, a persistent overreaching bound into the fabric of the human that is able both to 'be' and to 'have' itself; comedy shows how 'our finitude is always-already a *failed finitude* – one could say a finitude with a leak in it' (52). Of course, one should note that this sense of the human is also determined by an insistent underachievement and an interrupted transcendence. And it is, indeed, precisely this fissure in finitude (which offers the implication that there is a view on to it from elsewhere), and the hole in infinitude that ensures its contamination by the leaky pratfalls of matter, which offers the place of passage or a temporal movement between states that produces the comic. Perhaps Beckett is not quite right, then, to say that one must be in two places at once in his work. Almost at once might be more accurate. In terms of comic objects, I see something as one thing and then, while retaining a memory of that state, I see it interruptively shuddering into being something else. Comedy may make disjunctive spaces appear almost at the same time, but if temporal contraction is absolute, both the comic and indeed the human find themselves deformed in a humorless, amnesiac and finally inhuman grace.

'Kindly Tune Accordingly'

So a significant structural aspect in the sensation of the comic in an observer is the retention of a sense of disjunction in the comic object as body and soul, matter and transcendence, seem to trip on each other's traces. But, of course, this sensation is also dependent on this observer being out of time with a comic object who seemingly has almost none of its memory, or awareness, or at least feigns not to have it. For Bergson, duration is the ground for life and time and it produces a thickening of the present precisely because it retains the past:

> Our duration is not merely one instant replacing another; if it were, there would never be anything but the present – no prolonging the past into the actual, no evolution, no concrete duration. Duration is the continuous pro-gression of the past into the future which gnaws into the future and swells as it advances. (Bergson 1911a: 4–5)

In Bergson's terms, as we have seen, the figures in *Quadrat I* and *II* are comic because they repeat the same movements, the same path, the same frightened reaction at the centre of the quincunx in a slow progression towards a projected inert state – they resist the attributes of the living.

Although he never draws out the specific ways in which comedy and temporality might be thought together, in *Time and Free Will* (1889) Bergson states that the self should be 'an ever advancing boundary between the future and the present' (1910: 101) capable of integrating past action and the possibilities in front of it – two different spaces and times – into the fullness of time as duration. Ungraceful or jerky move-ments have insufficient past or future in them, they 'do not announce those which are to follow' (Bergson 1910: 12), and consequently they appear humorous to an observing consciousness possessed of the memory they lack. Of course, Beckett's characters, in their stiffness, manias and submission to mechanical forces, often seem to be assum-ing such an incipient mechanisation. For the 'puppets' in *Quad* there is indeed no escaping the force of their 'motor ritornello'; if they have any consciousness at all (for the women in *Come and Go* do have memo-ries) – perhaps a sudden awareness of something to be avoided – there is clearly no synthesis of the past and the future within the present moment of their tramping. They do not remember that they have been here before or recall until the very last moment the dangers of the 'danger zone' (*CDW*: 453).

In one sense, this is distinct from the conception of time for the characters in *Endgame*. There, memory and duration obtained through their pained awareness of being bound in a loop, as time decanted itself into space: 'Moment upon moment, pattering down like the millet grains of ... that old Greek, and all life long you wait for that to mount up to a life' (*CDW*: 126). Caught in spatialised present with almost no residue of the past or presentiment of the future, however, the players of *Quad* repeat excessively – come and go, to and fro – producing a form that is concussively rhythmic rather than gracefully melodic. If the figures seemed to pace acrobatically or danced to a melody, it would imply their ability to synthesise past tones and projected rhythms into their present movement.[12] But for these figures there is no freedom of movement or awareness of a diachronic form or the elapse of dance. The diachronic serial form is only visible to the audience: the scene is thus only potentially comic for us; there is no humour in it for them.

So if the *Quad* plays resemble a gag, it remains a profoundly attenuated and decelerating one. The sudden shift between the frantic primary and the exhausted da capo is unexpected, jerky and potentially slightly comic, but also seems to mark the last syncopation of this reduced universe – its last humorous moment. For *Quadrat II* beats out a rhythm that is profoundly rallentando: all percussion that might gather up the movement of the players has been evacuated from the scene and the players move as if in the final stages of a decrescendo that is the very antithesis of a drum roll. Not that *Quadrat I* is much more secure in its comic structure. Abraham usefully explains that an unchanging, fast or 'unadorned' rhythm, whose repetitiveness one might imagine would produce a comic object, actually runs the risk of spiriting a listener away from Bergsonian duration or lived time. It fixes them, like the repeating player, to a spatialised time that does not advance and from which, by implication, the comic cannot be marked:

> Unadorned rhythm appears in *succession*. But it is a succession that *does not advance*: the same cycle is constantly repeated, and duration – the very environment of consciousness, marches in place. For this duration has split off from itself, become alien to itself, in the service of objective, measurable time. It may take a momentary pleasure in this activity, of course, but the tick-tock of the pendulum soon becomes monotonous. If a consciousness were to remain within time continuously, it would ultimately annihilate itself – sinking into sleep or catalepsy. (1995: 22–3)

The consciousness enthralled to such a rhythm is a '*fascinated* consciousness, subjected to an inevitable, horizonless future' (84).[13]

As Bergson suggests, the comic appears in the other as a '*fundamental absentmindedness*, as though the soul has allowed itself to be fascinated and hypnotized by the materiality of a simple action' (1911b: 25). But if the viewer/listener falls into an unchanging rhythm, automaticity cannot be marked as other to the self: instead, 'duration . . . continually contracts, increasingly makes itself into time; and this temporification – more and more intense, more and more fatal – imposes on duration a suffocating tension, a tension that ultimately freezes into an ecstatic spasm' (Abraham 1995: 23). And as the viewer/listener of *Quadrat I* becomes momentarily synchronised with its mechanical rhythm and the gag thus begins to beat or draw out duration, the affect of the comic will not be felt. As the viewer and players march to the same beat, the viewer/listener is no longer allowed to inhabit the putative ease of their own time; they are, instead, nailed to spatialised time's seeming interminability.

Perhaps, though, the rhythm of *Quad* and its comic stamina is not quite as invariant as this characterisation implies. As the playscript tells us, '[e]ach player has a particular percussion, to sound when he enters, continue while he paces, cease when he exits' (*CDW*: 452), which means that there are four different instruments ('two Javanese gongs . . . an African wood block and an African talking drum, and a "wonderful wastepaper basket – from Rathmines" Beckett added whimsically' (Fehsenfeld 1982: 360)) resounding intermittently within the scene. There are thus increases and decreases in noise level as the series progresses from one to four players and back again. Even more significantly, the percussion is 'intermittent in all combinations to allow footsteps alone to be heard at intervals' (*CDW*: 452). In the middle of *Quadrat I*, then, there are a few seconds when the noisy percussive cacophony is suddenly aborted into a tense silence in which only the shuffling of feet can be heard. Equally, because the rhythmic beating of the percussion is somewhat erratic, syncopated and irregular, while nevertheless remaining synchronous with the general rhythm of the figures' pacing, there are shades of crescendo and decrescendo that begin to punctuate this exhausting uniformity. So it is possible to notice minor increases in the pace and timbre of the percussion as the figures race towards their deflected collision and small decrescendos as they move away from the centre of the quincunx. These sounds perhaps add a little syncopation, then – points of resistance and points of rest – in the inhuman perfection of the players' mechanical movement that is winding very slowly down. And if the comic insists in the interference of the living and the mechanical, in these small moments of gathering, in the minimised marking of this frantic repetition in which the disjunction between mechanical force and imperfect form can be perceived by an audience, *Quadrat I* evokes and retains a peculiarly passing set of pleasures.

So *Quadrat I* demands a consistent and heightened attention to the speed and the tempo of its elapse, to the points of inflection within its repeated series that enable the perception of the comic to appear and fade from view. Where in the early work affective indeterminacy was closed down by the laughter of superiority, only then to be opened up by the unexpectedly leaky uncertainties structurally implicated into the comic, in this scene of near maximal structural determinacy there is a paradoxical unfurling of the space and time of affective indeterminacy. *Quadrat I* indeed uses its weak and fading formal incongruities to produce shades of modal difference – differences of degree or intensity – that in turn produce wrinkles in the affective experience of an observer.

One of the difficulties, however, in describing the affective states that *Quad* produces is that the work seems to stage a peculiar deadening of the ability of mind and senses to gather themselves towards a comprehensibly perceptible affect. As we have seen, *Quad* is not easily markable as comic. But nor does it simply gather up the viewer into transcendent, annihilating ecstasy or drop them into a disinterested shrug, as amusement, surprise, boredom and anxiety phase and fade into the audience's affective arena. *Quad* indeed inaugurates distinctively uncertain affects in its surprisingly noisy and then shockingly etiolated pacings – its gatherings, deflections and hyperactive wheelings of unconscious matter that become predictable as they are drawn out over time and yet remain obtusely resistant to either conceptualisation or perception in terms of secure states of feeling. Although she does not mention *Quad*, Ngai has described a particular affect of astonishment and boredom that seems to insist in a whole strand of late modernist artworks. In this peculiarly indeterminate affect, the rapidly increasing neural excitement that is suddenly released of astonishment, and the low yet distended neural firing of boredom (Ngai 2005: 261), are layered next to one another in time. But this shuddering between states, between rhythms, precipitates a somewhat meta-feeling, an 'open feeling', that 'lacks the punctuating "point" of an individuated emotion' (Ngai 2005: 84) but remains a condition in which, Ngai suggests, 'difference' or distinction might be 'perceived prior to its qualification or conceptualization' (2005: 261). Left puzzling over whether it is in or out of time with the object of perception – oscillating between being a laughing subject and having its leg pulled by the strings of the gag – the audience watching *Quad* is indeed forced into overlaying sometimes abrasively distinct forms of temporal attention in response to the same, repeated space. This 'doing time' may sometimes feel like forced labour, as the affected subject is hauled through exhaustive and exhausting permutations that mirror how the players find themselves moved. And yet the audience is not simply imprisoned. Despite comedy's tendency to funnel affective experience into preconstituted structures of feeling marked out in humour's compact with 'suddenness', mastery and contraction into a sensation of presence, a gag without a punchline and the affective tremors it produces holds open the possibility that modes of experience and manners of response to the world that currently find little adumbration might also make a hesitant appearance.

Now it is perhaps ironic that Beckett uses comic forms that persist in falling away from themselves, showing their structural underpinnings, to prise open the relationship between the human, temporality and affective experience that is central both to comedy and to his own aesthetic concerns. For comedy works precisely by not showing its workings, by moving with the quickness of wit rather than with the tempered slowness and explicating ponderousness of certain modes of critical or philosophical thought. Freud indeed suggests that often it is the psychical energy spent on critical reason that is discharged in laughter; consequently, comic pleasure tends to drown out critical considerations of form, and indeed the paradoxes of comic structure, in its insistence that pleasure pays for all paradox to be tolerated. By denuding the comic of its payoff, of its occulting pleasure, however, Beckett's late plays insist on pursuing, on working through, the central paradoxes of comic form and affect that remain curiously analogous to the long-standing aesthetic and thematic concerns of the *oeuvre*. If, as Serres suggests, 'time makes contradiction possible' (1995: 50), the limping gag through which the passage of time is obtrusively staged allows paradox and incongruity, such as the texts' insistence on figuring the human at this particular moment of modernity as a site of leaky finitude and hobbled transcendence rather than absolute grace, to be thought and felt through rather than simply tolerated, skated over or reconciled in a finally determinable affect.

Despite an emphasis on the production of logic and philosophical certainty, Bergson's deeply unfunny, rather drawn out essay on laughter also finds it revealingly difficult to nail down its subject or hold it to a determined affective response. Seemingly despite himself, Bergson seems remarkably unable to decide that laughter or the comic are completely on the side of forms of languid life and the experience of duration. As we have seen, laughter, which seems to preserve a certain sudden and lively idea of 'life' by policing automaticity, risks the sensation of self-coincidence it so desires and requires by mirroring the mechanical in its laughter. If, as Bergson insists, laughter is 'the result of a *mechanism* set up in us by nature or, what is almost the same thing, by our long acquaintance with social life. It goes off spontaneously and returns tit for tat' (1911b: 198, my italics), then laughter is not graceful any more than the comic object is; it does not flow in time with the *élan vital*. But if laughter is paradoxically a 'mechanism set up in us by nature or, what is almost the same thing, by social life', perhaps 'life' itself is not gracefully self-identical. As Weller puts it in his thorough reading of the vicissitudes of the comic in Bergson, '[w]ere there no fall into alterity, were life to remain unremittingly mindful of itself, purely self-identical, there would be nothing comic, no laughter at all' (2006: 90), for 'laughter, as a mechanical effect, is always laughing at itself, and in so doing dividing itself from itself, producing or being produced as its own other' (2006: 96). But it might also be true, as Weller implies, that were life to remain unremittingly mindful, if it were absolutely reducible to itself, it would not be life at all, or certainly not human life.

Weller is correct in suggesting that Bergson does not articulate the peculiar logic at work here; instead he leaves the reader with an interruptive and highly paradoxical model of a living self-consciousness that emerges through a temporal process of *dédoublement*, of demonstrating its potential to lose itself, to take itself as its own other. And perhaps it is precisely in this moment of self-differentiation, which replicates what is laughable in the act of laughing, but repeats it with at least the potential for some critical distance inserted, that a particularly modern account of human life, which seems to inhabit the interstices between total mechanicity and fully symmetrical self-consciousness and self-coincidence, appears. For Bergson's account of laughter and the comic returns us to Kleist's model of the human lodged between the equal grace of absolute consciousness and total mechanisation, which are elided in a coincidence of contraries. But if this process of *dédoublement* and uncertainty as to the locations of sameness and otherness is always immanent within the comic, a structure of humour that is constructed explicitly as a temporary, passing affect, always fading out and in as it plays with complex materialisations of sensations of self-coincidence and alterity, will bring this capacity of the human subject to risk its own loss into centre stage. In one sense, such a method will produce the conditions under which a lack of reconciliation will traumatically be felt, in all its material specificity. But perhaps it is also in just this 'open' affect of the comic that processes of self-differentiation that could enable a little critical distance, even a shard of freedom, from the painful experience of the ever-same might minimally appear. For it is precisely in the uncertainty of affect elicited in a play like *Quad*, its resistance to pre-existent structures of feeling that could be named as distinct passions and quantifiable emotions, it is precisely in the stolid and yet ungraspable difficulty of describing what is going on in affective terms where there is no predigested lexicon to outline its distinctions, that tuning oneself accordingly to the play might necessitate the adumbration of as yet unnamed possibilities of thought, feeling and action.

'Like Something Out of Beckett'

So the trace of comedy in these late plays is structurally uncertain, close to petering out for good. Like the slow fading of the illuminated head in *That Time*, there may indeed be moments when an audience would find it hard to decide whether an object or an affect is still there at all, or whether all that remains is an after-image, shimmering on the surface of the retina. As Beckett's work shifts into its final bleached aesthetic, it folds temporisation and affective 'openness' into what seems otherwise to be a pure, abstracted and highly determined form, according to a seeming consciousness of the fact that there is always a subject to measure and witness stilling repetitions as such. This implication of temporal extension into the plays is not, however, simply confined to the experience of watching a single play, as though the spectator were held in the same void as the players. As the late plays become increasingly meta-theatrical, there is the clear sense that a spectator might begin to recognise the particular kinds of repetitions involved here and might find them funny in their echoing of what by now is an explicitly 'Beckettian' theatrical performance of skilled diminution. As an audience member at a Beckett play, one is often conscious of being part of a community engaged in a recognisable 'scene', and Beckett certainly seemed aware of the process of habituation. In an early version of *That Time*, Beckett ironically has the narrator address the figure on stage, referring, as if remembering, to 'the old scenes you lived in so long and the people stopping to look at you like something out of Beckett sitting there on the step' (1974: 2). Suggesting a return to a set of theatrical conventions that are now clearly recognisable to an audience as Beckett's own, these recognisable repetitions become drawn out, become expected or even habitual for the subject, both within a single performance and across the *oeuvre* as a whole.

Now this sense of habituation and the oddly indeterminate affects it elicits have consequences for the excavation of ethical articulations within Beckett's work. It is clear that these late plays are not interested in presenting ethical prescriptions with which rational subjects might choose to align themselves. Significantly, though, the idea of producing an audience traced through with certain habits, expectations and orientations does not simply sit outside the purview of philosophical ethics. For in *The Nicomachean Ethics*, Aristotle defines ethics as the formation of good character. He casts aside the Platonic 'idea of the Good', determining instead that moral excellence and ethical action emerge from the practice of virtue. But such moral virtue does not inhere naturally within the subject; instead, it requires the repetition and cultivation of certain bodily and mental attitudes – attitudes that become, in due course, habitual, or a kind of second nature. For Aristotle, then, 'moral excellence [ethics] comes about as the result of habit [*ethos*], whence also its name is one formed by a slight variation from the words for "habit"' (1984a: 1742).

In 1936 the young Beckett encountered a critique of such habits of virtue in the *Ethics* of the seventeenth-century occasionalist philosopher Arnold Geulincx. There, Geulincx specifically counters Aristotle's account of an ethics of habit, which Beckett noted down: 'we do [things] not because they are prescribed by custom and habit, or established by the consensus and authority of men, but only because God commands and Reason requires them' (2006: 322). Geulincx suggests that it is only by orientating one's reason to God's – a will which precedes and outlasts any human intention – that an ethical life can be led. But Beckett's persistent fascination with this Geulingian formulation '[u]bi nihil vales ibi nihil velis' ('wherein you have no power, therein neither should you will' (Geulincx 2006: 316)), is surely not to be related, in any straight way, to Geulincx's sense of binding oneself to a law of Reason which is a reflection of the goodness of God's will – a willing of what has already been willed. Indeed, when Beckett wrote to Sighle Kennedy in 1967, suggesting that a point of departure for studying his work would be the quotation '[u]bi nihil vales' found in *Murphy*, he conceded that such a position is not 'very rational' (*D*: 113). Nevertheless, this Geulingian ethics of withdrawal, this quietist relinquishment of will, intention and an autonomous form of rationality, does resound across Beckett's work, and it also resonates with Beckett's interest in habit. Extracted from the Geulingian frame of an interventionist God, the idea of an ethical orientation manifesting itself below the threshold of the rational subject of modernity and suspicious of any personal power to will ethical ideas or acts emerges in Beckett's long-standing fascination with semi-conscious, half intentional habits of being which one can detect at a level of content in his lectures to students in the 1920s,[14] in his interest in Pavlov and conditioned reflexes in the 1930s, through the obsessions with peristalsis in the mid-period and as far as his late fascination with Kleist. Denuded of the power bound to what Geulincx termed (and Beckett transcribed) as '[t]hat sorry little word that with them is frequently on their lips and ever in their minds: *Mine*' (Geulincx 2006: 315), it is a hesitantly staged suggestion of an ethics linked to certain aesthetic habits of going on, rather than any idea of good linked to 'value judgements' or decision procedures, that inheres in the evanescent 'open' affects of Beckett's late work.

As we have seen, *The Unnamable* uncertainly suggests, for of course it insists it can't quite know it, that one can only hold back from judgement in a space below the awareness of a knowing subject bound to cognitively determinable affirmations and negations: 'Can one be ephectic other than unawares? I don't know. With the yesses and noes it is different' (*T*: 293–4). From this particular historical moment compulsively bound to a fear of the 'knowing' and possessive subject, Beckett indeed uncovers an uncertain ethics that precisely materialises itself within the semi-automatic, the half-intentional – something paradoxically felt in an individual but nevertheless experienced below the brink of what is securely '*mine*'. And although it is certainly easier in critical terms to draw out the occasions in the work where the texts speak of habits of going on, in the late plays where commentary and dialogue are sloughed off in favour of forms that produce profoundly uncertain yet habitual affects that tread the threshold of what can securely be brought into the conscious awareness, the trace of an 'ephectic' ethics finds its shadowy articulation.

Habit, of course, is no stranger to accounts of the comic. For Bergson the person who falls to the floor in the place where he expected his chair to be is a comic victim of habit: 'Habit has given the impulse: what was wanted was to check the movement or deflect it. He did nothing of the sort, but continued like a machine in the same straight line' (Bergson 1911b: 9–10). In *Matter and Memory* of 1896, however, Bergson has already offered up a version of habit that is not simply other to the self and to life; instead, and perhaps surprisingly, habitual modes of going on are taken into the very core of subjectivity and its relations to temporality. Here, the 'law of life' is no longer 'the complete negation of repetition': instead, something called 'habit-memory', which allows the body to learn, for example, how to play a musical instrument, becomes part of the subject's orientation towards the living. Although the violinist first has to think consciously where to place her fingers on the finger board and how and where to draw the bow across the strings, as her actions are laid down over time in the plastic material of the nervous system, habit emerges through 'prolongation' that contracts and retains an initial perceptual image by repeating its useful effects. The role of 'prolongation is merely to utilize, more and more, the movements by which the first [image] was continued, in order to organize [the movements] together and, by setting up a bodily mechanism, to create a bodily habit', Bergson suggests (1994: 83–4). '[S]eated in the present and looking only to the future' (Bergson 1994: 82), habit memory's comportment towards adaptation, evolution and progression, enables it to appear under the auspices of 'life', even though it accumulates in the body as a 'series of mechanisms' (82). Caught in an archetypally modern uncertainty about the relationship between nature, mechanical reproduction and life, Bergson strangely represents 'habit-memory' as 'more natural' (Bergson 1994: 83) than conscious or voluntary memorisation. Just as laughter turns out to be a 'mechanism set up in us by nature or, what is almost the same thing, by social life' (Bergson 1911b: 198), for Bergson repeated 'habit memories' begin to seem innate (1994: 85) – to become a form of second nature.

In modernity, as Beckett's early *Proust* has demonstrated, habit is commonly figured as the opposite of human freedom. Trotsky writes in 1923 that '[c]onscious creativeness in the domain of custom and habit occupies but a negligible place in the history of man' (1973: 25), and a strong part of Bergson's position on habit also insists that bodies or minds infected by a form of 'obstinacy, by *rigidity* . . . [that] persists in the habit it has contracted' (1911b: 25), need to be brought back to the supple intuitive adaptability of life. As Slavoj Žižek puts it, with 'the shift from Aristotle to Kant, to modernity with its subject as pure autonomy, the status of habit changes from organic inner rule to something mechanic, the opposite of human freedom' (2009: 99), for the rational, autonomous subject is threatened by the automatic, by ill-fitting matter and by what occurs seemingly mindlessly. But for Bergson, as we can see, habit is not simply a mortification. Bergson almost certainly formed his complex and paradoxically doubled attitude to life and habit from reading the 1838 essay *Of Habit* by Félix Ravaisson, and Ravaisson's argument is significant not simply for its influence on a major strand of twentieth-century French vitalist thought, but because it effects a suggestive synthesis of ancient and modern accounts of habit. Ravaisson describes habit as a middle term that can effect a continuity between putative dualisms – mind and body, activity and passivity, will and nature – and he restores to modernity a sense of habit as proper to life. Following Aristotle, Ravaisson insists that '[h]abit is an acquired nature, a *second nature*' (Ravaisson 2008: 59), although habit also 'supposes a change in the disposition, in the potential, in the internal virtue of that in which change occurs, which itself does not change' (2008: 25). As something able to turn 'voluntary movements into instinctive movements' (2008: 59), Ravaisson's account of habit offers modernity a relationship of the human to *ethos* that suggestively demands being thought outside of ethics bound to an autonomous willing and willed subject.

According to Aristotle in the *Eudemian Ethics*, habit precisely implies that an experiencing subject has the possibility of and aptitude for change while maintaining the potential for preserving the alterations inherent in that change – a dialectic of mutability within the subject's experience of itself as continuous. In her reading of Hegel as part of a tradition that links Ravaisson and Aristotle (Ravaisson 2008: vii), Catherine Malabou suggests that organic beings and humans, even more specifically, are precisely determined by their ability to contract habits. An organic being has the capacity for self-differentiation, to perceive and even to contemplate within a form of unity the heterogeneous elements – impressions, perceptions, sensations – from which it is constituted: 'The organic being is characterized by its effort in maintaining its own unity through the synthesis of differences: the difference between the organism and its environment and the difference between the heterogeneous elements which make up the organism' (Malabou 2005: 58). Through this contraction, 'the individual feels the weight of its own existence' (64), appropriating the content of the world to itself without becoming identical with it or immersed in it, but nevertheless remaining interested and involved in it. In her reading of Hegel, habit is taken into and determines the form of the human because that subject is plastic: it has 'a capacity to receive form and a capacity to produce form' (9), in Malabou's terms. The subject is plastic because it is supple, flexible enough to receive the impressions of the world and to be formed by forces both exterior to it and those emanating from its inside. But it is also plastic because it is not polymorphous or infinitely malleable. Once moulded into a shape, something that is plastic will hold and retain impressions.

For Hegel, Malabou contends, this emergence of an individual subject represents a disturbance of a form of primary unity. This seems to echo Kleist's account of the human, which is reasonably contemporaneous with Hegel's, as something that emerges from a disturbance of the elided extremes of absolute mechanicity (pure otherness) and the ideal unity of pure self-coincidence (pure sameness). Emergent individuality represents, for Hegel, a form of alienation and dispossession – a fallen state, in Kleist's Christian terms:

The gradual formation of the 'I' is paradoxically accompanied by a loss of fluidity, leading to 'ruin and disaster within the conscious spirit'. This crisis results from the fact that the subject, being constituted in a free relation to the self, feels at the same time like 'an other', and this tension pushes it into a state of 'trembling'. (Malabou 2005: 32)

For Hegel, then, there is a derangement, a madness that haunts the subject from the very beginning, because there is a taking of otherness – the determinations of the external world and internal sensations which it experiences as discontinuous – into its nature, into its own way of being. This forces a state of 'trembling': a lack of coincidence in a self that is nevertheless continuous. In his early essay on Proust, Beckett approvingly quotes what seems like the older author's suspicion of habit's tendency to denude the human of its ability to possess pure self-identity: 'If Habit . . . is a second nature, it keeps us in ignorance of the first' (1999: 22), he writes. Even at this point, however, Beckett, like Proust himself, holds out a little hope for habit, for second nature is also 'free of [the] cruelties and [the] enchantments' (1999: 22) of 'first nature'. Beckett seems aware that habit mercifully kills the intolerable specificity of the absolute present in producing a second nature just as, for Proust, habit allows experience to become an object of regard in which pain is possessed by the subject and can thus be represented as art rather than experienced as nothing but subjection. Alongside the destitution caused by habit, then, there is a hope of restitution in which the subject might be able both to be and to have itself.

For Malabou, Hegel's individual subject emerges as a being which senses in its encounters with external objects but experiences these sensations as its own, as part of its self-continuity; it also experiences its own internal states as sufficiently discrete to be felt and known as such, as things it can represent to itself according to its inner processes of self-differentiation. The emergence of the individual subject is thus a process through which externality and otherness are contained and interiorised as part of the core of subjectivity, as part of its own habit of being. So habit becomes, in Malabou's reading, 'a liberating process, saving the soul from two forms of dissolution – either lost in the emptiness of ideality or absorbed in a determinate part isolated from the whole' (2005: 37). Habit is what allows the subject to appropriate its body for itself, alongside that which comes to it from the outside; habit turns the subject's corporeality and sensations into a reflection of its inner purposes. In Malabou's account of Hegel, it is thus habit that enables a reconciliation of the subject with the world that is exterior and other to it.

This unity within human nature, between the will and the body, self and the external world is only possible in a reflection which occurs seemingly naturally and mindlessly – without the lack of fit between intentional willing and an unyielding, materiality which lags behind it, tripping up its plans. For Hegel the truth of human nature, then, is that it is 'always and already "second nature"' (Malabou 2005: 66), appearing when human will is actualised in the body as an automatic reaction and becoming a reflection of an ideal unity between subject and object, consciousness and material world, which is untroubled by the self-consciousness that turns the mind into something out of phase with so much unresponsive flesh. This 'unreflective spontaneity' allows an external change to be repeated and turned into a tendency that is internal to the subject; as such, it turns the contingent into what is essential: 'The change itself is transformed into a disposition, and receptivity, formerly passive, becomes activity. Thus habit is revealed as a process through which man ends by *willing* or choosing what came to him from outside' (Malabou 2005: 70–1). Habituation allows the subject to maintain its unity by internalising an externally imposed change, moulding it into a way of being that enables the subject to deal with such changes. In a distorted echo of Geulincx, habit enables a willing of what has already been willed.

So habit requires a relationship with the past, but, as Bergson and Malabou insist, it also invokes a relationship with the future. 'Habit makes it possible to *retain* the changes that occur and expect that they will recur. Invoking the past and the future, habit brings becoming to life', writes Malabou (2005: 64). To contract a new habit involves a complex temporal reflexivity for subjectivity, then, for although habit allows the subject to perceive of its unity across time, to grasp past, present and future as one of its own ways of being, the subject still recognises itself as fundamentally constituted by the potential within repetition to insert difference into the heart of something that experiences itself as continuous and unified. Habit is something towards which I can orientate myself, but what produces my 'second nature' is never exactly 'mine'. Although habit enables something of a colonisation of the future, and a holding in reserve of the subject's potential by rendering future change as that towards which it is already habituated, it also evokes the possibility of a future event that could appear, altering the constitution of the subject totally – its past, present and future – and producing of a new habit of being.

By the time that Beckett had given up essays like *Proust* for aesthetic works, it is clear that the disempowered will of habit has considerable compensations. In *Godot* Vladimir laments that the 'air is full of our cries', but he goes on to state that, perhaps luckily, perhaps not, 'habit is a great deadener' (*CDW*: 84). Vladimir and Estragon certainly use their habits to ensure that they can muster enough energy to carry on. Crucially, though, for Beckett's figures there is no escape into a synthesising ideal of 'second nature' in which dualisms are overcome. For perceiving a continuity over time, as the being of habits does, also intensifies pain, in that it allows it to be felt as belonging to the subject stuck on the flywheel of repetition. This sensation of time passing is clearly felt by Vladimir, which the awareness of being observed by an audience that sees their repetitions only intensifies: 'At me too someone is looking, of me too someone is saying, he is sleeping, he knows nothing, let him sleep on. [*Pause*]. I can't go on!' (*CDW*: 84–5). Without any sense of a subject that persists over time or a subject of memory or habit, the torturous scenarios of *Godot* would appear as an ever-repeated present where, for better and for worse, pain might manifest itself in all its material immediacy but would not be recalled. Whether this would represent an increase or decrease of pain, however, is not easy to determine. Imagining a series of experiments along the lines of Pavlov's, who used pain as well as the more firmly remembered sound to test the relationship between excitation and inhibition in conditioned reflexes (1927: 188–203), the Unnamable owns that the 'problem is delicate . . . The affair is thorny', for an excess of severity might cause the creature to suffer less, according to the 'dulling effect of habit' (*T*: 370). But it is also perfectly possible that he would 'suffer as much, precisely as the first day', or suffer 'more and more, as time flies, and the metamorphosis is accomplished, of unchanging future into unchangeable past' (370). In *The Unnamable*, as in *Godot*, in the contraction of habit there is both an inuring and a sensitising. Pain is taken into the subject as one of its own ways of being, therefore effecting a form of resistance to what is imposed from without. But the persistence of the pain is experienced as belonging, in all its inexorable intensity, to a self that is continuous across time.

What seems of most interest to Beckett, however, is the potential for a particular sense of habit to enact the fact that human life is not reducible to either pure self-coincidence or pure automaticity – absolute freedom or total subjection. Consequently, he resists the overcoming of dualisms that Malabou finds in Hegel, revolting against synthesis by ensuring that the habits his work invokes and evokes remain inefficient, partial, incompetent – retaining the trace but not the power and coincidence that Hegel's 'automatically' reconciled being of habit is able to draw to itself. For Beckett is hardly concerned with determining a process of reconciliation, or the achievement of Spirit or Absolute Knowing in Hegelian terms. As the early *Murphy* reminds us, 'the beautiful Belgo-Latin of Arnold Geulincx: *Ubi nihil vales, ibi nihil velis*' (Beckett 1993: 101) which offers an answer to the question of how to 'tolerate, let alone cultivate the occasions of fiasco' (101), suggests hope – a certain protection and even restitution; nevertheless, 'it was not enough to want nothing where he was worth nothing' (102), for '[t]hese dispositions and others ancillary ... could sway the issue in the desired direction, but could not clinch it' (102). There is insufficient power in 'will-less' will (there is no Geulingian God or Hegelian Pure Spirit here) because Murphy is 'not of the big world, I am of the little world' (102); he remains desiring, 'divide[d]', 'as witness his deplorable susceptibility to Celia, ginger, and so on' (102). He remains a figure of somewhat incompetent habits rather than a graceful recipient of his own 'second nature'. As we have seen, comedy inheres in Beckett's work precisely because of persistent asymmetries, its insistent and vibrantly implicated dualisms, which have not been lifted into any absolute reconciliation. Murphy indeed remains, finally, a comic figure in whom 'occasions of fiasco' are not simply tolerated; they are staged.

But if characters are both inured and sensitised by the semi-conscious force of habit in Beckett's aesthetic work, it is revealing to note that it is in Bergson's account of comic art that the laughing spectator's experience and that of the characters are moved into shuddering echoes of one another. Here, the oscillating uncertainties of whether the comic is living or mechanical between which Bergson's argument finds itself incessantly clattering find their most forceful articulation. He suggests that the comic object in art must present itself as 'absentminded' to an audience if it is to be perceived as funny. But if it really is absent-minded, such clowning will be denuded of its element of performance and thus will no longer be art. To experience the comic within art, then, the spectator has also to demonstrate a capacity for doubling positions that mirrors that of the object; they must forget that what is being seen is skilled, is representation, but they must also remember if the comic is to be lifted above the simple derision, the mechanical 'tit for tat' return. In his account of comic representation through language, Bergson has already warned his readers that language, which provides the raw materials of representation here, turns out to be as immanently doubled and split, as displaced from pure grace, as the humans that use it:

> If this life of language were complete and perfect, if there were nothing of the stereotype in it ... [if] it were an absolutely unified organism ... it would evade the comic as would a soul whose life was a harmonious whole, unruffled as the calm surface of a peaceful lake. There is no pool, however, which has not some dead leaves floating on its surface, no human soul upon which there do not settle habits that make it rigid against itself by making it rigid against others, no language, in short, so subtle and instinct with life, so fully alert in each of its parts as to eliminate the ready-made and oppose the mechanical operations of inversion, transposition, etc., which one would fain perform upon it as on some lifeless thing. (1911b: 129–30)

So there is no comic representation that does not immanently partake of division or produce a highly interruptive oscillation of sameness and otherness. And to be the audience of comic art is explicitly to be subject to an immanent process of *dédoublement* in which the affected subject and the comic representation find themselves shuddering in and out of phase with themselves and each other, persistently marking themselves and their others as mechanical/living, mechanical/living, according to a syncopated and interruptive rhythm. But if this is so, it is hardly surprising that the uncertainty inherent within all comedy, an uncertainty connected to this *dédoublement*, is brought into heightened relief, and repeated with redoubled concentration, within particular kinds of aesthetic text that seem to play with processes of conscious unconsciousness. This mode indeed becomes part of a recognisably 'Beckettian' way of going on, with the evanescent comedy of the late plays interpellating an audience into a position of finding itself moved according to a recognisable set of affective habits as it faces the seemingly anaesthetised players that are precisely 'unwilled' (as laughter and affect always are, at least when they begin), but might be able, nevertheless, in their capacity to be taken into the self, to preserve the merest glimpse of freedom and restitution.

The capacity of these late plays to elicit and work with affects that are registered as habitually 'Beckettian', even as they do not submit to easily determinable or recognisable structures of feeling, might seem worrying for a philosopher like Adorno, who initially seems quite clear that in a culture dominated by late capitalism, habit just subtends the logic of the administered world. The habituated audiences of 'hit songs', for example, offer up an 'arrogantly ignorant rejection of everything unfamiliar' (1991: 45), and Adorno opines that such '[r]egressive listeners behave like children. Again and again and with stubborn malice, they demand the dish they have once been served' (45). Even Beckett is not completely immune. For Adorno notes that the habituation in Beckett's plays also becomes one of its precipitates – part of an infantilised experience which feeds the audience on pacifying pap. 'Even in Beckett's plays, the curtain rises the way it rises on the room with the Christmas presents' (Adorno 1992b: 248), he admits. For Alain Badiou, however, within both the form and the reception of Beckett's plays this habit of going on, staged somewhere below decision procedures, is something that resists things as they are: 'the true destination of the comical emerges: neither a symbol nor a metaphysics in disguise, and even less a derision, but rather a powerful love for human obstinacy, for tireless desire, for humanity reduced to its stubbornness and malice', he writes (2003: 75). If 'stubborn malice' is a bad habit for Adorno, it is one that orients itself towards a different world for Badiou. But maybe this could be the point for Adorno too. For although habit is part of the logic of the world of modernity and surely to be filed under identity-thinking as it can consist of fitting things into pre-existing categories (as the Beckett of *Proust* reminds us (1999: 23)), habit is nevertheless carved from a space of reflection and representation, from *dédoublement* and the capacity of the human both to be and to have itself. Habit may only be what Adorno would term a 'hair's breadth' (1974: 247) away from replicating the world as it is, but it nevertheless preserves a space in which the 'distortion and indigence' of the world one might seek to escape can be represented to the self as sufficiently distinct and retainable that it could be perceived as such.

For Adorno, as we have seen, Beckett's work represents the possibility that an autonomous art could replicate the abstraction of the administered world, materialising it in all its violence. In *Quad* and in *Come and Go*, there is indeed the appearance of an infernal, abstracted repetition, which is made to feel like the very opposite of any human freedom for the players, and indeed in places for the audience. Nevertheless, perhaps in such duplication, in clearing the space for an audience to see the world going on and on, in soliciting the perception of such repetitions in an affected spectator who becomes habituated to the scene – who feels its affects and yet neither possesses nor is possessed by them sufficiently that they can be lifted securely into the light of knowledge – there is, in these late texts, a hollowing out from the crevice of postwar abstracted aesthetics, the possibility of seeing how the world might be perceived and materialised otherwise. In one sense, as Beckett himself implies, characters like Hamm and Clov cannot be other than where they are: they persist in a world that is just as it is: 'Hamm as stated, and Clov as stated, together as stated . . . in such a place, and in such a world, that's all I can manage, more than I could' (Harmon 1998: 24). And yet in *Company*, the narrator offers up a suggestive echo of this phrase in what becomes a refrain, as it tells of the voice saying to a figure '[y]ou first saw the light on such and such a day' (*NO*: 5). The absolute specificity of 'such' is replaced by 'such and such', and the narrator is able to see that the voice's repeated attempts to nail the figure to a scene become infected by uncertainty. The narrator perceives the aim to pin the birth of the figure to 'such and such a day', but begins to observe the idiomatic vagueness of what seems like particularity. It can see that, in truth, there isn't much real difference between one 'such and such a day' and another– 'that bloody awful day' from 'this bloody awful day' (*CDW*: 113), as Clov would have it. All just goes on and on coming and going. But in being given time enough to see the repetition *as such* – for habit preserves the subject's orientation towards the future rather than allowing it to be nailed to pure subjection – a minimal difference appears in the witnessing narrator/spectator and specificity finds itself renewed.

The presentation of this minimal freedom (which for Adorno inheres in the purposelessness of all art) removes something of the subjection from habituation because it allows the audience to orientate itself towards the repetition, to see it in the present and to see it coming, in a way that suggests a resistance to absolute passive submission. Of course, there is something much more modest at work here than Malabou's rather heroic Hegelian reconciliation of subject and object world, for the subject that has fully achieved its 'second nature' would necessarily be graceful, unsyncopated, untroubled by dualism and therefore uncomic. But what remains in the humour that insists is something that borrows from habit the capacity for retention and anticipation that allows the asynchronicity of the world to be perceived and for the comic to be marked as such. Consequently, the subject of habits is able to orientate itself towards the world it in a way that refuses the kind of knowledge that this particular moment in the history of ideas fears will always lead to domination.

What appears is something more akin to an inoculation of the affected spectator with a resistance to be found in art. Inoculation is the impregnation of a subject with a pathogen in order to produce a mild version of the disease that will create antibodies to render it immune to future attack. Etymologically, it is derived from the notion of engrafting, of inserting a bud into a plant for the purposes of propagation, which later becomes wedded to the idea of uniting two things to produce a continuity of substance. An inoculated subject takes something damaging into its essential self, and, by doing so, it produces resistance as a very habit of its existence, as part of its paradoxically innate 'second nature'. The inoculation found in the affect elicited by Beckett's late plays is not a reasoned position, then; it does not produce resistance by forging attachments to ideas of truth to which a subject could bind itself. It is more as though the form of the late plays, the abstracted persistence, has, through a kind of reverberative contagion, infected the affective state of the spectator in such a way as to produce of a habit of going on that can take minimal gasps of difference into its own plastic form. As such, it can separate itself, by just a hair's breadth, from the usual carry on sufficiently to see, and only then perhaps to understand in a way that is not completely alien to an attenuated form of comic mastery, the incongruity of really how it is. This Beckettian habit, though only as the 'meremost minimum', gives resistance a form that can be retained.

Significantly, just after telling Juliet that it is not possible to find an ethics based on value judgements in his art, Beckett states that there is, nevertheless, a minimal hope – a hope to be found in form: 'Paradoxically, it is through form that the artist can find some kind of way out. By giving form to formlessness. It is only in that way, perhaps, that some underlying affirmation may be found' (Juliet 2009: 24). This shaping of form in the plastic material of art becomes, at the same time, the shaping of an affected, habituated spectator who has, as part of their second nature, the resistant realism of a witness. This resistant realism, taken into the spectator as an affective habit that is neither completely cognitive/intentional nor totally corporeal/automatic, is certainly not straightforwardly ethical. Indeed, in 1977 Beckett explicitly tells Juliet that his work cannot make what might be thought of as policing moral pronouncements, even as it remains aware of injustice: 'Everything in this damned world calls for indignation . . . But as far as the work goes . . . What can be said? Nothing is sayable' (Juliet 2009: 39). Alien to the kind of ethics that can be fully lifted up into cognition, the affect of the uncertain comedy produced by Beckett's limping gags nevertheless offers both an experience and a stubborn refusal of subjection by producing a powerfully driven yet incongruous art that will not simply be at one with the world as it stands. This is the minimal hope materialised within the untranscendent specificity of an affected subject, which feels the pain of being a subject of habits, of being nailed to 'such a day', but is able to 'have' itself and its environment sufficiently that it can perceive that world *as such*, as something that with minimised mastery it can orientate itself towards. So although the late plays and the last laughs they offer are certainly not the loudest of the Beckett canon, the muted and mutable effects that fade in and out as a function of this compulsive compact initiated by the comic between the formal and the affective, the aesthetic and the ethical, might yet be understood as forms that offer up an awareness of a lack of reconciliation, and the residual hope that sits alongside them that things might and should change. There remains the sensation of an incongruity that can be felt and powerfully recognised as such and the sound of a mistimed gag, ringing in the ears or resounding with sudden clarity, even in this final dim interference.

Notes

1. Redfern explains that a 'Joe Miller' is a 'stale joke, a chestnut' (1998: 104).
2. See, for example, Cohn (1962: 5, 211), Iser (1993: 161), Bersani and Dutoit (1993: 35–6) and Badiou (2003: 75). Bryden (2010) also offers an extensive analysis of clowning in Beckett.

3. Knopff uses the term 'pure gag' to indicate a comic routine that is not subordinated to any wider narrative purpose.
4. As Gidal puts it: 'The figures in the Beckett-directed Schiller Theatre production of *Waiting for Godot* are gesturised throughout so that there is neither a moment of pause when the going is a slow back and forth (whether it be monologue, dialogue or silent sections) nor a moment of speeding-up, when the going is dialectically jagged quickness' (1986: 188–9).
5. I am using this phrase in a mathematical sense to mean 'a change of curvature from concave to convex at a particular point on a curve' (*OED*).
6. Beckett increased the formal symmetry of *Godot* by placing both Vladimir and Estragon on stage at the beginning of the play in order that their appearance at the beginning of the second act should mirror this first image (Knowlson 1993: xviii).
7. This is Connor's suggestion (2001: 154).
8. See, for example, Kenner (1968: 117–32) and Michael Robinson (1969: 86–91). Feldman (2006: 41–57) offers a rigorously archival suspicion of the tendency for Beckett criticism to concern itself with Cartesian influences in Beckett's work
9. Baudelaire's 'On the Essence of Laughter' also states: 'Neither laughter nor tears can show themselves in the paradise of bliss' (1972: 143). The capacity to see himself as an object in his post-lapsarian state enables the comic and it is thus 'one of the clearest marks of Satan in man' (145). Laughter is thus 'at one and the same time a sign of infinite greatness and infinite wretchedness, infinite wretchedness in relation to absolute being, of whom man has an inkling, infinite greatness in relation to the beasts. It is from the constant clash of these two infinites that laughter flows' (148). Weller also offers a reading of comedy, concentrating on its relationship to alterity, which considers Bergson's, Kleist's and Baudelaire's texts alongside one another (2006: 83–110).
10. See also Wulf (1995: 144–5) and Gidal (1986: 187–9) on the relationship between Beckett and Kleist.
11. Although Beckett wrote to Schneider that the women in *Come and Go* should be like puppets, they are clearly not like Kleist's graceful marionettes; they are instead '[s]tiff, slow, puppet-like' (Harmon 1998: 417).
12. Bryden similarly notes that 'the movements of the bent, scurrying figures, while indubitably athletic, seem too uniform, too devoid of vocabulary, too literally pedestrian, to qualify the piece as either dance or acrobatics' (1995: 119).
13. There is, however, a strong and problematic primitivism at work in Abraham's assertion that the drumming of 'most African tribes' (1995: 83) or their 'purely toneless music' (84) produces rhythms that fascinate or render passive, while the 'creative rhythmizing consciousness' is engaged by the poetry of Goethe or Edgar Allan Poe.
14. Rachel Burrows recalls that her teacher emphasised that pure unconscious states should not be used in literature. Beckett noted, presumably with Surrealism in his sights, that such states 'destroy the integrity of the real'; instead, she averred that '"liminal consciousness", the half of

consciousness, that was the thing he really wanted' (Burrows, quoted in Le Juez 2008: 53). Coming at the question from the other end, Burrows's notes also reveal that Beckett's admiration for Gide stemmed from the latter's interest in what could not 'be translated consciously – *abîme* to be respected' (Le Juez 2008: 37).

Conclusion

In 1985, Desmond Egan wrote to Beckett asking a question that had been posed by many of his readers. Beckett was asked whether he thought more highly of tragedy or comedy. His answer was characteristically equivocal: 'Democritus laughed at Heraclitus weeping + Heraclitus wept at Democritus laughing. Pick yr. fancy' (quoted in Welch 1993: 162). '[L]ike something out of Beckett', this late statement has that signature swing of the chiasmus of which the author seemed inordinately fond. The Democritus/Heraclitus tremor of implicated contraries, in which comedy seems always to be sheering away from itself, or being folded into its own tragic other, is indeed a restatement of a point made in a number of different places across Beckett's *oeuvre*. In a letter to Nuala Costello fifty-one years earlier, the young Beckett sardonically yet similarly described his place as a rather depressive, unsuccessful artist: 'Well I might do worse than find myself as it were polarised between Democritus and Heraclitus for eternity . . . I would be familiar with the position' (*LSB*: 185). In the early story 'Yellow', however, Beckett makes and takes a little artistic capital from the idea, with Belacqua grimly noting, 'laughter or tears? It came to the same thing in the end' (Beckett 1970: 175). And in *Molloy*, the old narrator who is unable to distinguish between the sound of crying and of laughing also writes, with a comic shrug: 'perhaps I was mistaken and she was really crying, with the noise of laughter. Tears and laughter, they are so much Gaelic to me' (*T*: 37). Never quite able to be at one with itself, laughter in Beckett never emerges without an acknowledgement that it is a serious, uncertain, even a painful business.

This conscious acknowledgement that laughter might have a compact with gravity and perhaps form part of the work's central concerns persists through Beckett's *oeuvre* and, from the beginning, has marked an important theme in the criticism. Over the decades, such serious laughter has been taken to subtend Beckett's most essential thematics, whether marking out a humanist heroism that describes a stoic yet weary acknowledgement of the absurdity of the human condition, an awareness of the limitedness and finitude of the human, or a profound resistance to all authority, internal or external. But if Beckett's work, and its comedy, is indeed interested in ontological doctoring, it is certainly not prepared to write out prescriptions. Beckett put the problem to Juliet of being caught between what we might term tears and laughter in these terms:

> Negation is not possible. Nor affirmation. It is absurd to say that it is absurd. That's still passing a value judgment. There can be no protest, no agreement ... One must stand where there is no pronoun, no solution, no reaction, no tenable position ... That's what makes work so diabolically difficult. (Juliet 2009: 39)

For Beckett's work remains suspicious of anything that seems like a solution, of incorporating into the texts in any smooth way something that could be turned into the stability of an idea. Although so much is on the move in the work, Beckett's deep-seated and long-standing aesthetic and ethical resistance to the production of an art that is neatly explicable never wavers.

This book has argued that Beckett's ethical questioning, materialised through the potential of the comic both to render and resist violence, and to register experience both at the level of cognition and somatic affect, emerges from a historically specific anxiety about the potential violence within intellection, idea and representation, even as the work refuses their simple disavowal. And it is for this reason that Beckett's late statement to Juliet that his work turns towards a concern with form and the resistance of shape speaks to this historically specific hope for an ethics found within the aesthetic rather than in articulations of ideas as content – ideas that can be turned into 'value judgements'. This mirrors something Beckett said years previously to Harold Hobson:

> I take no sides. I am interested in the shape of ideas even if I do not believe in them. There is a wonderful sentence in Augustine. I wish I could remember the Latin ... 'Do not despair; one of the thieves was saved. Do not presume; one of the thieves was damned'. That sentence has a wonderful shape. It is the shape that matters. (Hobson 1956: 153)

Again, the chiasmus appears: despair and hope, damnation and salvation, to sit alongside tragedy and comedy, negation and affirmation, protest and assent. But if it is the shape of ideas that matters rather than the ideas themselves which could be ripped from their context and circulated in the world, this perhaps explains why Beckett's texts remain so compulsively attached to the priority of form. Within the concreteness of form, things seem, at least momentarily, to be just what they are rather than a synecdoche for something else: 'Hamm as stated, and Clov as stated, together as stated' without any 'headaches among the overtones' (Harmon 1998: 24).

But it is not quite that simple: it turns out that form doesn't offer any uncomplicated solace. It is significant that the shape to which Beckett's work remains bound is that of 'perhaps', of 'strong weakness', of tremor – a shape that emerges and describes itself within the texts' particular and paradoxical comedy that appears over time, indeed often as time. For these are shapes that are necessarily constructed and deformed by questions of power, obligation, compulsion, and they are shapes that fold the unpredictability of time's passage into themselves. As such, they always run the risk of reverberating beyond their seeming limits, of shuddering into one another or transmitting themselves as affect – of producing implications and 'overtones'. So if it is the shape that matters, perhaps it is because shape resists any notion that it could simply be a cipher for ideas or the technical neutrality of reason; although, at the same time, shape is not purely form, it is not just matter. Shape is instead matter brought into contact with force, matter subjected to movement. Shape is matter incarnated and reformed according to demands and pulsions that would otherwise be invisible.

What the texts produce, then, is not a collection of ideas about how things should go on; rather, it is a shape, a form modulated by force, that describes and materialises over time, according to what can best be described as a '[t]empo rubato'– a tempo that demands '[h]old back; but go ahead' (Bryden 1998: 36) – the insistence of powerful and compulsive demands. These demands that the world as it is should be taken into the form of the text retain echoes of an anxiety about the immanent violence within representation and even thought itself, offering it the space and time to resound. But the vital resistance of matter in the work, of the sometimes resinous, sometimes gritty materiality of words or of actors' bodies and the stolid stage, nevertheless strongly inheres, retaining and revealing the shape of, but not totally breaking under, a concussive contact with force, desire and perhaps even hope. In bringing force together with matter to produce shape, then, something remains that will not be transformed, lifted up and circulated as if it were so much thin air, for matter both deforms demands, reveals their weakness, but also makes their force visible as such.

So this tremor, this shape of 'strong weakness', that describes itself as a comic movement across Beckett's texts is not an empty formalism; instead, it describes the impact and impression of power, of domination and violence and gentleness and resistance, giving a shape to what in the end are determinedly uncertain ethical demands and questions, without offering up ideas of ethics or prescriptions. But the shape of tremor is not simply a back and forth, like an imagined perpetual motion machine; rather, it proceeds through time, registering change, entropic decline, the impact of external forces, even if it could hardly be said to articulate progression. In one sense, the shudders the texts describe and perform are like death throes – the movement towards a final cessation. And these throes reverberate. Adorno asserts that for both a 'philistine' and an admirer of abstract art, the tremors of Beckett's 'dialectics at a standstill' become like pathological infections; they materialise affect as a shudder. Adorno states that Beckett's works

> enjoy what is today the only form of respectable fame: everyone shudders at them, and yet no-one can persuade himself that these eccentric plays and novels are not about what everyone knows but no-one will admit . . . Beckett's *Ecce Homo* is what human beings have become. As though with eyes drained of tears, they stare silently out of his sentences. (1980a: 190)

Shuddering is an anxious form of mimesis, in Adorno's particular sense of the mimetic, because it involves an assimilation to the world, an expressive and affective affinity with it.[1] The affected person shudders because the world is shuddering. The death throes of human life, reduced and abstracted, are mimed by the abstract artwork and materialised in all their painful particularity in a spectator.

But if something is shuddering, it is not necessarily dying. An engine that is shuddering is as likely to be shaking itself into life as it is to be grinding to a halt. If something reverberates, it is not necessarily a predictable replication of what has gone before. It is precisely in shuddering's potential to move something into being beside itself, and it is in this potential to illuminate the shape and operation of force within the material that something gets seen for what it is. Within this moment of purchase on the way everything goes on, trembling enables a reader or spectator who has been a little thrown, moved to the side of where they normally are, to sense the merest impression of something else, something new, as it might emerge. This is hardly a grand gesture, but perhaps it is as much as an art that refuses to write out ethical prescriptions can do. For these texts, bound as they are to a historically specific suspicion of rationality, have 'worked around the limits of our logical concepts' (Kearney 1984: 112), as Derrida puts it in one of his rare comments on Beckett; they produce cryptically expressive, resistant and yet finally descriptive shapes rather than just ideas. But by tracing out the shapes of a funny/peculiar comedy and the uncertain ethics that mould them, it is possible to see something of the way Beckett's abstract forms move beyond themselves. We begin to see how it is that Beckett, in Derrida's terms, makes 'the limits of our language tremble' (112), while forcing and permitting the world to shudder alongside it.

Note

1. Adorno writes in *Aesthetic Theory*, 'the shudder is the mimetic comportment reacting mimetically to abstractness' (2002: 20). There is, however, potential in the shudder for Adorno. In places shuddering is figured as a primal, visceral reaction to undifferentiated and potentially engulfing otherness, and consequently on the side of 'identity thinking'; but the shudder produced by modern art is also felt, in its embodied particularity, to be an authentic reaction. As Gordon Finlayson puts it, the shudder is 'a spontaneous and somatic response of revulsion at the world of "universal fungibility," i.e. at a world which has been systematically denuded of intrinsically valuable ends and activities, and in which everything of value is only valuable as a means for something else' (2003: 81).

Works Cited

Abraham, Nicolas (1995) *Rhythms: On the Work, Translation, and Psychoanalysis*, trans. Benjamin Thigpen and Nicholas T. Rand. Stanford: Stanford University Press.

Acheson, James (1980) 'Chess with the Audience: Samuel Beckett's *Endgame*', *Critical Quarterly*, 22 (2): 33–45.

Ackerley, C. and Gontarski, S. E. (2004) *The Grove Companion to Samuel Beckett*. New York: Grove.

Adorno, Theodor W. (1974) *Minima Moralia*, trans. E. F. N. Jephcott. London: Verso.

Adorno, Theodor W. (1980a) 'Commitment', in Ronald Taylor (ed.), *Aesthetics and Politics: Theodor Adorno, Walter Benjamin, Ernst Bloch, Bertolt Brecht, Georg Lukács*, trans. Francis McDonagh. London: Verso, pp. 177–99.

Adorno, Theodor W. (1980b) 'Letter to Walter Benjamin, 1936', in Ronald Taylor (ed.), *Aesthetics and Politics: Theodor Adorno, Walter Benjamin, Ernst Bloch, Bertolt Brecht, Georg Lukács*, trans. Francis McDonagh. London: Verso, p. 123.

Adorno, Theodor W. (1990) *Negative Dialectics*, trans. E. B. Ashton. London: Routledge.

Adorno, Theodor W. (1991a) 'On the Fetish Character in Music and the Regression of Listening', in J. M. Bernstein (ed.), *The Culture Industry: Selected Essays on Mass Culture*. London: Routledge, pp. 26–52.

Adorno, Theodor W. (1991b) 'Trying to Understand *Endgame*', in Rolf Tiedemann (ed.), *Notes to Literature*, vol. I, trans. Shierry Weber Nicholsen. New York: Columbia University Press, pp. 241–75.

Adorno, Theodor W. (1992a) 'Commitment', in Rolf Tiedemann (ed.), *Notes to Literature*, vol. II, trans. Shierry Weber Nicholsen. New York: Columbia University Press, pp. 76–94.

Adorno, Theodor W. (1992b) 'Is Art Lighthearted?', in Rolf Tiedemann (ed.), *Notes to Literature*, vol. II, trans. Shierry Weber Nicholsen. New York: Columbia University Press, pp. 247–53.

Adorno, Theodor W. (2002) *Aesthetic Theory*, in Gretel Adorno and Rolf Tiedemann (eds), trans. Robert Hullot-Kentor. London: Continuum.

Adorno, Theodor W. (2010) 'Dossier: Adorno's Notes on Beckett', *Journal of Beckett Studies*, 19: 157–78.

Adorno, Theodor W. and Horkheimer, Max (1997) *Dialectic of Enlightenment*, trans. John Cumming. London: Verso.

Aristotle (1984a) *Nicomachean Ethics*, in Jonathan Barnes (ed.), *The Complete Works of Aristotle: Revised Oxford Translation*, vol. II. Princeton: Princeton University Press, pp. 1729–867.

Aristotle (1984b) *On the Parts of the Animals*, in Jonathan Barnes (ed.), *The Complete Works of Aristotle: Revised Oxford Translation*, vol. I. Princeton: Princeton University Press, pp. 994–1086.

Armstrong, Isobel (2000) *The Radical Aesthetic*. Oxford: Blackwell.

Armstrong, Tim (1998) *Modernism, Technology and the Body: A Cultural Study*. Cambridge: Cambridge University Press.

Badiou, Alain (2001) *Ethics: An Essay on the Understanding of Evil*, trans. Peter Hallward. London: Verso.

Badiou, Alain (2003) *On Beckett*, ed. Nina Power and Alberto Toscano. Manchester: Clinamen.

Bair, Deirdre (1978) *Samuel Beckett: A Biography*. London: Jonathan Cape.

Baker, Phil (1997) *Beckett and the Mythology of Psychoanalysis*. Basingstoke: Macmillan.

Bakhtin, Mikhail (1981) *The Dialogic Imagination: Four Essays*, trans. Caryl Emerson and Michael Holquist. Austin: University of Texas Press.

Banfield, Ann, (2003) 'Beckett's Tattered Syntax', *Representations*, 84: 6–29.

Baudelaire, Charles (1972) 'On the Essence of Laughter', *Selected Writings on Art and Literature*, trans. P. E. Charvet. Harmondsworth: Penguin.

Baudelaire, Charles (1975) *Oeuvres Complètes 1*. Paris: Gallimard.

Beckett, Samuel (1930s) 'Whoroscope Notebook', Reading University Library, MS 3000, © The Estate of Samuel Beckett.

Beckett, Samuel (1932) 'Letter to Thomas MacGreevy, 26 January', Trinity College Dublin, MS 10402, © The Estate of Samuel Beckett.

Beckett, Samuel (1934–5) 'Psychology Notes', Trinity College Dublin, MS 10971, © The Estate of Samuel Beckett.

Beckett, Samuel (1948) '*Molloy* Holograph Notebook', Harry Ransom Center, Austin, Texas. Box 4, Folder 5–7, Notebook 3, © The Estate of Samuel Beckett.

Beckett, Samuel (1951a) *Molloy*. Paris: Editions de Minuit.

Beckett, Samuel (1951b) *Malone Meurt*. Paris: Editions de Minuit.

Beckett, Samuel (1953) *L'Innomable*. Paris: Editions de Minuit.

Beckett, Samuel (1965) 'Good Heavens (inscribed by Beckett 'Before *Come and Go*)', Reading University Library MS 1227, © The Estate of Samuel Beckett.

Beckett, Samuel (1970) *More Pricks Than Kicks* [1934]. London: Calder & Boyars.

Beckett, Samuel (1972) *Film: Complete Scenario/Illustrations/Production Shots*. London: Faber & Faber.

Beckett, Samuel (1974) '*That Time* Draft', Reading University Library MS 1477, © The Estate of Samuel Beckett.

Beckett, Samuel (1976) *Watt* [1953]. London: John Calder.

Beckett, Samuel (1977) *Collected Poems in English and French*. New York: Grove.

Beckett, Samuel (1980) '*Quad* Draft', Reading University Library, MS 2100, © The Estate of Samuel Beckett.

Beckett, Samuel (1983) *Disjecta: Miscellaneous Writings and a Dramatic Fragment*, ed. Ruby Cohn. London: John Calder.

Beckett, Samuel (1990) *The Complete Dramatic Works*. London: Faber & Faber.

Beckett, Samuel (1992) *Nohow On: Company, Ill Seen Ill Said, Worstward Ho*. London: Calder Publications.

Beckett, Samuel (1993) *Murphy* [1938]. London: Calder Publications.

Beckett, Samuel (1994) *Molloy, Malone Dies, The Unnamable*. London: John Calder.

Beckett, Samuel (1995) *The Complete Short Prose: 1929–1989*, ed. S. E. Gontarski. New York: Grove Press.

Beckett, Samuel (1996) *Dream of Fair to Middling Women*. London: John Calder.

Beckett, Samuel (1999) *Proust and Three Dialogues with Georges Duthuit*. London: John Calder.

Beckett, Samuel (2002) *Poems: 1930–1989*. London: Calder Publications.

Beckett, Samuel (2006) 'Letter to Georges Duthuit, 9–10 March 1949', in S. E. Gontarski and Anthony Uhlmann (eds), *Beckett After Beckett*. Gainesville: Florida University Press, pp. 15–21.

Begam, Richard (1996) *Samuel Beckett and the End of Modernity*. Stanford: Stanford University Press.

Ben-Zvi, Linda (1980) 'Samuel Beckett, Fritz Mauthner, and the Limits of Language', *PMLA*, 95: 179–94.

Bergson, Henri (1910) *Time and Free Will: An Essay on the Immediate Data of Consciousness*, trans. F. L. Pogson. London: George Allen & Unwin.

Bergson, Henri (1911a) *Creative Evolution*, trans. Arthur Mitchell. London: Macmillan.

Bergson, Henri (1911b) *Laughter: An Essay on the Meaning of the Comic*, trans. Cloudesley Brereton and Fred Rothwell. London: Macmillan.

Bergson, Henri (1994) *Matter and Memory*, trans. Nancy Margaret Paul and W. Scott Palmer. New York: Zone.

Bersani, Leo and Dutoit, Ulysse (1993) *Arts of Impoverishment: Beckett, Rothko, Resnais*. Cambridge, MA: Harvard University Press.

Bhabha, Homi K. (1994) *The Location of Culture*. London: Routledge.

Brater, Enoch (1987) *Beyond Minimalism: Beckett's Late Style in the Theater*. New York: Oxford University Press.

Bryden, Mary (1993) *Women in the Prose and Drama of Samuel Beckett: Her Own Other*. Basingstoke: Macmillan.

Bryden, Mary (1995) '*Quad*: Dancing Genders', in *The Savage Eye/L'Oeil Fauve: New Essays on Beckett's Television Plays*. Amsterdam: Rodopi, pp. 109–22.

Bryden, Mary (1998) *Samuel Beckett and Music*. Oxford: Oxford University Press.

Bryden, Mary (2010) 'Clowning with Beckett', in S. E. Gontarski (ed.), *A Companion to Samuel Beckett*. Oxford: Wiley-Blackwell, pp. 358–71.

Büttner, Gottfried (1984) *Samuel Beckett's Novel 'Watt'*, trans. Joseph P. Dolan. Philadelphia: University of Pennsylvania Press.

Cabanne, Pierre (1971) *Dialogues with Marcel Duchamp*, trans. Ron Padgett. New York: Viking.

Caputo, John D. (1993) *Against Ethics: Contributions to a Poetics of Obligation with Constant Reference to Deconstruction.* Bloomington: Indiana University Press.

Carey, John (1992) *The Intellectuals and the Masses: Pride and Prejudice amongst the Literary Intelligentsia, 1880–1939.* London: Faber & Faber.

Caselli, Daniela (2005) *Beckett's Dantes: Intertextuality in the Fiction and Criticism.* Manchester: Manchester University Press.

Childs, Donald J. (2001) *Modernism and Eugenics: Woolf, Eliot, Yeats, and the Culture of Degeneration.* Cambridge: Cambridge University Press.

Coe, Richard N. (1962) *Beckett.* New York: Grove Press.

Cohn, Ruby (1962) *Samuel Beckett: The Comic Gamut.* New Brunswick, NJ: Rutgers University Press.

Cohn, Ruby (1970) 'The Laughter of Sad Sam Beckett', in Melvin J. Friedman (ed.), *Samuel Beckett Now: Critical Approaches to His Novels, Poetry and Plays.* Chicago: Chicago University Press, pp. 185–98.

Cohn, Ruby (1973) *Back to Beckett.* Princeton: Princeton University Press.

Cohn, Ruby (2001) *A Beckett Canon.* Ann Arbor: University of Michigan Press.

Conley, Tom (1993) 'Foreword: A Plea for Leibniz', in Gilles Deleuze, *The Fold: Leibniz and the Baroque*, trans. Tom Conley. London: Athlone Press, pp. ix–xx.

Connor, Steven (1988) *Samuel Beckett: Repetition, Theory and Text.* Oxford: Basil Blackwell.

Connor, Steven (1992) *Theory and Cultural Value.* Oxford: Blackwell.

Connor, Steven (1998a) 'Art, Criticism and Laughter'. Online: http://www.bbk.ac.uk/eh/eng/skc/artlaugh.htm.

Connor, Steven (1998b) 'How He Was: Samuel Beckett's Lives', *Bullán: An Irish Studies Journal*, 4 (1): 121–6.

Connor, Steven (2000) 'The Shakes: Conditions of Tremor'. Online: http://www.bbk.ac.uk/eh/eng/skc/shakes.

Connor, Steven (2001) 'Slow Going', *Yearbook of English Studies*, 31: 153–65.

Cornell, Drucilla (1992) *The Philosophy of the Limit.* New York: Routledge.

Coughlan, Patricia (1995) 'The Poetry is Another Pair of Sleeves: Beckett, Ireland and Modernist Lyric Poetry', in Patricia Coghlan and Alex Davis (eds), *Modernism and Ireland: The Poetry of the 1930's.* Cork: Cork University Press, pp. 173–208.

Critchley, Simon (1997) *Very Little . . . Almost Nothing: Death, Philosophy, Literature.* London: Routledge.

Critchley, Simon (1999a) *Ethics-Politics-Subjectivity: Essays on Derrida Levinas and Contemporary French Thought.* London: Verso, pp. 217–38.

Critchley, Simon (1999b) *The Ethics of Deconstruction: Derrida and Levinas*, 2nd edn. Edinburgh: Edinburgh University Press.

Critchley, Simon (2000) 'Demanding Approval: On the Ethics of Alain Badiou', *Radical Philosophy*, 100: 16–27.

Critchley, Simon (2002) *On Humour.* London: Routledge.

Critchley, Simon (2007) *Infinitely Demanding: Ethics of Commitment, Politics of Resistance.* London: Verso.

Cronin, Anthony (1996) *Samuel Beckett: The Last Modernist.* London: HarperCollins.

Culik, Hugh (1989) 'Neurological Disorder and the Evolution of Beckett's Maternal Images', *Mosaic*, 22: 41–53.

Cunningham, David (2002) 'Trying (Not) to Understand: Adorno and the Work of Beckett', in Richard Lane (ed.), *Beckett and Philosophy*. Basingstoke: Palgrave, pp. 125–39.

Damisch, Hubert (1979) 'The Duchamp Defense', *October*, 10: 5–28.

Davies, Christie (1996) *Ethnic Humor Around the World: A Comparative Analysis*. Bloomington: Indiana University Press.

De Man, Paul (1983) 'The Rhetoric of Temporality', in *Blindness and Insight: Essays in the Rhetoric of Contemporary Criticism*, 2nd edn. London: Methuen, pp. 187–228.

Deleuze, Gilles (1994) *Difference and Repetition*, trans. Paul Patton. London: Athlone Press.

Deleuze, Gilles (1998) 'The Exhausted', trans. Anthony Uhlmann, in *Essays Critical and Clinical*, trans. Daniel W. Smith and Michael A. Greco. London: Verso, pp. 152–74.

Derrida, Jacques (1978) 'Violence and Metaphysics: An Essay on the Thought of Emmanuel Levinas', in *Writing and Difference*, trans. Alan Bass. London: Routledge & Kegan Paul, pp. 79–153.

Derrida, Jacques (1987) 'To Speculate – on "Freud"', in *The Post-Card: From Socrates to Freud and Beyond*, trans. Alan Bass. Chicago: University of Chicago Press, pp. 259–409.

Descartes, René (1985a) *Meditations on First Philosophy*, in *The Philosophical Writings of Descartes*, Vol. II, trans. John Cottingham, Robert Stoothoff and Dugald Murdoch. Cambridge: Cambridge University Press, pp. 1–62.

Descartes, René (1985b) *The Passions of the Soul*, in *The Philosophical Writings of Descartes*, Vol. I, trans. John Cottingham, Robert Stoothoff and Dugald Murdoch. Cambridge: Cambridge University Press, pp. 325–404.

Descartes, René (1985c) *Treatise on Man. The Philosophical Writings of Descartes*, vol. I, trans. John Cottingham, Robert Stoothoff and Dugald Murdoch. Cambridge: Cambridge University Press, pp. 99–108.

Docherty, Thomas (1996) *Alterities: Criticism, History, Representation*. Oxford: Oxford University Press.

Driver, Tom (1979) 'Beckett by the Madeleine', in Lawrence Graver and Raymond Federman (eds), *Samuel Beckett: The Critical Heritage*. London: Routledge & Kegan Paul, pp. 217–23.

Eaglestone, Robert (1997) *Ethical Criticism: Reading After Levinas*. Edinburgh: Edinburgh University Press.

Elam, Keir (1994) 'Dead Heads: Damnation-Narration in the "Dramaticules"', in John Pilling (ed.), *The Cambridge Companion to Beckett*. Cambridge: Cambridge University Press, pp. 145–66.

Eliot, T. S. (1920) 'Tradition and the Individual Talent', in *The Sacred Wood: Essays on Poetry and Criticism*. London: Methuen, pp. 1–18.

Ellman, Richard (1983) *James Joyce*. London: Oxford University Press.

Ellman, Richard (1989) *A Long the Riverrun: Selected Essays*. Harmondsworth: Penguin.

Esslin, Martin (1986) 'Dionysos' Dianoetic Laughter', in *As No Other Dare Fail*. London: John Calder, pp. 15–23.

Fehsenfeld, Martha (1982) 'Beckett's Late Works: An Appraisal', *Modern Drama*, 25: 355–62.

Fehsenfeld, Martha Dow and Overbeck, Lois (eds) (2009) *The Letters of Samuel Beckett, Vol. 1: 1929–1940.* Cambridge: Cambridge University Press.

Feldman, Matthew (2006) *Beckett's Books: A Cultural History of Samuel Beckett's 'Interwar Notes'.* London: Continuum.

Finlayson, Gordon (2003) 'Adorno: Modern Art, Metaphysics, and Radical Evil', *Modernism/Modernity*, 10 (1): 71–95.

Foucault, Michel (1980) 'Preface to Transgression', in Donald F. Bouchard (ed.), *Language, Counter-Memory, Practice: Selected Essays and Interviews*, trans. Donald F. Bouchard and Sherry Simon. Ithaca, NY: Cornell Uiversity Press, pp. 29–52.

Frank, Joseph (1991) 'Spatial Form in Modern Literature', in *The Idea of Spatial Form.* New Brunswick, NJ: Rutgers University Press, pp. 6–66.

Freud, Sigmund (1905) *Jokes and Their Relation to the Unconscious*, in *The Standard Edition of the Complete Psychological Works of Sigmund Freud*, Vol. VIII, pp. 1-247. London: Hogarth Press and Institute of Psychoanalysis.

Freud, Sigmund (1911) 'Formulations on the Two Principles of Mental Functioning', in *The Standard Edition of the Complete Psychological Works of Sigmund Freud*, Vol. XII, pp. 213–26. London: Hogarth Press and Institute of Psychoanalysis.

Freud, Sigmund (1915) 'Instincts and Their Vicissitudes', in *The Standard Edition of the Complete Psychological Works of Sigmund Freud*, Vol. XIV, pp. 109–40. London: Hogarth Press and Institute of Psychoanalysis.

Freud, Sigmund (1920) *Beyond the Pleasure Principle*, in *The Standard Edition of the Complete Psychological Works of Sigmund Freud*, Vol. XVIII, pp. 1–64. London: Hogarth Press and Institute of Psychoanalysis.

Freud, Sigmund (1927) 'Humour', in *The Standard Edition of the Complete Psychological Works of Sigmund Freud*, Vol. XXI, pp. 159–66. London: Hogarth Press and Institute of Psychoanalysis.

Gershon, Michael (1998) *The Second Brain: A Groundbreaking New Understanding of Nervous Disorders of the Stomach and Intestine.* New York: HarperCollins.

Geulincx, Arnold (2006) *Ethics: With Samuel Beckett's Notes*, trans. Martin Wilson, ed. Han van Ruler, Anthony Uhlmann and Martin Wilson. Leiden and Boston: Brill.

Gibson, Andrew (1999) *Postmodernity, Ethics and the Novel: From Leavis to Levinas.* London: Routledge.

Gibson, Andrew (2006) *Beckett and Badiou: The Pathos of Intermittency.* Oxford: Oxford University Press.

Gibson, Andrew (2010) *Samuel Beckett.* London: Reaktion.

Gidal, Peter (1986) *Understanding Beckett: A Study of Monologue and Gesture in the Works of Samuel Beckett.* Basingstoke: Macmillan.

Gillies, Mary Ann (1996) *Henri Bergson and British Modernism.* Montreal: McGill-Queen's University Press.

Gontarski, S. E. (1985) *The Intent of Undoing in Samuel Beckett's Dramatic Texts.* Bloomington: Indiana University Press.

Gontarski, S. E. (ed.) (1992) *Endgame: With a Revised Text*, The Theatrical Notebooks of Samuel Beckett, Vol. II. London: Faber & Faber.

Gontarski, S. E. (ed.) (1999) *The Shorter Plays: With Revised Texts for 'Footfalls', 'Come and Go', and What Where*, The Theatrical Notebooks of Samuel Beckett, Vol. IV. London: Faber & Faber.

Graver, Lawrence (1992) 'Homage to the Dark Lady: *Ill Seen Ill Said*', in Linda Ben-Zvi (ed.), *Women in Beckett: Performances and Critical Perspectives*. Urbana: University of Illinois Press, pp. 142–9.

Gunn, Dan (2006) 'Until the Gag Is Chewed', *Times Literary Supplement*, 21 April, p. 15.

Haerdter, Michael (1968) *Materialen zu Becketts Endspiel*. Frankfurt: Suhrkamp Verlag.

Harmon, Maurice (ed.) (1998) *No Author Better Served: The Correspondence of Samuel Beckett and Alan Schneider*. Cambridge, MA: Harvard University Press.

Harvey, Lawrence (1970) *Samuel Beckett: Poet and Critic*. Princeton: Princeton University Press.

Heidegger, Martin (1962) *Being and Time*, trans. John Macquarrie and Edward Robinson. London: Blackwell.

Henning, Sylvie Debevec (1988) *Beckett's Critical Complicity: Carnival, Contestation, and Tradition*. Lexington: University Press of Kentucky.

Hiebel, Hans. H. (1995) '*Quadrat 1* and 2 as a Television Play', in *The Savage Eye/L'Oeil Fauve: New Essays on Beckett's Television Plays*. Amsterdam: Rodopi, pp. 335–43.

Hill, Leslie (1990) *Beckett's Fiction: In Different Words*. Cambridge: Cambridge University Press.

Hobbes, Thomas (1839) *Leviathan*, in William Molesworth (ed.), *The English Works of Thomas Hobbes*, Vol. III. London: John Bohn.

Hobson, Harold (1956) 'Samuel Beckett: Dramatist of the Year', *International Theatre Annual*, 1: 153–5.

Hugill, Andrew (1992) 'Beckett, Duchamp, and Chess in the 1930s'. Online: http://www.mti.dmu.ac.uk/~ahugill/writings/chess.htm.

Huizinga, Johan (1955) *Homo Ludens: A Study of the Play Element in Culture*. Boston: Beacon Press.

Hutcheson, Francis (1994) 'Reflections Upon Laughter' [1725], in R. S. Downie (ed.), *Philosophical Writings*. London: Everyman-Orion Publishing, pp. 45–63.

Iser, Wolfgang (1993) 'The Art of Failure: The Stifled Laugh in Beckett's Theater', in *Prospecting: From Reader Response to Literary Anthropology*. Baltimore: Johns Hopkins University Press, pp. 152–93.

James, William (1890) *Principles of Psychology*, Vol. I. New York: Henry Holt.

Jay, Martin (1994) *Downcast Eyes: The Denigration of Vision in Twentieth-Century French Thought*. Berkeley: University of California Press.

Jolas, Eugène et al. (1929) 'Proclamation: Revolution of the Word', *transition*, 16/17: 13.

Jones, Ernest (1920) *Treatment of the Neuroses*. London: Ballière, Tindall & Cox.

Jones, Ernest (1923) *Papers on Psychoanalysis*. London: Ballière, Tindall & Cox.

Juliet, Charles (2009) *Conversations with Samuel Beckett and Bram van Velde*, trans. Tracy Cooke and Axel Nesme. Champaign, IL and London: Dalkey Archive Press.

Kant, Immanuel (1987) *The Critique of Judgement*, trans. Werner S. Pluhar. Indianapolis: Hackett.

Katz, Daniel (1995) *Saying I No More: Subjectivity and Consciousness in the Prose of Samuel Beckett*. Evanston, IL: Northwestern University Press.

Katz, Daniel (2003) 'Beckett's Measures: Principles of Pleasure in *Molloy* and "First Love"', *Modern Fiction Studies*, 49: 246–60.

Kearney, Richard (1984) *Dialogues with Contemporary Continental Thinkers: The Phenomenological Heritage*. Manchester: Manchester University Press.

Kearney, Richard and Dooley, Mark (eds) (1999) *Questioning Ethics: Contemporary Debates in Philosophy*. London: Routledge.

Kenner, Hugh (1962) *The Stoic Comedians: Flaubert, Joyce and Beckett*. Berkeley: University of California Press.

Kenner, Hugh (1968) *Samuel Beckett: A Critical Study*. Berkeley: University of California Press.

Kenner, Hugh (1973) *A Reader's Guide to Samuel Beckett*. London: Thames & Hudson.

Kern, Edith (1970) 'Black Humour: The Pockets of Lemuel Gulliver and Samuel Beckett', in Melvin J. Friedman (ed.), *Samuel Beckett Now: Critical Approaches to His Novels, Poetry and Plays*. Chicago: Chicago University Press, pp. 89–102.

Kleist, Heinrich von (1981) 'On the Marionette Theatre', in Idris Parry (ed.), *Hand to Mouth and Other Essays*. Manchester: Carcanet, pp. 13–18.

Knopff, Robert (1999) *The Theater and Cinema of Buster Keaton*. Princeton: Princeton University Press.

Knowlson, James (ed.) (1985) *Happy Days: The Production Notebook of Samuel Beckett*. London: Faber & Faber.

Knowlson, James (ed.) (1992) *Krapp's Last Tape: With a Revised Text*, The Theatrical Notebooks of Samuel Beckett, Vol. III. London: Faber & Faber.

Knowlson, James (ed.) (1993) *Waiting for Godot*, The Theatrical Notebooks of Samuel Beckett, Vol. I. London: Faber & Faber.

Knowlson, James (1996) *Damned to Fame: The Life of Samuel Beckett*. London: Bloomsbury.

Knowlson, James and Pilling, John (1979) 'Beckett and Kleist's Essay "On the Marionette Theatre"', in *Frescoes of the Skull: The Later Prose and Drama of Samuel Beckett*. London: John Calder, pp. 277–85.

Knox, Norman (1961) *The Word Irony and its Context, 1500–1755*. Durham, NC: Duke University Press.

Lacan, Jacques (1993) *The Seminar: Book III, The Psychoses, 1955–56*, trans. Russell Grigg. London: Routledge.

Lacan, Jacques (1994) *Le séminaire. Livre IV. La relation d'objet*. Paris: Seuil.

Lacan, Jacques (1998) *The Four Fundamental Concepts of Psycho-Analysis*, trans. Alan Sheridan. London: Vintage.

Lawley, Paul (1992) 'Adoption in *Endgame*', in Steven Connor (ed.), *Waiting for Godot* and *Endgame: New Casebooks*. Basingstoke: Macmillan, pp. 119–27.

Le Juez, Brigitte (2008) *Beckett before Beckett: Samuel Beckett's Lectures on French Literature*. London: Souvenir Press.

Levinas, Emmanuel (1969) *Totality and Infinity. An Essay on Exteriority*, trans. Alphonso Lingis. Pittsburgh: Duquesne University Press.

Levinas, Emmanuel (1985) *Ethics and Infinity: Conversations with Philippe Nemo*, trans. Richard A. Cohen. Pittsburgh: Duquesne University Press.

Levinas, Emmanuel (1987) *Time and the Other [and additional essays]*, trans. Richard A. Cohen. Pittsburgh: Duquesne University Press.

Levinas, Emmanuel (1988) *Existence and Existents*, trans. Alphonso Lingis. Dordrecht: Kluwer.

Levinas, Emmanuel (1996) 'Is Ontology Fundamental?', in Adriaan T. Peperzak, Simon Critchley and Robert Bernasconi (eds), *Basic Philosophical Writings*. Bloomington: Indiana University Press, pp. 1–10.

Levinas, Emmanuel (1998) *Otherwise than Being or Beyond Essence*, trans. Alphonso Lingis, Pittsburgh: Duquesne University Press.

Locatelli, Carla (1990) *Unwording the World: Samuel Beckett's Prose Works After the Nobel Prize*. Philadelphia: University of Pennsylvania Press.

McCabe, John (1978) *Charlie Chaplin*. Garden City, NY: Doubleday.

McMullan, Anna (1993) *Theatre on Trial: Samuel Beckett's Later Drama*. London: Routledge.

Magalini, Sergio I., Magalini, Sabina C. and de Francisi, Giovanni (1990) *Dictionary of Medical Syndromes*, 3rd edn. Philadelphia: J. B. Lipincott.

Malabou, Catherine (2005) *The Future of Hegel: Plasticity, Temporality and Dialectic*, trans. Lisabeth During. Abingdon: Routledge.

Massumi, Brian (2002) 'The Autonomy of Affect', in *Parables for the Virtual*. Durham, NC: Duke University Press, pp. 23–45.

Maude, Ulrika (2009) *Beckett, Technology and the Body*. Cambridge: Cambridge University Press.

Maude, Ulrika (2012) 'Pavlov's Dogs and Other Animals in Samuel Beckett', in Mary Bryden (ed.), *Beckett and Animals*. Cambridge: Cambridge University Press (forthcoming).

Maxwell, James Clerk (1872) *Theory of Heat*. New York: Appleton.

Mercier, Vivian (1962) *The Irish Comic Tradition*. London: Oxford University Press.

Miller, Jonathan (1987) 'Jokes and Joking: A Serious Laughing Matter', in John Durant and Jonathan Miller (eds), *Laughing Matter: A Serious Look at Humour*. Harlow: Longman, pp. 5–16.

Miller, Tyrus (1999) *Late Modernism: Politics, Fiction, and the Arts Between the World Wars*. Berkeley and Los Angeles: University of California Press.

Mooney, Sinéad (2005) 'Kicking Against the Thermolaters: Beckett's "Recent Irish Poetry"', *Samuel Beckett Today/Aujourd'hui*, 15: 30–42.

Mooney, Sinéad (2010) 'Beckett in French and English', in S. E. Gontarski (ed.), *A Companion to Samuel Beckett*. Oxford: Wiley-Blackwell, pp. 196–208.

Moorjani, Angela (2003) 'Diogenes Lampoons Alexandre Kojève', in Linda Ben-Zvi (ed.), *Drawing on Beckett: Portraits, Performances, and Cultural Contexts*. Tel Aviv: Asaph, pp. 69–88.

Morreall, John (ed.) (1987) *The Philosophy of Laughter and Humor*. Albany, NY: SUNY Press.

Nabokov, Vladimir (1990) *Strong Opinions*. New York: Vintage International.

Nadeau, Maurice (1965) 'Samuel Beckett: Humor and the Void', in Martin

Esslin (ed.), *Samuel Beckett: A Collection of Critical Essays*. Englewood Cliffs, NJ: Prentice Hall.

Ngai, Sianne (2005) *Ugly Feelings*. Cambridge, MA: Harvard University Press.

Nietzsche, Friedrich (1968) 'Homer's Contest', in Walter Kaufman (ed.), *The Portable Nietzsche*. Harmondsworth: Penguin, pp. 32–41.

North, Michael (2009) *Machine-Age Comedy*. Oxford: Oxford University Press.

Parkinson, James (1817) *Essay on the Shaking Palsy*. London: Wittingham & Rowland, for Sherwood, Neely & Jones.

Pavlov, Ivan P. (1927) *Conditioned Reflexes: An Investigation of the Physiological Activity of the Cerebral Cortex*, trans. G. V. Anrep. London: Oxford University Press.

Pfister, Manfred (2001) 'Beckett's Tonic Laughter', in Angela Moorjani and Carola Veit (eds), *Samuel Beckett: Endlessness in the Year 2000*. Amsterdam: Rodopi, pp. 48–53.

Pilling, John (1997) *Beckett Before Godot*. Cambridge: Cambridge University Press.

Pilling, John (ed.) (1999) *Beckett's 'Dream' Notebook*. Reading: Beckett International Foundation.

Pilling, John (2003) *Companion to 'Dream'*, *Journal of Beckett Studies*, 12: 1–393.

Pilling, John (2006) *A Samuel Beckett Chronology*. Basingstoke: Palgrave.

Plato (1997a) *Philebus*, in *Plato: Complete Works*, trans. Dorothea Frede. Indianapolis: Hackett, pp. 398–456.

Plato (1997b) *Republic*, in *Plato: Complete Works*, trans. Dorothea Frede. Indianapolis: Hackett, pp. 971–1223.

Purdie, Susan (1993) *Comedy: The Mastery of Discourse*. Hemel Hempstead: Harvester Wheatsheaf.

Putnam, Samuel et al. (eds) (1931) *European Caravan*. New York: Brewer, Warren, & Putnam.

Rabaté, Jean-Michel (2010) 'Philosophizing with Beckett: Adorno and Badiou', in S. E. Gontarski (ed.), *A Companion to Samuel Beckett*. Oxford: Wiley-Blackwell, pp. 97–117.

Rank, Otto (1929) *The Trauma of Birth*. London: Kegan Paul, Trench, Trubner.

Ravaisson, Félix (2008) *Of Habit*, trans. Claire Carlisle and Mark Sinclair. London: Continuum.

Ravez, Stéphanie (2002) 'From Cythera to Philautia, an Excursion into Beckettian Love', in Daniela Caselli, Steven Connor and Laura Salisbury (eds), *Other Becketts*. Talahassee: Journal of Beckett Studies Books, pp. 136–51.

Redfern, Walter (1998) 'A Funny-Bone to Pick with Beckett', *Journal of Beckett Studies*, 8: 101–17.

Restivo, Guiseppina (1997) 'The Iconic Core of Beckett's *Endgame*: Eliot, Dürer, Duchamp', in Marius Buning, Matthijs Engelberts and Sjef Houppermans (eds), *Samuel Beckett: Crossroads and Borderlines*. Amsterdam: Rodopi, pp. 111–24.

Ricks, Christopher (1995) *Beckett's Dying Words: The Clarendon Lectures, 1990*. Oxford: Oxford University Press.

Robbe-Grillet, Alain (1975) 'Samuel Beckett, or Presence on the Stage', in

Snapshots and Towards a New Novel, trans. Barbara Wright. London: Calder & Boyars.

Robbins, Jill (1999) *Altered Reading: Levinas and Literature*. Chicago: University of Chicago Press.

Robinson, Michael (1969) *The Long Sonata of the Dead: A Study of Samuel Beckett*. London: Rupert Hart-Davis.

Sacks, Oliver (1991) *Awakenings*. London: Picador-Macmillan.

Salisbury, Laura (2011) 'Bulimic Beckett: Food for Thought and the Archive of Analysis', *Critical Quarterly*, 53 (3): 60–80.

Schlegel, Friedrich (1991) *Philosophical Fragments*, trans. P. Firchow. Minneapolis: University of Minnesota Press.

Schneider, Alan (1972) 'On Directing *Film*', in *Film: Complete Scenario/ Illustrations/Production Shots*. London: Faber & Faber.

Schopenhauer, Arthur (1966) 'On the Theory of the Ludicrous', in *The World as Will and Representation*, trans. E. F. J. Payne, Vol. II. New York: Dover, pp. 91–101.

Schwab, Gabriele (1992) 'On the Dialectic of Closing and Opening in *Endgame*', in Steven Connor (ed.), *Waiting for Godot* and *Endgame: New Casebooks*. Basingstoke: Macmillan, pp. 87–99.

Serres, Michel and Latour, Bruno (1995) *Conversations on Science, Culture, and Time*, trans. Roxanne Lapidus. Ann Arbor: University Michigan Press.

Sharkey, Rodney (1994) 'Singing in the Last Ditch: Beckett's Irish Rebel Songs', *Samuel Beckett Today/Aujourd'hui*, 3: 67–76.

Sheehan, Paul (2002) *Modernism, Narrative and Humanism*. Cambridge: Cambridge University Press.

Sheehan, Paul (2008) 'A world Without Monsters: Beckett and the Ethics of Cruelty', in Russell Smith (ed.), *Beckett and Ethics*. London: Continuum, pp. 86–101.

Shenker, Israel (1956) 'Moody Man of Letters: An Interview with Samuel Beckett', *New York Times*, 5 May, section 2, p. 3.

Taylor, Mark C. (1987) *Altarity*. Chicago: University of Chicago Press.

Terada, Rei (2001) *Feeling in Theory: Emotion after the 'Death of the Subject'*. Cambridge, MA: Harvard University Press.

Tönnies, Merle (1997) *Samuel Beckett's Dramatic Strategy: Audience Laughter and the Postmodern Debate*. Trier: Wissenschaftlicher Verlag.

Topsfield, Valerie (1988) *The Humour of Samuel Beckett*. Basingstoke: Macmillan.

Trezise, Thomas (1990) *Into the Breach: Samuel Beckett and the Ends of Literature*. Princeton: Princeton University Press.

Trotsky, Leon (1973) 'Habit and Custom', in *Problems of Everyday Life and Other Writings on Culture and Science*. New York: Momand Press, pp. 25–30.

Uhlmann, Anthony (1999) *Beckett and Poststructuralism*. Cambridge: Cambridge University Press.

Uhlmann, Anthony (2006) *Samuel Beckett and the Philosophical Image*. Cambridge: Cambridge University Press.

Wade, W. C. (1987) *The Fiery Cross*. New York: Simon & Schuster.

Walton, Jean (2010) 'Modernity and the Peristaltic Subject', in Laura Salisbury and Andrew Shail (eds), *Neurology and Modernity: A Cultural History of Nervous Systems, 1800–1950*. Basingstoke: Palgrave, pp. 245–66.

Watson, David (1991) *Paradox and Desire in Samuel Beckett's Fiction*. Basingstoke: Macmillan.

Weber, Samuel (1985) 'Literature – Just Making It', in Jean-François Lyotard and Jean-Loup Thébaud, *Just Gaming*, trans. Wlad Godzich. Manchester: Manchester University Press, pp. 101–20.

Weisberg, David (2000) *Chronicles of Disorder: Samuel Beckett and the Cultural Politics of the Modern Novel*. Albany, NY: SUNY Press.

Welch, Robert (1993) *Changing States: Transformations in Modern Irish Writing*. London: Routledge.

Weller, Shane (2006) *Beckett, Literature and the Ethics of Alterity*. Basingstoke: Palgrave.

Weller, Shane (2008) 'The Anethics of Desire: Beckett, Racine, Sade', in Russell Smith (ed.), *Beckett and Ethics*. London: Continuum, pp. 102–17.

Weller, Shane (2009) 'Preface', in Samuel Beckett, *Molloy*. London: Faber.

Williams, Raymond (1989) 'Metropolitan Perceptions and the Emergence of Modernism', in *The Politics of Modernism*. London: Verso, pp. 37–48.

Windelband, Wilhelm (1931) *A History of Philosophy*, trans. James H. Tufts. New York: Macmillan.

Wittgenstein, Ludwig (1980) *Culture and Value*, ed. G. H. Von Wright. Oxford: Blackwell.

Wood, Michael (1998) 'The Comedy of Ignorance', in *The Children of Silence*. New York: Columbia University Press, pp. 44–54.

Woodworth, Robert S. (1931) *Contemporary Schools of Psychology*. London: Methuen.

Worth, Katherine (1999) *Samuel Beckett's Theatre: Life Journeys*. Oxford: Oxford University Press.

Wulf, Catharina (1995) 'La Voie de la Über-Marionette: L'acteur en Marge', in *The Savage Eye/L'Oeil Fauve: New Essays on Beckett's Television Plays*. Amsterdam: Rodopi, pp. 139–48.

Ziarek, Ewa P. (1996) *The Rhetoric of Failure: Deconstruction of Skepticism, Reinvention of Modernism*. Albany, NY: SUNY Press.

Žižek, Slavoj (2009) 'Discipline Between Two Freedoms – Madness and Habit in German Idealism', in Markus Gabriel and Slavoj Žižek (eds), *Mythology, Madness and Laughter: Subjectivity in German Idealism*. London: Continuum, pp. 95–121.

Zupančič, Alenka (2008) *The Odd One In: On Comedy*. Cambridge, MA: MIT Press.

General Index

Index of Authors and Works